# COURSE IN CRYPTOGRAPHY

## TRANSLATED FROM THE ORIGINAL "COURS DE CRYPTOGRAPHIE"

by
**General Marcel Givierge**

ISBN: 0-89412-028-X

PUBLISHED by AEGEAN PARK PRESS
P.O. BOX 2837, LAGUNA HILLS, CALIFORNIA 92653
TEL. (714) 586-8811

Manufactured in the United States of America

# FOREWORD

The following English translation of General Givierge's classic work "Cours de Cryptographie" is offered to the public for the first time. Certain comments are in order. For those that possess the French edition, it will be noticed that the syntax is for the most part periodic. In the exposition of a complicated science like that of modern cryptography and cryptanalysis, such a style, though the individual sentences are long, condenses the total subject matter considerably. However, it must be remarked that in the process of integrating sentences so as to subordinate ideas correctly, clarity is often sacrificed. This observation will, it is felt, explain many passages which the author himself calls "meticulous and bewildering." In this translation no attempt has been, in any case, to simplify the original work.

It is to be noted that the meanings of technical words, as used by General Givierge, are often at variance with the definitions given in French dictionaries and those popularly accepted. Also, General Givierge employs terms such as "cipher" and "code", for example, with somewhat different meanings from those given in technical cryptographic publications in the U.S. But, since he is consistent in his use of the terms as defined by him, the reader will encounter no confusion.

Such a surprisingly large portion of this course is taken up with examples of the solution of problems in French that it has been deemed impractical, if not impossible, to substitute corresponding English examples.

In checking the problems, incidentally, a certain number of errors, most of then probably typographical, have been found and corrected. Indulgence, of course, is asked for inevitable mistakes in translation.

AEGEAN PARK PRESS

# TABLE OF CONTENTS

## PREFACE

The results of the labors of cryptanalysts, even the object of these labors, and the existence of cryptanalytic offices were of old left in the dark by the governments or private interests that profited by them. In fact, they endeavored to keep from drying up the spring of information furnished them through this channel. They avoided scaring off their unsuspecting informants by disclosing the possibility of danger in connection with the secrecy with which they desired to enshroud their correspondence. In our epoch of "daylight diplomacy", there has been allowed to filter through certain fairly precise information on the services which agencies charged with the study of cryptography have been able to render. Thus, in the course of the war and afterwards, frequent allusions, sometimes covert and sometimes perfectly clear, have been made with reference to the translations of telegrams enciphered by the warring powers. In the *Revue Militaire française*, of July 1, 1921, we may read how the Tannenberg maneuver was singularly facilitated for Ludendorff by a knowledge of the Russian cipher, which made it possible to translate all the orders of the armies that this general was fighting. The communications of these armies were made by wireless only, and the radiotelegrams were intercepted and translated in sufficient time for Ludendorff to formulate his orders, taking those of the enemy into account (*Revue Militaire française*, Librairie Chapelot, Paris, no. 1, pp. 14 and 15). *L'Intransigeant*, of September 5, 1920, contains an article, entitled "The Battle of the Marne Told by the Radios of the Enemy Command", in which the text of a certain number of the translations of these enciphered radiotelegrams is given.[1]

We may add that the secrecy of our decipherments was pretty poorly guarded during the war. The censors, poorly informed on matters to be kept secret, allowed the press, as much at home as among the Allies, to give out information which drew our enemies out of their initial self-confidence. Consequently, the enemy reduced their military radiotelegraphic correspondence, and made it harder to translate. A polemic between the *Œuvre* and the *Action française*, in November 1919, moreover, alludes to some translations of enciphered diplomatic correspondence, certain portions of which appeared in a newspaper of the same month (*La Voix Nationale*, Paris Press). But already, even in the course of the war, the question of the translations of enciphered diplomatic dispatches had been discussed by the world-wide press, with reference to certain telegrams addressed to the German representatives, Bernstorff and Luxburg, in America, and the disclosures relative to the conduct of these diplomats in countries at that time still neutral may be regarded as one of the factors contributing to the declaration of war by the United States and Brazil.

It cannot be hoped that the governments whose correspondence was translated ignored the publication of information relative to this translation. So the secrecy with which cryptographic services were of old enveloped has been betrayed. We may, nevertheless, deplore the fact that the censors, sharing the public's general ignorance, except in the cases of rare specialists, on matters of cipher, let notes get by them that were of practical value to the adversary. Too much secrecy is sometimes undesirable; because of hiding what is known about cryptography, a well-informed personnel is wanting, while knowledge of a general nature extending over certain questions—that of transports, for example—does not prevent the staff from concealing the details, a knowledge of which would interest the enemy. Too much has

---

[1] However, this article contains an historical discrepancy: it leaves the impression that these radios were translated at the time of the Battle of the Marne, and that they could, therefore, come to the aid of our command. As a matter of fact, they were not translated until later, and it was several weeks after this battle that our generals were in the position of Ludendorff described above.

been said about it for the existence of services of deciphering to be kept under cover. Controversial newspapers, such as *Aux Écoutes*, the *Cri de Paris*, and even the *Journal* have given out details that make it possible for an informed man to acquaint himself with our organization. Under these conditions, it is better to increase the number of persons having practicable ideas on this subject.

Without needing to go back to historical examples (see Josse and Bazeries) and to recall the importance that ministers used to attach to the researches of Viète under Henry IV and of Rossignol under Louis XIII, we can say, supporting ourselves on the foregoing considerations, that in all epochs cryptographic studies have been useful to all nations, and that all nations need expert cryptanalysts.

It seems to us to the interest of the nation to try to awaken cryptographic talent. A few talented individuals were discovered in the course of the war, thanks to happy chances which caused some persons thitherto ignorant of this type of study to enter the Cipher Service, where, because they were so well endowed, they came up with the most brilliant success. However, it is wise not to count only on such improvisation to reinforce, at the time of mobilization, services that function in time of peace.

We will fancy that we have fulfilled a part of the task that we set ourselves if the exposition that we give further on, in spite of its dryness, can interest some persons—up to the time of reading it strangers to cryptographic problems, but desirous of devoting themselves to the study of a science as interesting as geometry—with the seasoning of curiosity which can encourage them to discover the content of communications desired secret by their authors.

While, at the end of the last century, it would have required extraordinary circumstances to permit individuals to get possession of authentic cryptograms like those which passed over telegraph wires, and which were protected against every indiscretion by the secrecy enshrouding this kind of communication, the wide use of wireless telegraphy permits us at the present time to harvest cryptograms of every nature, some enciphered with relatively simple systems, others with the most complicated systems of diplomacy.

The other aim that we have visualized is to facilitate for our pupils the research of more or less classic methods, described sometimes at lengths that appear useless to us for an understanding of the principle, but which, being available only in certain collections, are today almost unobtainable, the editions being exhausted. Consequently, we do not pretend to have contributed an original work. We have composed a manual enabling our pupils to study here exercises which we will set for them elsewhere. We have left aside certain classic systems, because their present importance from a practical point of view seemed to us negligible, judging by documents that have come under our scrutiny, and because they did not appear to us to afford any interesting information.

So, like a bee, we have hummed pilfering right and left, endeavoring not to forget to cite our authors. Bazeries regrets not knowing the names of cryptanalysts after the epoch of Louis XIV; there will be found, in this compilation, the names of those who, among many others, worked on cipher matters around 1920. We would add thereto, with quite an especially affectionate feeling, those of Mr. Ancel and Mr. Haverna, cryptanalysts as wise as modest, who, in 1907, had the kindness to guide our first steps in the cryptographic career. We also add thereto those of Colonels of Artillery Thévenin and Olivari. In spite of the interesting studies of these two remarkable cryptanalysts, their names have not come under our pen in the course of the pages that are going to follow, beside those of other officers, who, in the course of the war, either in staff offices or during the hours of leisure left them from the exercise of command at the front, strove, and often with success, to penetrate the puzzles of enemy transmissions to discover therein the disclosure of attacks against our country, and to make it possible to ward them off quickly enough.

# COURSE IN CRYPTOGRAPHY

CHAPTER I

## GENERAL IDEAS

To encipher a document is to transform a *clear* text, that is to say written so that any reader who knows its language may be able to understand its meaning, into an *enciphered* text, whose meaning is understandable only to those who can decipher it—those who know the key.

If a *code* be used, the text may present a meaning, but this is not the meaning that the addressee will give it. So we may conceive that the telegram, "I send you three tons of arachis on the S.S. Cap Vert", means: "Three German torpedo boats arrived at Cape Verde Isles." Certain codes are very complicated. We give the following example: A certain number of expressions giving important information are adopted and numbered. Let us suppose that in the series of these expressions, those that represent numbers are enumerated from 1 to 10; those which designate arrivals and departures, from 11 to 20; those which specify kinds of boats, from 20 to 30. Let us also suppose that in these categories the expression 11 means: Leaves this morning; the expression 23 means: Armored ships.

We wish to send to our correspondent, under a form inspiring no suspicion, the numbers 11, 7, and 23, which he will interpret as meaning: "Leaving this morning 7 armored ships." We will telegraph him: "Cours du café au Havre cent douze soixante quinze", or "Cotons filés Roubaix quatre vingt quatre trente", and our telegram will be read in three parts: The number of letters (1) in the name of the commodity, (2) in the name of the place, and (3) in the price of the commodity, i.e., 11, 7, and 23, respectively.

The placing of stamps on envelops may also constitute quite an extensive enumeration, corresponding to a catalog of phrases. This is a kind of code where the text, seemingly innocent enough, is in some fashion determined by the envelop and its address. Frequently, and particularly in connection with telegraphic service, messages written in a language with words belonging to that language, but presenting no sense to a reader ignorant of the key because the words of the telegram represent other words of the language, are said to be in conventional language. For example: Send to the bear five monuments delivered cows pretty to blacks (Send to Fox and Co. five full suits black cloth 115 to 135 francs). Sometimes the expression "conventional language" is extended to a message in which words of the telegram, vaguely resembling French, belong to foreign tongues or fictitious languages. In my own opinion, it is better to keep the term "conventional language" for messages that are easily read with an obvious meaning, and to treat other documents, which appear at first glance to have undergone a deformation to hide the sense, as enciphered documents or cryptograms.

We will not undertake the study of documents in conventional language. Before passing on to the study of cryptograms, and especially of the different classical systems of cryptography, we will reject also, while mentioning their existence, a rather important series of documents of a rather special nature. They are those which can be studied only in the texts written by their author, or on photographs of this text, and which, strictly speaking, may be classified as conventional language.

(1)

Inventors, in fact, propose to call the attention of the addressee of a missive to certain letters chosen in a document, the meaning of which is self-sufficient. So we may, as described by About in his novel "Trente et Quarante", underline certain letters in a newspaper or on a poster in such a way that these letters give words and sentences. But, if we underline, we risk attracting the attention of a third party interested in knowing the communication. We may, however, use less visible signs: faint links between the letter and its neighbors, letters slightly out of line, etc., or, in printed texts, particularly in sections devised for certain propaganda and which must pass as insignificant, certain special kinds of type presenting a peculiar form, such as gaps in the body of the letter, systematic typographical imperfections, etc. We will no more than mention documents of this kind. However, it is to be remarked that the series of letters thus marked for the addressee may not give plain text, but a cryptogram whose study will come under a subject treated further on.

Having rejected from our subsequent studies things that pertain to conventional language, we are going to commence the study of cryptograms, that is to say, documents that reveal by their very appearance the fact that they are not intended to be read by the addressee without the knowledge of a prearrangement or a key.

To make our language easy, we are going to define "to encipher" as meaning to transform a clear text into an enciphered text; "to decipher" will apply to the task of the addressee who, having already made an agreement with the sender (this constitutes the key), will transform the cipher text into clear text. As to the work of the prying third party, the "cryptanalyst" [1] by avocation or vocation, who seeks to discover the key and to translate a document that is not meant for him, we will call it "decryptment", although certain authors call it "perlustration." Cryptograms are not to be confused with cryptographs, which are instruments for making cryptograms—cipher machines.

In the development of a cryptographic system, people usually try to make the enciphering and deciphering as simple and rapid as possible, while causing the cryptanalyst a maximum of difficulty. While we are on the subject of things to be considered in devising a cryptographic system, let us turn the attention of the reader to the following point: The first thing to be considered in making a choice of processes is the use to which the system is to be put. The same dangers are not to be feared, the same precautions are not to be taken, if two experienced cryptographers working in their offices are corresponding, as when the units on the battlefront wish to correspond by wireless with the commanding officers in the rear. This is a point that many inventors lose sight of and take advantage of in order to criticize official methods. They wax angry because the government does not adopt their inventions. Perfectly fine razors are, for all their quality, quite dangerous in the hands of a monkey, and certain delicate revolution counters would function pretty poorly on a wheelbarrow. So it is with cryptographic systems devised for the use of thousands upon thousands of officers of high and low ranks who are anything in the world but cryptanalysts. They must encipher in dark shelters with their nerves more or less tense and are likely to forget details, however full of ingeniousness. It cannot be hoped to keep secret the general system, which these men are required to apply. The secret elements must be reduced to a few indicators or keys.

Enciphering in diplomatic posts is susceptible to slips which the general theory cannot foresee. This is frequently true when the duty of enciphering increases too much, and consequently a very inexperienced personnel is employed. Such is the proof of experience to the great joy of cryptanalysts.

---

[1] Those who find that the word "cryptanalyst" does not, by its construction, give sufficient indication of dealing with secret *writing*, might use the word "crypto*graphist*."

A theoretically excellent system may yield much more readily to cryptanalysis than processes scorned by authors who have a too-limited and too-theoretical knowledge of cipher work. This frequently happens when excellent systems are exploited extensively and placed in the hands of too many correspondents. In addition to this element to be considered in the choice of a system, account must be taken of transmission requirements. The use of telegraphy imposes rules from which we are free in letters or in telephone messages. The "Administration" charges for cryptograms by counting the number of letters, except in the case of the words of those languages that belong to a repertory published under the auspices of the Conference at Berne. If the cryptogram can be divided up into sets of ten letters giving pronounceable words, even though they belong to no language, each set is charged for as a word. When the letters give only a random mixture of consonants and vowels, five letters count for a word. It is the same in the case of numbers: Groups representing a word must contain a maximum of five digits. Finally, a mixture of letters and digits is not permitted in a five-letter word. These are elements which cannot be neglected in the preparation of a system for enciphering telegrams, as much for the price of sending as for the ease with which it can be used, and for avoiding errors.[1] We will not dwell upon the qualities to be looked for in a system in each particular case. We will abandon these preliminary questions and will approach the technical definitions of cryptographic systems.

**Classification of cryptographic systems.**—Cryptographic systems can be brought under two heads: *substitution* and *transposition*.

Sometimes also a distinction is made between syllabic and alphabetic systems on one hand and dictionaries or codes on the other.

Substitution systems yield cryptograms in which the elements of the clear text—namely, letters, syllables, words, and even parts of sentences—are replaced by an equivalent, differing from the clear element, but in which the order of the equivalents conforms to the order of the elements of the clear text. Thus, for example, if the same syllable is found at the beginning and the end of the clear text, the element at the beginning and the element at the end of the cipher text represent the same syllable in clear. These are sometimes called conversion systems.

Transposition systems are those where the elements of the clear text keep their identity but in which their order is changed. Thus, for example, if a clear text contains the letter A 10 times, including one appearance at the beginning and one at the end, the cipher text will contain 10 A's, but these A's may be grouped side by side, and the first and last letter of the cryptogram may have nothing in common with A.

These two systems may be combined in such a way that the elements of the clear text are replaced by equivalents, and then these equivalents are mixed up to destroy any order in their succession.

Syllabic or alphabetic systems appertain only to the elements of words. Certain systems give rise to dictionaries or codes, but they are only, properly speaking, substitution systems. They are systems where words in clear are replaced by groups of digits, groups of letters, or French or foreign words, and where the number of words or expressions having equivalents of this kind is so great that the lists of words and their equivalents form material for a whole book.

---

[1] The International Telegraph Conference of Madrid in 1932 completely revised the regulations governing the construction of code words.

## CHAPTER II

## SIMPLE SUBSTITUTION WITH SINGLE EQUIVALENTS

Under the category of substitution, we will also bring together all ciphers in which the letters of the clear text are replaced by signs differing from those ordinarily used in the language of the document, and in which the signs succeed each other in the order of the letters that they represent.

The writing of the text in the Morse code or in the Braille writing for the blind is substitution. So is the transliteration of text into the characters of another tongue. When these characters are little known, cryptanalysts often treat them as they would treat any sort of artificial writing. At the end of the war, the Cipher Bureau received for study many letters written in German by means of cursive Hebrew writing which had been ignored by the French censors. The works of Edgar Allan Poe and Arthur Conan Doyle allude to artificial writing in which, for example, small manikins replace the 24 letters of the alphabet, their arms and legs occupying 24 different positions. Substitution alphabets have been made with music notes, using in certain positions in the scale, whole notes, half notes, quarter notes, etc. Then the cryptogram assumes the innocent aspect of a love song or a fox trot. In works on cryptography, there are numerous examples of artificial writing for use among members of secret orders: for example, the Masonic script. We will not dwell on these rather historical curiosities. We will leave them in favor of substitutions which may be subjected to telegraphic transmission, that is to say, in which the letters and digits are used as in French. Systems of this sort are sometimes defined as literal systems or numerical systems. Those in which the conventional signs are neither letters nor digits are called steganographic systems.

To compose a cryptogram by substitution, the letters of the clear may be replaced by other letters in whose combinations there is no obvious sense. In the simplest case, one cipher letter, and one only, will correspond to each letter of the clear. If the letters of the clear are written out in a list in the normal alphabetical order, and opposite each of them the corresponding cipher letter, together they constitute a substitution alphabet. Thus, we get a system of two alphabets—the clear alphabet and the cipher alphabet. These correspond to one another and may be called the correspondence table relative to the cryptogram. A certain number of technical terms which we are going to indicate below are applied to substitution alphabets for facility of language.

An alphabet in which the letters follow thus: A, B, C, D, . . . Z, beginning with A, is called a *normal* or a normally ordered alphabet. If, however, we are considering an alphabet in which the letters follow in this same order, but which does not begin with A, we will call this alphabet a *regularly ordered* one. When the alphabet is not regularly ordered, it is *mixed*, but there may exist certain relations between the letters. If none exists, and if chance alone has determined the correspondence of the clear and cipher letters, the alphabet is called *random*. When the clear and cipher letters are so grouped in pairs, that if clear M is replaced by cipher X, clear X is replaced by cipher M, then such an alphabet is called *reciprocal*. Often the correspondence table of a reciprocal alphabet is written on two lines, the letters on one line corresponding to those on the other.

```
A B C D E F G H I J K L M
N O P Q R S T U V W X Y Z
```

A=N, N=A, B=O, O=B, etc.

If the last letter of one of the alphabets corresponds to the first of the other, they are sometimes called *reversed* alphabets.

```
A B C D E F G H I J K L M
Z Y X W V U T S R Q P O N
```

In certain works, the name *complementary* alphabets is applied to those in which the total of the alphabetical rank of the clear letter and the cipher letter is constant, as in the example of the ordered, reversed alphabet above. (A, first letter, + Z, twenty-sixth letter, = 27; B, second letter, + Y, twenty-fifth letter, = 27, etc.)

Finally those which are such that the difference between the alphabetical ranks of a letter in one of them and that of the cipher letter which corresponds to it in the other is constant,[1] are called *parallel* alphabets. The expression "sliding" is used with regard to parallel alphabets, meaning that one is slid *n* letters with respect to the other. The alphabet M N O P Q . . . is slid two letters with respect to K L M N O . . . , that is to say, any letter in the first corresponds to that one letter in the second which is two in front of it in the sequence considered.

We have given these definitions only to enable the reader to follow certain works or the description of certain systems. In themselves, they are of no special interest. The chief interest lies in the formation of a substitution alphabet and the manner of devising the key of the system.

When only regularly ordered alphabets are used, we will have a substitution table of the following kind:

```
Clear___ A B C D E F G H I J K L M N O P Q R S T U V W X Y Z
Cipher__ C D E F G H I J K L M N O P Q R S T U V W X Y Z A B
```

and the clear word ENNEMI will be enciphered GPPGOK. The key may be indicated either by the difference of alphabetical order between the cipher letter and the clear letter, that is, +2, or by marking the cipher letter which corresponds to clear A, that is, C.

A substitution system in which the cipher alphabet is an alphabet ordered like that of the clear, but only slid along a certain number of letters, is called the system of Julius Caesar.

Hence, the following observation: If, under each of the cipher letters, we write the entire alphabet in order, always recommencing with A after Z, we will reproduce the clear when all the letters have been changed the same number of times:

```
G P P G O K
H Q Q H P L
I R R I Q M
. . . . . .
. . . . . .
D M M D L H
E N N E M I
F O O F N J
```

The decipherment of cryptograms enciphered by this means is, hence, one of the easiest. It is well to try this process on the beginning of a cryptogram when we are dealing with a document that looks like a substitution, and when it might have come from noncryptanalysts such

---

[1] This statement is not true when a mixed alphabet slides against itself although the author also calls alphabets, obtained in this way, "parallel."

as prisoners, or troopers (we will see further on how opinions are formed on this point). Often long labor and vain pryings are thus avoided.

If random alphabets are used, the key is constructed by the correspondence table. Now, though it may be easy to remember one of the lines of this table—to wit, the clear, ordered alphabet—it may be difficult to remember the other. Moreover, we may have reasons for not keeping it in writing, and for resorting to reconstructing it only when needed. Several means exist for reestablishing mixed alphabets by means of keys easy to recall. We will point out a few of them:

Let the key word be I N F A N T E R I E.

Let us write out in their proper order, on the first line, the letters of the key, setting down each of them only the first time it appears:

I N F A T E R

and let us write under them in lines of the same length (except the last) the other letters of the alphabet in normal order:

```
I N F A T E R
B C D G H J K
L M O P Q S U
V W X Y Z
```

Transcribing this table by columns, we have a mixed alphabet yielding the following correspondence table:

Clear_____A B C D E F G H I J K L M N O P Q R S T U V W X Y Z
Cipher_____I B L V N C M W F D O X A G P Y T H Q Z E J S R K U

and the word ENNEMI will be enciphered NGGNAF.

Let the key word be C O M M I S S I O N   D E   D É L I M I T A T I O N.

Let us write on one line the letters of the key word with no repetitions

C O M I S N D E L T A

and on another line underneath, let us write the rest of the alphabet in normal order:

```
C O M I S N D E L T A
B F G H J K P Q R U V W X Y Z
```

We will consider these two lines as forming a reciprocal alphabet, in which the last letters, W, X, Y, Z, having no equivalents, will not be changed by enciphering. (When using alphabets of this sort, it might be a good idea sometimes to reverse the order of the second line, so that it would not always be the last letters of the alphabet that remain unchanged.)

The word CHAMEAUX will be enciphered BIVGQVTX.

As we have said, instead of replacing clear letters by other letters in substitution, they may be replaced by groups of digits, or of letters, or even by any symbols at all. When we represent the 26 letters of the French alphabet by the 26 letters of an alphabet which may or may not be mixed, taken from this same French alphabet, we usually get but one equivalent for each letter.

If *groups* of letters or digits were used to represent the normal letters of the alphabet, several of these groups could be made to correspond to each letter, since more than 26 groups of this nature can be formed. It is the same if symbols are invented.

Substitutions, in which each clear letter or syllable has but one single equivalent in the correspondence table—be it a single character or a group of characters—will be set apart under the title of simple substitutions. We will add no adjectives to this name, though we sometimes hear simple substitutions with single equivalents.

We are going to continue the study of the simple substitution with single equivalents without any longer considering substitutions in which a single clear letter may have several equivalents. Now we will pass from the systems where one letter is represented by one letter to those in which it is represented by a group.

When groups of letters or digits are used to represent clear letters, we have a substitution table which may be complicated, and, if we do not wish to keep it in writing, we must resort to tricks. We have already spoken about these above with reference to the formation of mixed alphabets in time of need.

A frequently used artifice is that of forming a table of 25 cells. In this, the alphabet, less one letter (usually W which is replaced by two V's), is written in any order. However, this order must be known to the two correspondents (either by rows or columns in natural order, or in mixed order resulting from a key word).

A letter or a digit is made to correspond to each row and each column of such a table. It is agreed to represent each cell by a group of two letters—for example, the letter of the row followed by that of the column (or the reverse—but a prearrangement must be chosen which gives only one equivalent in each case, and not two). The key may be used to fix the letters representing rows and columns.

Example: Key— I N F A N T E R I E

I write in the square a mixed alphabet composed of I N F A T E R followed by the rest of the alphabet. Above the box, I write the first five letters of I N F A T E R; to the left, the last five letters

|   | I | N | F | A | T |
|---|---|---|---|---|---|
| F | I | N | F | A | T |
| A | E | R | B | C | D |
| T | G | H | J | K | L |
| E | M | O | P | Q | S |
| R | U | V | X | Y | Z |

and I agree to represent a clear letter by the letter of the row followed by that of the column.

ENNEMI is replaced by AI FN FN AI EI FI.

In designating rows and columns by digits, all different, agreeing always to place the larger of the two digits first, and forming the table of 25 by inscribing the normal alphabet parallel to a diagonal, the table below

|   | 0 | 2 | 4 | 6 | 8 |
|---|---|---|---|---|---|
| 1 | A | C | F | J | O |
| 3 | B | E | I | N | S |
| 5 | D | H | M | R | V |
| 7 | G | L | Q | U | Y |
| 9 | K | P | T | X | Z |

will yield the following equivalent for the word ENNEMI: 32 63 63 32 54 43.

We might go on making up systems of this kind, but they always imply one rule—to construct the table with the help of a key. Advantage might be found in not fixing any rule, but by choosing the equivalents of each letter by chance, the succession of numbers of the two digits used to represent the letters being, for example, in no wise ordered. During encipherment the clear letter will be easily found in the correspondence table in its alphabetical position and opposite it the cipher number which equals it may be read. Upon decipherment, however, it will be necessary to seek out in the list of numbers without any guide, that one whose meaning we wish to find. To simplify this search, we may make two correspondence tables, one called *enciphering*, in which the clear letters are in alphabetical order and in which the substitution numbers form a random list, the other called *deciphering*, in which the numbers, which are read in the cryptogram, are in numerical order, and can be easily found, each having opposite it the letter to be written in deciphering.

Although groups of two letters or digits may seem sufficient to furnish an ample choice of equivalents for letters, sometimes longer groups have to be dealt with. In that part of cryptography which is more historic than anything else, the alphabet of Lord Bacon is found. In this alphabet, the only characters used are A and B, but each letter is represented by five characters (A=AAAAA, S=AABBB, etc.).

The use of telegraphy today would scarcely authorize such a waste. But by superimposing upon these combinations certain secret preagreements, we may perform certain curious operations upon old ciphers. We may use two forms of letters, for example, all the little letters might stand for A and all the capitals for B. Thus, the word "vingt" in little letters will represent A, while "viNGT" will represent S. An interesting example for study of this sort relative to Shakespeare was published in the *Mercure de France* from 1921 to 1923 by General Cartier, former Chief of the Cipher Section in the Ministry of War.[1] (See the Feb. 1, 1923, number of the *Mercure de France*.) Before pointing out other earmarks of simple substitution systems, we will speak of the decrypting of these systems. Our type will be the cryptogram in which clear letters are represented by cipher letters. It behooves us to observe that many cryptanalysts prefer to make certain changes in cryptograms. When they are dealing with writing they are not familiar with—for example, with steganographic systems—instead of working upon the text as it is, they replace each character by a letter or number. Their eyes are accustomed to these, and they can, thus, see certain peculiarities which would escape them in the original script. So we must be able to recognize and identify the different characters. We will suppose at first that they do not exist in excess of 26, which allows us to imagine that the text might be French, and we will go a step further by assuming that we are really dealing with a message in the French tongue.

Cryptograms are sometimes presented in letter groups of unequal length. This leads us to think that the author enciphered each letter of the clear text and let the word lengths remain intact, but more often and in conformity with telegraphic regulations we deal with series of groups of five letters or digits, in which nothing indicates the beginning and end of words, or, as in letters, with broken lines.

The decrypting of substitutions is based upon the consideration of frequencies.

If we count, in different messages of a given language, sufficiently long to yield fairly reliable probabilities, the number of certain components—such as letters; recurrences of two letters, called "digraphs"; and words frequently used, such as auxiliary verbs, conjunctions, preposi-

---

[1] The study here referred to deals with the "biliteral cipher" of Sir Francis Bacon and with the alleged decipherments obtained by Elizabeth Wells Gallup in applying the principles of that cipher to the Shakespearean First Folio. It is merely necessary to indicate here that the "decipherments" are purely subjective and have never been substantiated by cryptographic experts.

tions, etc.—we find that each one of these elements has an almost constant percentage for the whole number of elements of the same nature (letters, digraphs, words).

Thus, if we consider the number of times that a given letter recurs in a text of a hundred letters, we will find that the percentages or frequencies in French are as follows: [1]

| | | | |
|---|---|---|---|
| E=17 | N=8.7 | A=7.2 | I=6.8 |
| R= 6.8 | S=6.8 | T=6.7 | U=6.7 |
| O= 6.6 | L=4.9 | D=4.6 | C=3.5 |
| M= 3 | P=2.8 | V=1.8 | F=1.3 |
| B= 0.9 | G=0.7 | Q=0.7 | H=0.5 |
| X= 0.5 | J=0.3 | Y=0.3 | Z=0.3 |
| K= 0.01 | W=0.01 | | |

These figures are borrowed from Valerio. Other authors (Viaris, for example) give others which differ somewhat. For practical purposes it must be recalled that E has a normal proportion of from $\frac{1}{5}$ to $\frac{1}{7}$, and that the most frequent letters practically in their order are those which form a word of cabalistic turn, ERASINTULO. The S and the A in the calculations of Viaris actually reach a frequency of 8.0 and 8.2 percent, while N is only 7.2 percent. Another interesting point is the total percentage of the vowels among all the letters, which is 44 percent.

We will observe the frequency of letters in several foreign tongues:

### GERMAN

| | | | |
|---|---|---|---|
| E=18 | N=9.4 | R=7.6 | I=7.2 |
| T= 6.6 | S=6.3 | D=5.5 | U=5.1 |
| A= 4.6 | H=4.4 | L=3.7 | C=3.1 |
| G= 3.0 | O=2.5 | Z=2.4 | M=2.0 |
| B= 1.9 | W=1.6 | F=1.5 | K=1.3 |
| V= 1.0 | P=0.7 | J=0.6 | |

### ENGLISH

| | | | |
|---|---|---|---|
| E=13 | T=9.1 | O=8 | A=8 |
| N= 7.5 | R=7 | I=6.5 | S=6.5 |
| H= 6 | D=4 | L=3.5 | C=3 |
| F= 3 | U=3 | M=2.5 | P=2 |
| Y= 1.5 | W=1.5 | G=1.5 | B=1 |
| V= 1 | K=0.5 | X=0.3 | J=0.1 |
| Q= 0.1 | Z=0.1 | | |

### RUSSIAN (PRE-BOLSHEVIK)

| | | | |
|---|---|---|---|
| О=10 | А=8 | Н=7 | Е=6 |
| Т= 6 | И=5 | Р=5 | В=5 |
| С= 5 | Ь=4.5 | Л=4 | Д=3 |
| Я= 3 | П=3 | К=3 | М=2.5 |
| I= 2 | Ѣ=2 | Ы=2 | У=2 |
| З= 1.5 | Б=1.5 | Ъ=1.5 | Г=1 |
| Ч= 1 | Х=1 | Ж=1 | Ю=1 |
| Й= 1 | Ш=0.5 | Щ=0.3 | Ц=0.2 |
| Э= 0.2 | Ф=0.1 | | |

---

[1] The frequency of E in French is so much greater than in English, and stands so far above all the other letters, that its determination on the basis of frequency alone is made much simpler. This fact should be kept in mind, as the author will often determine E, with certainty, in cases when the corresponding amount of text in English would yield no definite information.

## SPANISH

| | | | |
|---|---|---|---|
| E=14 | A=12 | O=9 | N=7 |
| S= 7 | I= 7 | R=6.5 | L=5.5 |
| D= 5 | C= 5 | T=4.5 | U=3.5 |
| P= 3 | M= 3 | G=1.5 | B=1 |
| Y= 1 | V= 0.9 | F=0.7 | J=0.6 |
| Q= 0.5 | Z= 0.4 | H=0.3 | X=0.2 |
| Ñ= 0.1 | K= 0.0 | W=0.0 | |

## ITALIAN

| | | | |
|---|---|---|---|
| E=12.5 | I=10 | A=10 | O=9 |
| R= 7 | L= 6.5 | N= 6.5 | T=6 |
| S= 6 | C= 4 | D= 4 | P=3 |
| U= 3 | M= 2.5 | G= 2 | V=1.5 |
| H= 1 | B= 1 | Z= 1 | F=1 |
| Q= 0.5 | J= 0.0 | | |

Supplementary information will be found in the first volume of Valerio, on the principal languages (frequent digraphs and various peculiarities), and material of all sorts, as much on the above-mentioned foreign languages as on the French language.

Just as there is a characteristic frequency for letters, so also there is one for combinations of two letters or digraphs. We will again borrow from Valerio the frequency table of French digraphs obtained by picking out sequences of two letters from text of about 1,500 letters. The separation of words has not been taken into account, so that, in this fashion, initial or final Z's or final Q's (ending the word "cinq", for example) may form digraphs with letters that they would never be joined to within the body of a French word. The letters at the top of the table are the initial letters of the digraphs; those to the left, the second letters. Thus, AE is not met with; EA is encountered eight times. The numbers on the lowermost row are the frequencies of the individual letters in a total of 1,500. They differ by a few points from the total of the digits in the column, the initial or final letters of sentences having furnished no digraphs. (See the table just following.)

## TABLE OF DIGRAPHS

(About 1,500 letters)

| | A | B | C | D | E | F | G | H | I | J | K | L | M | N | O | P | Q | R | S | T | U | V | W | X | Y | Z |
|---|---|---|---|---|---|---|---|---|---|---|---|---|---|---|---|---|---|---|---|---|---|---|---|---|---|---|
| A | 1 | 4 | 8 | 12 | 8 | 4 | | 1 | 2 | | | 12 | 3 | 9 | | 6 | | 10 | 5 | 5 | 7 | 7 | | | 1 | 3 |
| B | 3 | | | | | | | | | | | 4 | 1 | 1 | | | | | | | 1 | | | | | |
| C | 4 | | 4 | 12 | | | | 1 | | | | | 10 | 3 | | | | 4 | 8 | | 6 | | | 1 | | |
| D | 1 | | 1 | 1 | 21 | | | 4 | | | | | 8 | 1 | | | | 4 | 13 | 13 | 1 | | 1 | | | |
| E | | 2 | 11 | 32 | 10 | 3 | 4 | 6 | 17 | 2 | | 32 | 19 | 24 | | 8 | | 25 | 19 | 21 | 8 | 9 | | 3 | | |
| F | 1 | | | | 5 | 2 | | 1 | | | | | 2 | | | 1 | | 1 | 1 | | 3 | | | 1 | | |
| G | 2 | | | | 3 | | | 4 | | | | | | | | | | 1 | | | | | | | | |
| H | | 3 | | 2 | | | | | | | | | | | | | | | 1 | | | | | 1 | | |
| I | 10 | 1 | 1 | 8 | 1 | 1 | 1 | | | | | 5 | 8 | 3 | 10 | 1 | | 11 | 12 | 17 | 8 | 4 | | 1 | | |
| J | | | | 1 | | | | | | | | 1 | | | | | | | 1 | | 2 | | | | | |
| K | | | | | | | | | | | | | | | | | | | | | | | | | | |
| L | 9 | 3 | | | 16 | | | | 7 | | | 10 | | 1 | 1 | 1 | | 8 | 6 | 5 | 2 | | | 2 | | 1 |
| M | 4 | | 1 | 1 | 20 | | | 3 | | | | | 1 | | 6 | | | 3 | 2 | 1 | 4 | | | | | |
| N | 18 | | | | 39 | | 4 | | 10 | | | 2 | | 12 | 28 | | | | 1 | 4 | 13 | | | | | |
| O | | 2 | 14 | 2 | | 6 | | | 10 | | | 4 | 6 | 10 | | 11 | | 12 | 6 | 5 | | 6 | | | | 1 |
| P | 8 | | | | 12 | | | | | | | | 4 | | 1 | 2 | | 4 | 3 | 2 | 6 | | | | | |
| Q | 1 | | | | 1 | | | | 1 | | | 1 | | 2 | | | | 1 | 2 | 1 | | | | | | 1 |
| R | 19 | 1 | 2 | 4 | 19 | 2 | 2 | | 7 | | | | 1 | 11 | 4 | | | 3 | 1 | 12 | 15 | 1 | | | | |
| S | 3 | 1 | | | 42 | | | | 8 | | | | 16 | 7 | 4 | | | 3 | 6 | 4 | 9 | | | | | |
| T | 10 | | 2 | | 17 | | | | 18 | | | | 25 | 1 | 1 | | | 7 | 8 | 3 | 8 | | | | | |
| U | 8 | | 6 | 8 | 13 | | 1 | | | | | 4 | 1 | 3 | 27 | 3 | 11 | 3 | 8 | 4 | | | | | | |
| V | 7 | | | | 6 | | | | 2 | | | | 2 | 1 | | | | 4 | 1 | | 5 | | | | | |
| W | | | | | | | | | | | | | | | | | | | | | | | | | | |
| X | | | | | | | | | 6 | | | | | | | | | | | 2 | | | | | | |
| Y | | | | | | | | | | | | 2 | | 2 | 1 | | | | | | | | | | | |
| Z | | | | 1 | | | | | | | | | | | | | | | | 3 | | | | | | |
| | 109 | 14 | 54 | 68 | 255 | 19 | 11 | 8 | 103 | 5 | 0 | 73 | 46 | 131 | 99 | 42 | 11 | 104 | 101 | 101 | 100 | 27 | 0 | 8 | 5 | 4 |

Among the systems that are often made easier by a few timely remarks, we must place that which consists in representing the frequency of a letter by a line whose length is proportional to this frequency. Let us, for example, draw up for French 26 equal lengths as abscissae, and let us, at each point, write a letter of the normal alphabet. Now erect ordinates at these points and lay off on the ordinate of A, a length equal to 7 arbitrary units; on that of B, one unit; on that of C, 3.5 units; D, 4.6 units; E, 17 units; etc. Thus, we get a drawing of characteristic appearance, which we can make still more precise by joining all the extremities of the ordinates by straight lines. This forms the normal graph of the French language. In the method of Julius Caesar, the cipher graph would be analogous to the normal graph displaced parallel to itself.

With the idea of frequency in mind, we will count each character of the cryptogram and determine its frequency on the basis of 100.

In the great majority of cases, and always if the cryptogram is rather long, and has not been forged to make a cryptographic curiosity, the most frequent character will correspond to the letter E.[1]  We remember that we are treating here the case of simple substitutions, and that, in this type of cryptogram, the E's should have a frequency of somewhere between 14 percent and 20 percent.  (If the most frequent letter does not fall between 1/7 and 1/5, we will suspect that we are not dealing with a simple substitution.)

Having determined the most frequent letter, we will replace it in our text by E.

If word lengths actually occur in the cipher, short words will next be considered in which E occurs, DE, LE, NE, EN, JE, ET, EST.  Guiding ourselves by letter frequencies, we will succeed in identifying a certain number of additional characters.  Thus, it will be noted that N is more frequent than D (NE, DE) and very much more frequent than J (JE).  We will also be guided by certain peculiarities of the French tongue: Isolated letters are probably A, J, L, M, N, S, T. A double letter within the body of a word is probably a consonant, while the letters which precede and follow this doublet are very likely vowels.  The discovery of "le" will bring with it the discovery of "les", and "la".  Words themselves present individual peculiarities which enable us to identify them when we know their lengths and one or two letters in them, by making use of lists prepared by great decrypting laboratories (words of $n$ letters having all their letters different, having two letters alike (called a repetition), three letters alike, two repetitions, a doublet, a triplet, no e's, two e's, three e's, etc.).  So, in general, we see that the decrypting of simple substitutions with word lengths is not an extremely difficult task. This is particularly true when we know what language is used, and when we are not dealing with eastern tongues which do not write the vowels.

If the words are not separated, the problem becomes much harder.

A good method to follow, when we have no preconceived idea about the subject of a cryptogram and when we wish to apply the analytical method, is, once having determined E, to write down the letters which precede and follow E, and consider the table of digraphs.

There we see that the digraphs into which E enters are most often consonant-vowel or vowel-consonant groups and much more rarely vowel-vowel diphthongs.  Now, certain vowels are very frequent.  Among the very frequent letters, those which rarely combine with E are very likely vowels.  Among the latter, A is placed only exceptionally before E (the ending of a word in A and the beginning of a word in E, aero, etc.).  IE is much more frequent than EI; the combination of O with E or E with O is very rare; the combination OU is relatively frequent. So, we have factors to study in determining vowels.  As soon as we have discovered a few vowels, we will make assumptions about the remaining ones.  We base these assumptions on considerations of the spacing of vowels in the language.  No French word contains a sequence of five consonants.  Such sequences can only be found by adding to three consonants at the end of a word (the last of which must be S) two consonants at the beginning of the following word.  In any six consecutive letters, one *must* represent a vowel.  The total percentage of vowels, we have said, has to be approximately 44 percent.  If the frequency of a letter, thought to be a vowel, is added to the total frequency of vowels already known, we should have a grand total not much above 44 percent, particularly if it is not the last vowel to be found.

Once the vowels are found, a consideration of digraphs will help in determining the consonants.

Thus, we get the following list for the frequent consonants:

|  |  |
|---|---|
| ES=42 | SE=19 |
| EN=39 | NE=24 |
| EL=16 | LE=32 |
| ER=19 | RE=25 |

[1] See note on p. 9.

S and N follow E oftener than they precede it, while the contrary is true of L and R.

In this way we succeed in establishing the translation of fragments of words, and when these translations allow hypotheses on the letters which precede or follow, these hypotheses are checked by a consideration of frequency.

The method indicated above need not necessarily be developed in a rigorous fashion, a seeking out of vowels, then, of consonants. Whenever an identification is possible, it ought to be assumed and tested. Indeed, it may well be that certain vowels cannot easily be found, but that attention may be attracted by digraphs beginning with E, which recur at intervals of less than a dozen letters. So we will fancy a series of feminine plurals, which will give us ES; the last letter of the message is to be considered from this point of view.

We will not try to discuss any further the procedure to take for these operations. Every cryptanalyst has his little "tricks" in the applications of general procedures. We will only give one example of the manner in which such a problem may be treated.

Let the cryptogram be 130 letters long:

```
YJXMG   XBXUF   JGECU   JEBZD   XAMNM   ZDFLG   FAFNJ   OFNDJ
GVJXE   FNNME   VRJZJ   KAFNB   FNZAG   NCUJE   BNRUX   OFNJG
NNXKX   FELGF   BJRVF   NOFUI   FXAAF   GTFVR   FAFKU   FNBJE
NADXN   VMXUF
```

The frequencies of the cipher letters are:—

A 8, B 6, C 2, D 4, E 7, F 20, G 8, I 1, J 12, K 3, L 2, M 5, N 16, O 3, R 4, T 1, U 7, V 5, X 11, Y 1, Z 4

F is the most frequent letter, 20 out of 130 gives 15½ percent. That is not entirely normal for E, but is a possible proportion, and, the cryptogram being brief, we must not demand too much of results based upon the calculation of frequencies alone.

We surmise that F=E.

Now we are going to count for each letter the digraphs it gives with E. We give below the cipher letters in the order of decreasing frequencies, indicating for each letter the number of times it precedes F by the number preceding the frequency. We will indicate the number of times it follows F by a number following the frequency.

| | | | |
|---|---|---|---|
| N=0–16–8 | J=0–12–1 | X=1–11–1 | G=2–8–1 |
| A=4– 8–2 | E=4– 7–1 | U=3– 7–1 | B=1–6–1 |
| M=0– 5–0 | V=1– 5–1 | D=1– 4–0 | R=1–4–0 |
| K=0– 3–1 | O=3– 3–0 | Z=0– 4–0 | C=0–2–0 |
| L=0– 2–1 | I=1– 1–0 | T=1– 1–0 | Y=1–1–0 |

J, X, and M are probably vowels, since they are frequent and give few digraphs with E.

Counting F, we have four probable vowels. Let us immediately seek to determine the others. The total frequency of F, J, X, and M is 48. Forty-four percent of 130 letters would give 57. The letter Y, being infrequent in the clear, would not augment the total much. It is the letters that occur eight times—that is to say, probably G or A, perhaps E or U—that we must examine for the sought-for vowel. A is to be disregarded. It occurs too often with E. Let us take G as our first assumption.

We may, however, follow another course in looking for our missing vowel. Let us underline in the message the letters F, J, X, and M, admittedly vowels.

```
YJXMG   XBXUF   JGECU   JEBZD   XAMNM   ZDFLG   FAFNJ   OFNDJ
GVJXE   FNNME   VRJZJ   KAFNB   FNZAG   NCUJE   BNRUX   OFNJG
```

Between the sixty-first and sixty-seventh letters we have a sequence of seven letters not underlined, NZAGNCU. One of them has to be a vowel. Now, N occurs too often with E, while Z and C are too infrequent to be a vowel other than Y. However, they are too frequent for Y. U and G remain; G gives fewer digraphs with E (3 out of 8, against 4 out of 7). Other arguments, not decisive when considered alone, when taken together point to G being a vowel. At the eightieth letter, G is in front of a doublet and doublets other than ÉE and rarely OO are consonants (unless we are straddling two words) and are contained between two vowels. If we count the digraphs of hypothetical vowels, F J, X, and M with U and G, we find less for G than for U.

We will, therefore, consider G a vowel. Let us notice that this process of vowel separation by considering intervals, as described in Valerio, is widespread and fruitful. Granting that the two digraphs of X with F disconcerted us, and that we admitted only F, J, and M as vowels, then this process applied to the cryptogram:

```
YJXMG   XBXUF   JGECU   JEBZD   XAMNM   ZDFLG   FAFNJ   OFNDJ
GVJXE   FNNME   VRJZJ   KAFNB   FNZAG   NCUJE   BNRUX   OFNJG
NNXKX   FELGF
```

would give the sequences GXBXU, EBZDXA, NZAGNCU, EBNRUXO, and GNNXKX (in which the frequency of X cannot fail to attract attention) to study. While we are hesitating among several letters in determining the last vowels, we may count for each doubtful letter the number and length of the intervals separating it from the vowels already found (for example, three intervals of length 1, four intervals of 2, one interval of 6), and determine the mean of these intervals, by forming the sum of the product of the number of intervals by their length (for example, $(3\times1)+(4\times2)+(1\times6)$), and by dividing it by the total number of intervals considered $(3+4+1)$. The letter for which this mean is the greatest is most likely the sought-for vowel.

Now let us try to identify our probable vowels, J, X, N, G. The table of digraphs (sequences with E) and the frequencies lead us to identify $J_c$ as A and $M_c$ as O, these two letters yielding few digraphs with E, and A being the more frequent. Similar considerations cause us to adopt $X_c$ as I and $G_e$ as U.

Now let us write these letters into the cryptogram:

```
YJXMG   XBXUF   JGECU   JEBZD   XAMNM   ZDFLG   FAFNJ   OFNDJ
.AIOU   I.I.E   AU...   A....   I.O.O   ..E.U   E.E.A   .E..A

GVJXE   FNNME   VRJZJ   KAFNB   FNZAG   NCUJE   BNRUX   OFNJG
U.AI.   E..O.   ..A.A   ..E..   E...U   ...A.   ....I   .E.AU

NNXKX   FELGF   BJRVF   NOFUI   FXAAF   GTFVR   FAFKU   FNBJE
..I.I   E..UE   .A..E   ..E..   EI..E   U.E..   E.E..   E..A.

NADXN   VMXUF
...I.   .OI.E
```

Let us look for the consonants. Among the frequencies, that of $N_c$ is the greatest. This letter follows E more often than it precedes it. It is the third of the group, presumably of five consonants, from the seventieth to the seventy-fourth letter. It yields series of digraphs $FN_c$ with E which correspond perfectly to possible ES's in a sentence. We conclude, therefore, that $N_c=S$, and we write the S's into the cryptogram.

$U_c$, because of its frequency and because it precedes E oftener than it follows, may correspond to R. If we try to replace $U_c$ by R, we are enabled to guess the beginning of the cryptogram: J'AI OUÏ DIRE. From this, we find that $Y_c=J$ and $B_c=D$. This final result is not contrary to frequencies, but let us notice that sequences of DE are less numerous in our text than usual. We have the digraph UE twice, preceded by $L_c$ which appears only these two times. We conclude then that $L_c = Q$.

To get the series of frequent letters in "ERASINTULO", we still lack NTL. The frequent cipher letters not yet identified are E, A, V — $E_c$ and $V_c$ follow E as often as they precede it, while $A_c$ precedes it one-half oftener than it follows. We will try $A_c$ as L, then relying upon the order of frequency, $E_c$ as N and $V_c$ as T. Having gone thus far with the solution it will become easy to fill in the words and find the clear text.

| | | | | | | | |
|---|---|---|---|---|---|---|---|
| YJXMG | XBXUF | JGECU | JEBZD | XAMNM | ZDFLG | FAFNJ | OFNDJ |
| JAIOU | IDIRE | AUNGR | ANDPH | ILOSO | PHEQU | ELESA | MESHA |
| | | | | | | | |
| GVJXE | FNNME | VRJZJ | KAFNB | FNZAG | NCUJE | BNRUX | OFNJG |
| UTAIN | ESSON | TCAPA | BLESD | ESPLU | SGRAN | DSCRI | MESAU |
| | | | | | | | |
| NNXKX | FELGF | BJRVF | NOFUI | FXAAF | GTFVR | FAFKU | FNBJE |
| SSIBI | ENQUE | DACTE | SMERV | EILLE | UXETC | ELEBR | ESDAN |
| | | | | | | | |
| NADXN | VMXUF | | | | | | |
| SLHIS | TOIRE | | | | | | |

It must be noticed that very often several theories, on the identification of certain letters, must be tried before finding the one that fits. One has just been described here for systematically directing our trials; it is a rather analytical method.

There is another one which is to this first method what the geometric method is to analysis in certain sciences, and, according to the whims of individuals, certain cryptanalysts prefer one to the other. Certain others, incapable of getting the answer with one of the methods in the solution of a difficult problem, conquer it by means of the other, with a disconcerting masterly stroke. This other method is that of the probable word. We may have more or less definite opinions concerning the subject of the cryptogram. We may know something about its date, and the correspondents, who may have been indiscreet in the subject they have treated. On this basis, the hypothesis is made that a certain word probably appears in the text. In the text, a series of letters is sought which reproduces the formula of this word—its peculiarities of spelling.

Let us suppose that after a conversation with the addressee of the preceding cryptogram, we imagine that the text contains the word PHILOSOPHE, or PHILOSOPHIE.

In the cryptogram, we will have to find a sequence in which a digraph corresponding to PH is repeated at a five-letter interval. P and H are rather infrequent letters. The three letters preceding the second digraph will be frequent, and O itself will be found twice. Certain cryptanalysts, just beginning on such a cryptogram, never start with a consideration of frequencies. But underneath their cryptogram, written out in such a fashion that all the letters are equally spaced, they move a piece of paper along, containing, at equal intervals, the letters of the word PHILOSOPH, which they will easily identify with ZDXAMNMZD. Having thus got a "break" into the cryptogram they will deduce the unknown letters from the known letters and from the text.

In certain classes of documents, military or diplomatic telegrams, banking and mining affairs, etc., it is not impossible to make very important assumptions about the presence of certain words in the text. After a cryptanalyst has worked for a long time with the writings of certain correspondents, he gets used to their expressions. He gets a whole load of words to try out; then the changes of key, and sometimes of system, no longer throw into his way the difficulties of an absolutely new study, which might require the analytical method.

# CHAPTER III

## SIMPLE SUBSTITUTION WITH VARIANTS

We have dwelt at length upon the solution of simple substitutions; for we must know the procedure perfectly in order to approach the solution of more complicated substitutions.

In fact, the methods of increasing the labor of the cryptanalyst in substitutions are very numerous.

We have seen that the basis of solution is the notion of frequency. The most frequent letter corresponds to E. We are going to try to mask these frequencies, so that the most frequent letter will no longer be E, and the cryptanalyst will be retarded.

We may, for example, distinguish between E accented (which has its place in the Morse alphabet) and E unaccented.

Another rather simple procedure which does not augment the number of equivalents in the correspondence table, and requires only the use of the 26 letters of the alphabet, is to give E several equivalents and to suppress those of rarely occurring letters. Clear J may be replaced by I, W by two V's, K by C or Q.

By these means the frequency of E is distributed among several characters.

The cryptanalyst must face the possibility of such a trick. If he is working along the lines of a probable word, he will not worry about various equivalents for E in the word he is trying. If he is following the analytical route, he will refer to a table of digraphs which he will draw up for his cryptogram according to the model of the normal digraph table given above. Then, he will notice that certain letters produce digraphs with many other letters of the alphabet, leaving but relatively few cells empty in their row and column. These letters are likely to be vowels, especially if they combine little among themselves, and thus more vowels may be discovered than the alphabet of the language used contains. Questions of doublets (probable consonants) and letters which precede and follow them (probable vowels) must be carefully examined. Finally, it would be a good idea to make a search for what we are going to speak of now for the first time but which we will mention very often in the course of these studies—namely, repetitions.

Let us suppose that "ENNEMI" is enciphered twice in the cryptogram.

Let us suppose that E has two equivalents and that these two encipherments are the following: FGGWNJ and FGGFNJ.

If the encipherer were very careful, this assumption would probably not appear, and "ENNEMI" would always be enciphered in the same fashion. But all encipherers are fallible. So we conclude (none too boldly) that W and F are two equivalents for the same letter of the clear. Then, replacing the second of the two equivalents, wherever it appears, by the first, we will reduce our cryptogram to the simple substitution that we know how to deal with. So, in the cryptogram, we will look for all the sequences that are almost identical. We will underline them with colored pencils, or we will transfer them to another sheet of paper so we can compare them. These comparisons may lead us to recognize that we are no longer dealing with a simple substitution proper but rather with a simple substitution with variant values. Moreover, they will serve at the same time to reduce the latter to a simple substitution proper.

This process, which may no longer work with a literal correspondence table, may assume a great extension if arbitrary characters, or groups of letters or digits, are used. In practice, we often have to study cryptograms enciphered by simple substitutions with variants; that is to say, with correspondence tables in which a given cipher character or digraph always stands for the same clear letter, but in which a clear letter may be represented by several cipher characters or polygraphs.

Such systems may be developed in two ways: By a correspondence table (or an enciphering and deciphering table), in which all the clear letters with their different equivalents opposite them appear in a column, or by tables of 25 cells, like those we spoke of, but in which we use several equivalents for each letter.

If we place the 25 letters in the 25 cells, and let each column and each row correspond to a letter or digit chosen so that the groups obtained by reading in the order row-column would never be formed in the order column-row, we would have two equivalents for each cell according to whether we let the row letter follow the column letter, or vice versa. (For example, the column indicators may be different from the row indicators.)

|   | 1 | 2 | 5 | 6 | 9 |
|---|---|---|---|---|---|
| 3 | A | F | H | J | N |
| 4 | G | B | L | P | R |
| 7 | I | M | C | T | V |
| 8 | K | G | U | D | Y |
| 0 | O | S | N | Z | E |

TABLE A

In the table above, L may be represented by 45 or 54 without fear of confusion. By permitting several equivalents for each column and each row the equivalents of the letters are multiplied

| | 1 2 | 3 4 | 5 6 | 7 8 | 9 0 |
|---|---|---|---|---|---|
| 1, 3 | Z | J | K | L | M |
| 5, 7 | Y | I | B | C | N |
| 9, 0 | X | H | A | D | O |
| 2, 4 | V | G | F | E | P |
| 6, 8 | U | T | S | R | Q |

TABLE B

| | I E | N R | F B | A C | T D |
|---|---|---|---|---|---|
| G, M | F | G | H | I | J |
| H, P | P | Q | R | S | T |
| J, Q | U | V | X | Y | Z |
| K, S | K | L | M | N | O |
| L, X | A | B | C | D | E |

TABLE C

In table B, depending upon the order column-row or row-column, we have likewise four equivalents per letter. For example, in row-column order, H is represented by 93, 94, 03, or 04. But the order must be fixed; for in column-row order 93 would represent M, and 04, P.

In table C, the column letters being different from those of the rows, we have eight equivalents per letter. Q may be replaced by HN, HR, PN, PR, NH, NP, RH, RP.

Cryptograms of this nature are complicated enough even though a single correspondence table is used for some time, and we are able to get an appreciable quantity of text for study.

The principle of cryptanalytic research is the study of repetitions. We must strive to lessen the number of equivalents for a given letter. In practice, this is often easier than theory would suggest. The infrequent letters offer information as useful as the letters of the "ERASINTULO" series, for which the frequencies have been diminished. Let us consider, then, table C just as constructed, and let us imagine a cryptogram enciphered by means of this table. The combinations equaling Z (T, D, J, Q)[1] will be infrequent or missing. On the contrary, (T, D, K, S)=O and (T, D, L, X)=E will be frequent. In the next column (A, C, J, Q)=Y are infrequent, (A, C, K, S)=N are frequent. Thus, we come to consider K, S as forming a part of a combination indicating a row or column other than J, Q, since these two last letters appear infrequently with A, C, T, D, while K and S frequently appear there. With sufficient data, we can identify among them certain ones indicating rows and columns, and reduce their number. But, as we have said, it is upon repetitions we must count when the encipherer uses certain given groups for some of the appearances of particular letters and different groups for the others.

Example: Let the beginning of two telegrams be

|     |       |       |       |       |       |       |       |       |
|-----|-------|-------|-------|-------|-------|-------|-------|-------|
| (1) | IPTSQ | IFPIX | HDTPE | LXBGF | TXSBA | MSNAG | HDXIM | CPFTX |
| (2) | EPSTQ | IPFEX | TPDPX | IXBMF | DLKBG | CNSAM | TPLIC | GBHTL |

Both of these, with table C, mean: "POUR ATTACHÉ MILITAIRE". By writing them one under the other and comparing them, it is seen that, in the fourth group, one of the sequences is XBGF while the other is XBMF. This leads us to suppose that M in the second message may be equivalent to G in the first. This assumption is checked in the sixth group (AG=AM). The general appearance of groups 1 and 2, in which TS corresponds to ST and FP with PF will attract the keen attention of an *experienced* cryptanalyst, and make him imagine a biliteral cipher, single letters being represented by digraphs *in which the order is immaterial*, (TS=ST). This fundamental observation having been made, the comparison of the two messages will make it possible to retrieve the elements determining rows and columns. (IP=EP, therefore I=E, strengthened by IX=EX; DP=TP=HD, whence D=T, H=P, etc.) In practice, to be sure, such things will certainly not be very often easy to recognize with only two messages, but numerous comparisons, assiduously made, sometimes at the end of a few days or several weeks, lead to the observation of a detail which results in identifications such as we have here imagined, and permits the cryptanalyst to recognize both the system and the elements of the solution.

The probable word method combined with frequencies should be used in these labors. We have used it in studies which gave results for many successive years in the following manner: The infrequent letters remain infrequent regardless of the system. We would determine the frequency of each digraph, and we would assume a probable word, such as the word PHILOSOPHE, cited earlier, in which infrequent letters are found at certain intervals. (We are not talking about a repetition, but only of *infrequent letters*, which may be different.) Foreign proper names such as WILHELM or SAZONOFF are often advantageous in this respect. After having underlined in

[1] By the notation (T, D, J, Q), the author means a cipher digraph with one letter chosen from the first two (T, D), and the other chosen from the last two (J, Q.).

different ways the very frequent digraphs and the very infrequent digraphs of the cryptogram, we would run a sheet of paper along underneath it, upon which the interval of the infrequent letters was marked. Each coincidence was examined, letter by letter, and checked with the frequencies. Then we would try to decrypt part of the telegram. Many trials were necessary, but often we reached happy results.

In practice, we have not often met with literal substitutions using variants. We have met with many in digits. Before the war, telegrams, thus enciphered, used to be transmitted most often in groups of five or four digits. A prime difficulty was to distinguish them from telegrams enciphered with codes, which are transmitted in the same way. First, the total number of the digits of the document had to be counted. If this number was even, and not a multiple of four or five, it was a first indication that the system was cipher and not code. Then the repetitions were attacked, and if, on this score also, repetitions were found whose lengths though even were still not multiples of four or five, the supposition was strengthened. Finally, repetitions having numerous coincidences of two digits were scarcely admissible in code. Thus, for example:

2432   1614   1846   2539   and   2432   8514   1872   8039

It is to be noticed that human nature is so constituted that it is extremely rare when an encipherer has several equivalents at his disposal for a letter or a word that he does not adopt certain ones, whose frequency is double or triple that of the others in the long run. This facilitates the task of cryptanalysts by making certain frequencies stand out.

The tables employed by encipherers can often be replaced by a square of 100 numbered cells, in which the clear letters are inscribed, giving more equivalents to frequent letters than to the others. This is true if the work is done by a cryptanalyst, but such a precaution is usually not taken if it is done by a layman. In either case, certain letters strike the eye more easily than others in these squares. That is one of the causes which prompt encipherers to use a given equivalent for a letter rather than other less noticeable equivalents for the same letter.

When the system employed by correspondents is known to be in groups of two digits or two letters, we begin by dividing up the cryptogram into sets of two characters to separate the letters and examine their frequencies. A given group of two always represents the same letter of the text. We may count the frequency of each one of these groups, and thus begin the study of the cryptogram on that basis.

However, it is often sought to throw the cryptanalyst off his track from the very beginning of his study, and there are methods of breaking this regular succession of groups of two. Thus, the cryptanalyst thinks he is reckoning with a group representing a clear letter, but he is really joining the second character of such a group and the first character of the following group, and his labor is in vain.

Among these processes, we may cite several:

(A) A correspondence table formed by numbers of one and two digits, such that the cryptographer immediately recognizes groups of one digit and those of two.

| A | B | C | D | E | F | G | H | I | J | K | L | M | N | O | P | Q | R | S | T | U | V | W | X | Y | Z |
|---|---|---|---|---|---|---|---|---|---|---|---|---|---|---|---|---|---|---|---|---|---|---|---|---|---|
| 1 | 2 | 3 | 4 | 5 | 60 | 66 | 67 | 68 | 69 | 70 | 76 | 77 | 78 | 79 | 80 | 86 | 87 | 88 | 89 | 90 | 96 | 97 | 98 | 99 | 00 |

(Preference should be given to a random alphabet, but the principle would be the same: Five of the digits are employed only in one-digit groups; the other five, only in two-digit groups.)

(B) A table of 25 cells formed with letters indicating rows and columns, all different from those of the first row of the table, for example, and the prearrangement that these letters of the first row will be enciphered by themselves (or by their neighbor to the right on the row instead of being enciphered by a group of two letters).

|       |     | A<br>E | D<br>H | G<br>V | U<br>C | B<br>F |
|-------|-----|--------|--------|--------|--------|--------|
|       |     | J      | K      | L      | M      | N      |
| I, X  |     | A      | B      | C      | O      | P      |
| O, Q  |     | D      | E      | F      | Q      | R      |
| S, Y  |     | G      | H      | I      | S      | T      |
| P, Z  |     | U      | V      | X      | Y      | Z      |

ITALIE will be enciphered GY BS EX L VY HO.

(C) The introduction of nulls, either digits or letters. Let us take, for example, a correspondence table from 00 to 99, in which we suppress all numbers beginning with 4. In the succession of cipher digits the group 44 cannot appear, since the 4 which ends 04, 14, 24, etc., will never be followed by the 4 of a group in the 40's, while 22, 33, etc., will occur, either by such successions (13 followed by 35, for example), or because 33 is in the correspondence table. If we write a null 4 following a cipher 4 before the group representing the next letter, we will have interpolated a digit that will break the cadence of groups of two and which the decipherer will know to be a null, since 44 does not exist otherwise. He will discard it, and pay no attention to it.

Example: Let a portion of the table be

| E  | I  | M  | N  | O  | P  | R  | S  | U  |
|----|----|----|----|----|----|----|----|----|
| 17 | 24 | 36 | 38 | 61 | 72 | 83 | 84 | 94 |
| 19 |    |    | 54 |    |    |    |    |    |
| 25 |    |    |    |    |    |    |    |    |

"ENNEMI REPOUSSÉ" may be translated by 17385 42536 24483 17726 19484 48419. The cryptanalyst, ignorant of the null, will divide it up thus: 17 38 54 25 36 24 48 31 77 26 19 48 44 84 19, and will find two groups 19, for example, when only one has been used (and two groups 48 when neither was actually gotten from the table).

We will not tarry with these procedures which complicate substitutions by variants. Even when many documents devised from the same table are at hand, decrypting is ordinarily difficult; the basis of solution is the comparison of the repetitions, making possible the elimination of the causes of confusion, and the consideration of frequencies.

It would be wise to arrive at the latter by series from 50 to 100 groups at most, so as to make sure that the general trend of the frequency graph does not change too much in the course of a document, a phenomenon which might be produced, by the methods noted above, to lead us astray on the formation of digraphs. Then, particularly by means of frequency graphs, we may be led to compare the frequencies obtained with shifts of one letter or digit in the succession of sets of two. The comparison of graphs, with or without shifts, revealing comparable parts, may put us on the track of the shifts in the cryptogram and the method used. In any case, we do not know any hard and fast rules to apply to cryptograms of this nature.

But, along these lines, we have better yet. We have seen how correspondents used the same system and the same table for a pretty considerable number of documents furnishing us with several elements for study. Now, there are systems where the alphabet changes with each cryptogram or even several times in the course of a single one. It is obviously quite easy to have quite a few cipher alphabets and to change them as frequently as is wished, indicating by an order number or a specially reserved group the alphabet used. Tables in which row or column indicators are changed at the correspondents' will, the correspondents having indicated the enciphering elements either by agreements as to the dates of documents or by special words at the beginnings of messages, will give the same results.

We will treat summarily an example of the use of a device giving a substitution with easily changeable variants.

Suppose we know that the enemy is using devices in which, between two series of digits variable only as the whole process changes, a strip of paper bearing the letters of the alphabet in keyed order is placed. Date and hour agreements fix the position of the movable strip with respect to the series of digits.

At the beginning of the operations, the position of the strip was rarely changed, and we had a chance to get several telegrams enciphered with the same equivalents (two for each letter). Among different telegrams intercepted on the third day, let us choose two of those whose beginnings offer striking similarities:

EM. groupe armées à 7ᵉ et 8ᵉ corps – 2 h. – 66316 13819 52575 32060 64593
82364 13663 03920 68501 55322 10381 73916 22642 06133 17321 16634
60303 93138 66206 43860 52596 12038 17206 06468 38356 45520 66605
86638 52381 96162 53201 45623 38236 61364 10392 06850 61105 35510
24226 65515 35645 62066 50

EM. groupe à 7ᵉ corps – 5 h. – 66386 13119 61573 92060 64683 11766 13643
03920 59502 32052 12615 51017 64162 26650 59535 52060 66593 13564
55346 66064 31926 41917 66525 61123 64561 21711 32662 06010 39313
86620 64316 06853 56206 06668 31146 45520 6660

If we count the frequencies of the two-digit groups in these two messages, we find:

| | 10 | 11 | 12 | 13 | 14 | 15 | 16 | 17 | 19 | 20 | 22 | 23 | 24 | 30 | 31 | 32 | 33 | 34 | 35 |
|---|---|---|---|---|---|---|---|---|---|---|---|---|---|---|---|---|---|---|---|
| First message | 4 | 1 | 0 | 2 | 1 | 2 | 1 | 3 | 2 | 10 | 3 | 3 | 1 | 2 | 2 | 1 | 1 | 1 | 2 |
| Second message | 2 | 2 | 2 | 1 | 1 | 0 | 1 | 4 | 2 | 8 | 1 | 2 | 0 | 1 | 7 | 1 | 0 | 1 | 1 |

| | 38 | 39 | 50 | 52 | 53 | 55 | 56 | 57 | 58 | 59 | 60 | 61 | 62 | 64 | 66 | 68 | 92 |
|---|---|---|---|---|---|---|---|---|---|---|---|---|---|---|---|---|---|
| First message | 10 | 4 | 3 | 3 | 4 | 3 | 2 | 1 | 1 | 2 | 5 | 5 | 1 | 8 | 9 | 3 | 0 |
| Second message | 2 | 3 | 2 | 2 | 2 | 4 | 3 | 1 | 0 | 3 | 6 | 4 | 0 | 9 | 10 | 1 | 1 |

These observations confirm our suspicions that the two messages have really been enciphered with the same key. The same groups are frequent, and, which is an even better indication, the same groups are infrequent. This is true since a frequent letter, which has several equivalents, may or may not give an infrequent group, but an infrequent letter yields only infrequent groups.

Then, if we examine the messages, we see that certain sets offer numerous similarities. We will go on the theory that they represent the same words.

First message beginning_____ 66 31 61 38 19 52 57 53 20 60 64 59 38 23 64 13
Second message beginning____ 66 38 61 31 19 61 57 39 20 60 64 68 31 17 66 13
First message group 28_____ 66 38 52 38 19 61 62 53 20 14 56 23 38 23 66 13

66 30 39 20 68 50
64 30 39 20 59 50
64 10 37 20 68 50

First message group 15_____ 17 32 11 66 34 60 30 39 31 38 66 20 64 38 60
Second message group 26_____ 17 11 32 66 20 60 10 39 31 38 66 20 64 38 60

First message group 23_____ 60 64 68 38 35 64 55 20 66 60
First message end_____           35 64 56 20 66 50
Second message group 16_____ 60 66 59 31 35 64 55 34 66 60
Second message end_____ 60 66 68 31 35 64 55 20 66 60

and we deduce the following sets of equivalents: 38=31, 61=52, 53=39, 66=64, 68=59, 62=57, 23=17, 32=11, 34=20, 30=10, 60=50.

A certain prudence is necessary in these guesses. Words very much alike, say like CHARMES and CHARLES, might give rise to an erroneous assumption, causing the group representing M to be confused with that equaling L. Also we will not consider differences bearing on more than one letter enframed between two given groups or two groups recognized otherwise as equivalents, and we will not take account of the 14, 56, 23 sequence in the thirty-first 5-digit group of the first message. When the soil is less fertile than in the example above, such observations as the following may be made: Group 31 is frequent in the second message and infrequent in the first. It is possible that the encipherer happened to use more particularly a different equivalent in each message; group 38, infrequent in the second and frequent in the first message, might quite possibly be coupled with 31 to give a constant frequency.

Let us now replace, in one of the cryptograms, the groups whose equivalency we think we know, taking in each case the smaller of the two numbers. We will get:

64 31 52 31 19 52 57 39 20 50 64 59 31 17 64 13 64 10
39 20 59 50 15 39 22 20 31 17 39 16 22 64 20 52 .. ..

Sixty-four is the most frequent group. It occurs 17 times in 106 letters. This frequency is rather weak for E. Substituting, we get:

E . . . . . . . . . E . . . E . E . . etc.

As we do not want to weary ourselves with this example, we will say that the address gave the cryptanalyst the idea of trying these three E's in the word "SEPTIÈME." Fitting in the letters thus obtained, we get:

64 31 52 31 19 52 57 39 20 50 64 59 31 17 64 13 64 10 39 20
 E  T     T                 S  E  P  T  I  E  M  E

59 50 15 39 22 10 31 17 39 16 22 64 20 52
 P              T  I           E

With the repetitions of 52 as confirmation, we guess the word "ÉTAT—MAJOR", and since 19 gives M, it has the same value as 13 which gave the M of SEPTIÈME. Likewise, by fitting in the newly found letters, we see the word FONCTIONNERA taking shape, and we conclude from this decrypting that N is given by 22 and 64.

Now we are able to retrieve the value of the two groups assigned to each letter, and get this sort of table:

| A | B | C | D | E | F | G | H | I | J | K | L | M | N | O | P | Q | R | S | T | U | V | X | Y | Z |
|---|---|---|---|---|---|---|---|---|---|---|---|---|---|---|---|---|---|---|---|---|---|---|---|---|
| 52 | 21 | 10 | 37 | 64 | ? | ? | 14 | 17 | 57 | 58 | 11 | 13 | 16 | 39 | 59 | ? | 20 | 50 | 31 | 55 | 12 | ? | 24 | ? |
| 61 | 69 | 30 | 92 | 66 | ? | ? | 35 | 23 | 62 | ? | 32 | 19 | 22 | 53 | 68 | ? | 34 | 60 | 38 | 56 | 33 | ? | ? | ? |

permitting the two messages to be translated:

      1°. État-major septième corps fonctionnera Villers-Cotterets à partir 7 heures.
K. État-major huitième corps à Coucy 9 heures.

      2°. État-major septième corps ira Vauciennes pour 7ʰ 1/2 au lieu Villers-Cotterets pour 7 heures.

There are some letters for which only one equivalent was found, or even none at all.

If, for example, on the morrow, the enemy changes the position of the movable strip, and we have enough telegrams, or rather telegrams advantageous for finding frequencies, we will again be able to decrypt the correspondence and we will get a new table.

| A | B | C | D | E | F | G | H | I | J | K | L | M | N | O | P | Q | R | S | T | U | V | X | Y | Z |
|---|---|---|---|---|---|---|---|---|---|---|---|---|---|---|---|---|---|---|---|---|---|---|---|---|---|
| 11 | 16 | 50 | 39 | 23 | 10 | 21 | ? | 64 | ? | ? | 24 | 14 | 52 | 31 | 24 | ? | 20 | 17 | 59 | 55 | 12 | 20 | ? | 33 |
| 32 | 22 | 60 | 53 | 71 | 30 | ? | ? | 66 | ? | ? | 54 | 35 | 61 | 38 | 54 | ? | ? | 23 | 68 | 56 | 33 | ? | ? | ? |

By comparison with the first table, we may complete the grouping of digits which go by two's, and write 34 under 20.

We will thus be capable of translating telegrams reduced to simple single-letter substitutions; however, each change of the position of the strip will make necessary painstaking labors, sometimes thorny with difficulties. Now we have a problem: to reconstruct a combination that will produce the same results as the device. This means one in which, by a simple shifting of the strip bearing the alphabet correctly reconstructed, between the rows of digits correctly arranged, we may pass from one decipherment to another. Thus, it is necessary to arrange letters and digits according to a rule, so that when A is shifted from 52 to 11, the letter B is shifted from 21 to 16, and so on. This means that the interval from 52 to 11 in the series of numbers written on the device is equal to the interval from 21 to 16, etc. In chapter 9 will be found the solution to this problem.

So then, having reconstructed a device enjoying the same properties as that of the enemy, to wit: such that, for a position of the letter A opposite any given group whatever, all the letters are found opposite the groups representing them, we can read the telegrams even with material insufficient to help us find a table analogous to those preceding. A diagram of frequencies for the letters of the strip in their order compared with a diagram of the digits of the cryptogram in order parallel with the numbers written on the device will permit us to find the position of the strip immediately. The crests and troughs of the two diagrams are made to coincide by simply slipping the strip along.

Such devices have been used. Those who used them would change the position of the strip frequently, but the position was shown by placing, at the head of the message, an indicator in the form of one of the two groups to be placed opposite a given letter, like A 11, or I 66, and so on. With a large number of messages, it was thus made possible to group those with the same indicator, and this information facilitated the segregation of cryptograms in the same key.

A system of the same kind is described in the treatise on cryptography by Carmona (Madrid, 1894). The device comprises a strip bearing a random alphabet sliding along a table in which each column, corresponding to a letter in each position of the strip, contained several equivalents. This problem, a little further complicated by the multiplicity of variants, would be attacked in the same manner.

But the device with two equivalents, just studied, which Fleissner says Carmona attributes to Austrian cryptanalysts, has to our knowledge been employed in yet another fashion. Starting with a given position on the strip, a series of say 10 letters was enciphered, then the strip was shifted a certain number of letters to encipher the next 10 letters, and so on. There is another way still: After any number of letters a change in the strip's position was indicated by means of an infrequent letter. As an indicator, the new position of this infrequent letter or of A was given, and another set of length different from the first was enciphered. In this wise, cryptograms quite secure from solution were devised, but they can no longer be properly spoken of as simple substitutions; for even in the course of one document, a given cipher group has different meanings. By reducing the lengths of successive sets to one single letter, we have a classic type of substitution known as polyalphabetic, a system which will be the object of the next chapter.

Before closing the discussion of variant substitutions, we will point out those made with the almost inexhaustible reservoir of a printed volume. By agreeing to use a certain work and a certain page, prearranged or indicated at the head of the cryptogram, we can replace each letter of the alphabet by an indicator of the line and of the place in the line where the letter occurs, thus changing the position indicators with each new occurrence. Often this system is recognized by the appearance of cryptograms formed by groups of two numbers. As there are no repetitions, in theory, such a process is absolutely secure, but letters are therein represented by three or four character groups and this is cumbersome. In practice, we have seen such cryptograms successfully solved. This is sometimes made possible by the laziness of encipherers who let repetitions slip in, or who do not separate the letters of conjunctions, articles, and so on, so that these short words are recognized by the presence of two neighboring letters on the same line. With a sufficient number of messages, we have seen cryptanalysts succeed in solving messages of this type.

# Chapter IV

# POLYALPHABETS: VIGENÈRE'S SYSTEM AND SIMILAR SYSTEMS

## GENERAL REMARKS

At the end of the preceding chapter we alluded to changes in the correspondence table in the course of a given cryptogram. Systems like this require, on the part of the decipherer, knowledge of two conventions: First, the formation of the correspondence tables; second, the order in which they are used. These agreements between encipherer and decipherer, we have said, constitute the keys of the system. Now we will take systems requiring two keys: They are called polyalphabetic substitutions. As will be seen in the course of this study, polyalphabetic systems are easy to invent and their diversity is great. A certain number of them are classic and have afforded interesting experiments. We will talk of them first, not so much because we meet with them frequently today as because it seems to us utterly indispensable to know perfectly how to solve them in order to approach the more complicated systems related to them.

First, we will make some study of alphabetic systems. Instead of using a given correspondence table between the clear and the cipher alphabets which yields a simple substitution, suppose we have several different correspondence tables, and that we use them successively, changing tables with each letter of the clear. The letter E of the clear, for example, will be given by a different letter in every one of these tables. Inversely, any cipher letter M will correspond to different clear letters according to the table. Thus, while in simple substitution proper, a clear letter was always given by the same cipher character which always stood for that letter alone, and while in simple substitution with variants, though a clear letter had different cipher equivalents, the latter each represented only this one letter, on the other hand, in polyalphabetic substitution, we will have different equivalents for a clear letter according to where it is placed in the cryptogram, and one cipher letter may represent successively different clear letters.

To make it clearer, let us take a simple example: Suppose we have three correspondence tables comprising three regularly ordered substitution alphabets opposite the normal clear alphabet. Suppose these substitution alphabets are slid along the normal alphabet through spaces of 1, 2, or 3 letters so that these tables, which we will in the future often designate by the initial letter of the substitution alphabet in them, (we will call, for example, alphabet 2, alphabet "c") are:

| Table 1 | Table 2 | Table 3 |
|---------|---------|---------|
| A–B | A–C | A–D |
| B–C | B–D | B–E |
| C–D | C–E | C–F |
| etc. | etc. | etc. |

We agree to use these tables successively in the order 1, 2, and 3.
The word ENNEMI will turn out to be FPQFOL.

# POLYALPHABETIC SUBSTITUTIONS USING NORMAL ALPHABETS

**Vigenère.**—In the classic systems that we are first going to examine, normally ordered alphabets are used. In order to avoid preparing for every cryptogram the tables to be used, the discovery of which on a bit of stray paper would lighten the cryptanalyst's task by stopping the search for the alphabets in question, what in France is called "Vigenère's square table" is used. This is named after the French cryptanalyst of the seventeenth century whom certain authors consider as the inventor of a system long regarded as extremely difficult to solve. Others trace the paternity of the system to Trithemius. We will not dwell on questions of inventions in cryptography; the secrecy that ordinarily hovers over the practical applications of this science is quite favorable to the competition of authors. The Vigenère table is presented herein.

As we see, it is composed of as many normally ordered alphabets as there are letters in the alphabet, each slid one letter with respect to the preceding one. Twenty-four- or twenty-five-letter tables may be made by suppressing W and one other letter, J or K.

In using this table,[1] we will agree to designate each alphabet by its first letter—the one which corresponds to clear A. If we have ENNEMI to encipher by successively using alphabets B, C, K, L, we proceed thus: At the intersection of row E and column B, we find the first letter, F; of row N and column C, the second letter, P; of N and K, the third letter, X; of E and L, the fourth letter, P. Then we begin again with alphabet B, and at the intersection of row M and column B we find the fifth letter, N; of I and C, the last letter, K. Thus: F P X P N K.

The letters in order designating the alphabets to be used are the only key afforded us, since none is necessary to form the alphabets. In this case, the key is B C K L. Usually, in order to facilitate memorizing, a key word or phrase in a known tongue is given. This is called a "clear" key. A key comprising a series of jumbled letters is called "random."

---

[1] The reader should observe that the column indicator designates the alphabet, and that the row indicator gives the letter to be enciphered.

## VIGENÈRE'S SQUARE TABLE

|   | A | B | C | D | E | F | G | H | I | J | K | L | M | N | O | P | Q | R | S | T | U | V | W | X | Y | Z |
|---|---|---|---|---|---|---|---|---|---|---|---|---|---|---|---|---|---|---|---|---|---|---|---|---|---|---|
| A | A | B | C | D | E | F | G | H | I | J | K | L | M | N | O | P | Q | R | S | T | U | V | W | X | Y | Z |
| B | B | C | D | E | F | G | H | I | J | K | L | M | N | O | P | Q | R | S | T | U | V | W | X | Y | Z | A |
| C | C | D | E | F | G | H | I | J | K | L | M | N | O | P | Q | R | S | T | U | V | W | X | Y | Z | A | B |
| D | D | E | F | G | H | I | J | K | L | M | N | O | P | Q | R | S | T | U | V | W | X | Y | Z | A | B | C |
| E | E | F | G | H | I | J | K | L | M | N | O | P | Q | R | S | T | U | V | W | X | Y | Z | A | B | C | D |
| F | F | G | H | I | J | K | L | M | N | O | P | Q | R | S | T | U | V | W | X | Y | Z | A | B | C | D | E |
| G | G | H | I | J | K | L | M | N | O | P | Q | R | S | T | U | V | W | X | Y | Z | A | B | C | D | E | F |
| H | H | I | J | K | L | M | N | O | P | Q | R | S | T | U | V | W | X | Y | Z | A | B | C | D | E | F | G |
| I | I | J | K | L | M | N | O | P | Q | R | S | T | U | V | W | X | Y | Z | A | B | C | D | E | F | G | H |
| J | J | K | L | M | N | O | P | Q | R | S | T | U | V | W | X | Y | Z | A | B | C | D | E | F | G | H | I |
| K | K | L | M | N | O | P | Q | R | S | T | U | V | W | X | Y | Z | A | B | C | D | E | F | G | H | I | J |
| L | L | M | N | O | P | Q | R | S | T | U | V | W | X | Y | Z | A | B | C | D | E | F | G | H | I | J | K |
| M | M | N | O | P | Q | R | S | T | U | V | W | X | Y | Z | A | B | C | D | E | F | G | H | I | J | K | L |
| N | N | O | P | Q | R | S | T | U | V | W | X | Y | Z | A | B | C | D | E | F | G | H | I | J | K | L | M |
| O | O | P | Q | R | S | T | U | V | W | X | Y | Z | A | B | C | D | E | F | G | H | I | J | K | L | M | N |
| P | P | Q | R | S | T | U | V | W | X | Y | Z | A | B | C | D | E | F | G | H | I | J | K | L | M | N | O |
| Q | Q | R | S | T | U | V | W | X | Y | Z | A | B | C | D | E | F | G | H | I | J | K | L | M | N | O | P |
| R | R | S | T | U | V | W | X | Y | Z | A | B | C | D | E | F | G | H | I | J | K | L | M | N | O | P | Q |
| S | S | T | U | V | W | X | Y | Z | A | B | C | D | E | F | G | H | I | J | K | L | M | N | O | P | Q | R |
| T | T | U | V | W | X | Y | Z | A | B | C | D | E | F | G | H | I | J | K | L | M | N | O | P | Q | R | S |
| U | U | V | W | X | Y | Z | A | B | C | D | E | F | G | H | I | J | K | L | M | N | O | P | Q | R | S | T |
| V | V | W | X | Y | Z | A | B | C | D | E | F | G | H | I | J | K | L | M | N | O | P | Q | R | S | T | U |
| W | W | X | Y | Z | A | B | C | D | E | F | G | H | I | J | K | L | M | N | O | P | Q | R | S | T | U | V |
| X | X | Y | Z | A | B | C | D | E | F | G | H | I | J | K | L | M | N | O | P | Q | R | S | T | U | V | W |
| Y | Y | Z | A | B | C | D | E | F | G | H | I | J | K | L | M | N | O | P | Q | R | S | T | U | V | W | X |
| Z | Z | A | B | C | D | E | F | G | H | I | J | K | L | M | N | O | P | Q | R | S | T | U | V | W | X | Y |

**Short-key cryptograms.**—In the study of a solution that we are going to take up, we will suppose that the key is short—that it contains much fewer letters than the cryptogram—which causes the following circumstance: When the alphabets corresponding to the length of the key have been used, we return to the alphabet employed to encipher the first letter, and so on. If, then, the key has $n$ letters, the letters numbered 1, $n+1$, $2n+1$, $3n+1$, etc., in the message are enciphered with the same alphabet. The letters 2, $n+2$, $2n+2$, etc., are all enciphered with a second alphabet, etc. The number $n$ being small for a short key, the same alphabet enciphers many letters which in the clear fall at equal intervals. It is on the assumption, quite often correct, that the key is brief that the decrypting method that we are going to describe is based. We believe that Kerckhoffs first presented this method, and that an observation of Kasiski (whose work in German dates from 1863) was taken up and developed by him.

Let the sentence to be enciphered be:

"QUELLES QUE SOIENT LES QUESTIONS QUE PUISSE SOULEVER L'ÉTUDE FAITE CI—APRÈS . . ."

with LYON as a key.

To carry out the encipherment practically, the message is usually divided up into sets of $n$ letters, $n$ being the length of the key. The key is written above each set. Then, in the Vigenère table, the first (second, etc.) alphabet to be used is marked off, say with a ruler. After that, all the letters to be enciphered with this alphabet, the first, $n+1$, $2n+1$, etc., are converted, instead of taking the letters in textual order, enciphering one by one, and changing alphabets each time. Thus, time is saved and errors avoided.

Working in such fashion, we get:

| LYON | LYON | LYON | LYON | LYON | LYON | LYON | LYON |
|------|------|------|------|------|------|------|------|
| QUEL | LESQ | UESO | IENT | LESQ | UEST | IONS | QUEP |
| BSSY | WCGD | FCGB | TCBG | WCGD | FCGG | TMBF | BSSC |

| LYON | LYON | LYON | LYON | LYON | LYON | LYON | LYO |
|------|------|------|------|------|------|------|-----|
| UISS | ESOU | LEVE | RLET | UDEF | AITE | CIAP | RES |
| FGGF | PQCH | WCJR | CJSG | FBSS | LGHR | NGOC | CCG |

First, in contrast to what happens in simple substitutions, clear-text doublets in no wise correspond to those in the cipher, and we may find cipher letters trebled. In fact, five or six identical cipher letters might occur in sequence. Such occurrences destroy any hypothesis as to a simple substitution (except in case where nulls are intentionally introduced).

Next, let us note the four QUE trigraphs in the clear text. The first and fourth are similarly placed with respect to the key and are enciphered with the same alphabets. The same letters are enciphered by the same alphabets. They are, hence, both enciphered by the trigraph BSS. Now, the second and third, occurring between them, are likewise placed similarly with respect to the key but in a position different from the others. They are both enciphered by DFC. From this, we conclude: *When two identical polygraphs are placed similarly with respect to the key, they yield identical cipher polygraphs.* The reciprocal, however, is not true; for: (1) Chance may cause keys to yield identical cipher polygraphs with different clear polygraphs placed differently with respect to the key (see BSS corresponding to DEF in ÉTU<u>DE FA</u>ITE), and (2) the key may present a partial repetition, causing the same alphabets to recur though they are not similarly placed with respect to the key (for example: Key, MARCEAU—MARSEILLE; text, QUELLES QUE SOIENT. The two QUE trigraphs will be enciphered with the same alphabets MAR, and will yield the same cipher trigraphs; yet they will not be similarly placed with respect to the key).

Despite these exceptions, the following assumption can be made in the great majority of cases: *Two identical cipher polygraphs come from two identical clear polygraphs, similarly placed with respect to the key, and, hence, the number of letters separating the initial letters of these polygraphs is a multiple of the number of letters of the key; for this number corresponds to an exact number of repetitions of the key.*

In our example, the intervals separating repeated polygraphs are:

| seven letters | WCGDFCG | 12 letters: $3 \times 2^2$ |
|---------------|---------|--------------------------|
| three letters | BSS | 28 letters: $7 \times 2^2$ |
| three letters | BSS | 21 letters: $7 \times 3$ |
| two letters | WC | 24 letters: $3 \times 2 \times 2^2$ |
| two letters | CJ | 3 letters: $3$ |
| two letters | GG | 11 letters: $11$ |

More weight is always given to long repetitions than to digraphs, which chance may often cause. The most frequent factor is $2^2$, that is to say 4, the length of our key.

Note, however, that we might hesitate before the frequency of the factor 3. When the message is long, the factors due to intervals resulting from fortuitous repetitions are usually eliminated easily in the face of the frequency of factors actually resulting from repetitions of polygraphs similarly placed. Nevertheless, when two solutions are possible, both must be tried successively.

If the key has four letters, the first, fifth, ninth, etc., letters of the document have been enciphered with a given alphabet, and, apart from the rest of the cipher, they may be treated as the components of a simple substitution, in which the most frequent letter is E. Likewise, the second, sixth, and tenth letters will give rise to analogous studies, and so on.

As a practical conclusion, when a cipher yields nothing in the way of letter frequencies which might lead us to conclude that it is simple substitution, we may suspect a polyalphabetic substitution (that is to say, when the most frequent letter does not occur with a percentage of nearly 17; when other letters do not appreciably approach the frequencies of RASIN; and when no letter is very infrequent, we may suspect a polyalphabetic substitution). Then the repetitions of polygraphs will be sought, and the number of intervening letters found. Next, we will try to find the common factor which is the length of the key or a multiple of this length. This length once established, the cryptogram is written in sets of this length, one set under the other, in such a way that if the key has $n$ letters, the 1st cipher letter, the $(n+1)$st, the $(2n+1)$st, etc., appear in the same column. Then, the frequencies of the letters in any column are studied: If E can be determined in one of the alphabets, the rest of the letters in that column can be translated, since the alphabet is normally ordered. The letter corresponding to A of the clear yields a letter of the key. If we cannot find E in one of the columns, it is rare that the context of the columns found and that of the key, which must not be lost sight of, do not yield letters in the columns in question. (If the key is clear, it often yields the solution as soon as the first few letters are obtained, because the rest may be guessed. If, however, the key is random, it helps us in no wise.) Again, a consideration of the frequency graph for each column might be advantageous in determining the position of the sliding alphabet even if E is not the most frequent letter.

We will not dwell on this system; it is fully described in Kerckhoffs and in Valerio, to cite those only; for polyalphabetic substitutions gave rise to remarkable works during the last quarter of the nineteenth century. We must be familiar with this system, because it is the foundation of the studies that follow. However, the author must say that, in the course of a career already long, he does not remember ever having seen a substitution in Vigenère's classic system outside of exercises made by himself during his studies, and certain inventions submitted to him by cryptologists full of good will but void of erudition.

**Decrypting by the use of the probable word.**—Here we have set forth the analytical method. The method of the probable word is also applicable. A whole school, following Bazeries, contending that intuition is the prime requisite of the cryptanalyst, declares that this method is the most general and almost always succeeds. And, in fact, we will see that we have to resort often to it amid the complexities of polyalphabetic substitutions. It is important, then, to know well how to apply it. When the occurrence of a word is suspected in a Vigenère-type cryptogram, we try to proceed backwards from the cryptogram to this word, and study the succession of alphabets that would have given the encipherment. If these alphabets show periodicity, we will know that the key (which corresponds to this periodicity) has been found. Then translation is extended by trying this key outside the probable word.

Let the cryptogram be:

```
AAUQN  XSZWF  EAIBA . . .
```

wherein we suspect the word DIVISION.

Suppose this word to be at the beginning. The first cipher letter, A, would then equal the letter D. Now, if we look for the alphabet in which A represents D in the Vigenère table, that is to say, if we follow the D row up to A, and see what the first letter of the column is, we will find that it is alphabet x. X would then be the first letter of the key. If AAUQNXSZ equaled DIVISION, the key would be XIZIVPEM. This result offers us nothing toward the solution of the problem. Let us make a trial on the next letter one space to the right. In order for AUQNXSZW to equal DIVISION the key would have to be XMVFFKLJ; nothing yet. Let us slide another space; UQNXSZWF will give DIVISION with the key RISPARIS. This time we have a periodicity, so continuing our trial with the key, PARIS, EAIBA upon decipherment gives PARTI. The key, then, is correct.

(To decipher a cryptogram with the Vigenère table, the letter of the key is taken, we go down the column until we find the cipher letter to be translated with this key, and we follow this row to the left of the table. The row letter in column A is the translation. Just as when enciphering, it is best to divide the text up into sets of length equal to that of the key which is written above the sets.)

Here we have a particularly nice key because it is in clear. However, a random key would betray itself by the repetition of a series of letters in the same order. The method does not succeed, however, except when the probable word is longer than the key. Otherwise, the repetitions in the latter would not appear.

**Long-key cryptograms.**—Whether we use the analytical method or that of the probable word, it is seen that long keys inconvenience the cryptanalyst. In the analytical method, with a long key, there will be fewer repetitions of the key. Therefore, there will be fewer chances for repetitions of similarly placed polygraphs and less elements for each alphabet comprising a series analogous to the first, $(n+1)$st, $(2n+1)$st . . . letters, since $n$ is greater. Thus, we find more difficulties in the way of reconstructing the alphabets and also of determining the length of the key. In a single cryptogram, these difficulties may be considerable, especially if it is short.

If several cryptograms in the same key are at hand, the search for the key length may be neglected. Unless the encipherer places nulls at the beginning of the cryptogram after having enciphered it, the first letters of these cryptograms are enciphered with the first of the key and, hence, with the same alphabet. By writing these cryptograms one under another, we may treat the first column of the table thus obtained just as we treated the first column of the cryptogram of the type that was divided up into sets, one written under the other. The column of second letters is treated in the same manner, and so on. The decipherment itself will give the key.

**Finding plain-text letters other than E.**—The difficulty that we may next encounter is that of not finding E in the different columns, because of the lack of sufficient text. This may happen even though we use a graph. In such a case, we may have recourse to a procedure which follows.[1] Like several other procedures in the pages to follow, it was described by Major Bassières, a member of the Military Cryptography Commission. Like other works of this distinguished cryptanalyst, we would point this out as an ingenious method. Doubtless we will not have the opportunity to apply it often, but it reveals perfectly the peculiarities of polyalphabetic systems, and may be of value in the study of the complicated systems arising from this class of ciphers.

---

[1] The method which the author is about to describe is similar to completing the plain component. The reader will observe that the latter method (see pp. 47-49 of *Elements of Cryptanalysis*) is much more general and much easier to apply than the former.

Let the beginnings of cryptograms enciphered in the same key with a Vigenère table be:

1. X Q Y B Y
2. N Q I T I
3. X W C A W
4. N Q W P R
5. Z V G Z E
6. Z V Y P Q

We will try and see if we can tentatively determine two letters in the first column, say E and S. Let us draw up the following correspondence table, composed of two normally ordered alphabets, E in one corresponding to S in the other; we will call them (e) and (s).

(e)  A B C D E F G H I J K L M N O P Q R S T U V W X Y Z
(s)  O P Q R S T U V W X Y Z A B C D E F G H I J K L M N

The two letters of any column of this table have the same interval between them as exists between E and S in the normal alphabet. If one of the letters of (e) represents the encipherment of E in an alphabet of the Vigenère table, the corresponding letter of (s) will represent the encipherment of S in the same alphabet. Let us examine the first column in our table of the beginnings of the six messages: It contains the letters X, N, Z. J, which is not one of these letters, corresponds in alphabet (e) to X in alphabet (s).[1] Z, which occurs there, corresponds to N. If Z=E, N=S in the same alphabet—alphabet v in the Vigenère table, where X=C. Thus, the first letters of our cryptograms in the order of the messages numbered from 1 to 6 will be:

C, S, C, S, E, E

enciphered with alphabet v. The first key letter would be V.

Let us try out the second column in the same way. It contains the letters Q, W, V. Q corresponds to C which is not in the column; W to I, V to H, neither of which is there. The column does not appear to contain E and S at the same time. Let us see if it does not contain another pair of letters, I and N, for example:

(i)  A B C D E F G H I J K L M N O P Q R S T U V W X Y Z
(n)  F G H I J K L M N O P Q R S T U V W X Y Z A B C D E

In the alphabets slid so that N coincides with I, Q yields L, which we do not have, and W yields R which we do not have, but V gives Q which we do have. So then, if Q=I, V will equal N; this corresponds to alphabet i, and the succession of our second letters is I, I, O, I, N, N. Placing this second column after the first, the beginning of the key will be VI and the beginnings of the messages will be the following digraphs:

CI
SI
CO
SI
EN
EN

which are quite acceptable in French.

---

[1] The correspondence of X to J is based on the assumption that X in alphabet (s) =S. Had it been supposed that X in alphabet (e) =E, then X and L would have been the proper pair to consider. This sort of omission occurs throughout the entire discussion—not every possible combination is mentioned by the author.

The third column contains the letters Y, I, C, W, G.

We assure ourselves easily that it contains neither of the pairs ES and IN. Let us see if it does not contain the pair NR.

(n)  A B C D E F G H I J K L M N O P Q R S T U V W X Y Z

(r)  E F G H I J K L M N O P Q R S T U V W X Y Z A B C D

In this column, we have Y, I, and W, which do not give any correspondence with another letter of the column; however, C corresponds to Y and G to C, both of which are found there. Which correspondence is to be chosen? Let us try them both by juxtaposing the results of our trials to the already translated part of the ciphers.

G=R and C=N in key P, which gives Y=J, I=T, W=H. Our key would now be VIP . . . and for our messages we would have the trigraphs written below to the left. If C=R and Y=N in key L (which gives VIL . .) we will have I=X, W=L, G=V, and the trigraphs to the right:

| Key VIP | | | | Key VIL | | |
|---|---|---|---|---|---|---|
| C | I | J | | C | I | N |
| S | I | T | | S | I | X |
| C | O | N | | C | O | R |
| S | I | H | | S | I | L |
| E | N | R | | E | N | V |
| E | N | J | | E | N | N |

On examination of these trigraphs, the series under the key VIL appears more pleasing than those under the key VIP (CIJ, ENJ); hence, we might reject the latter. Nevertheless, just to show how such a study unfolds, let us remain undecided about the matter, and go on to the next column. Trials on its letters B, T, A, P, Z, will show us that this column does not contain ES or IN or NR. We find EI with the following correspondences, in key L, T=I, P=E, B=Q, A=P, Z=O. Juxtaposing these results to both series of trigraphs, we get:

| Key VIPL | | | | | Key VILL | | | |
|---|---|---|---|---|---|---|---|---|
| C | I | J | Q | | C | I | N | Q |
| S | I | T | I | | S | I | X | I |
| C | O | N | P | | C | O | R | P |
| S | I | H | E | | S | I | L | E |
| E | N | R | O | | E | N | V | O |
| E | N | J | E | | E | N | N | E |

The tetragraphs of key VIPL are to be rejected (CIJQ, CONP). The key is VILL.

Now we will halt the development of this example.

**Very short cryptograms.**—In order to show yet another example of procedure that may whet the ingeniousness of persons fervent in cryptanalytical studies, we will take up another thesis by the same author on the solution of several very short cryptograms.[1] The supposition is that we are still working on Vigenère substitutions.

Let the messages be:

1. KAUVJ  VGVBI  GINAL  R
2. QRHWT  ECZPU  V
3. WEQIA  EQLBT  G
4. HAUHF  ZYSTF  OCOCV

We are going to hunt for the key by a mechanical procedure, so to speak, by continued trials.

---

[1] This method, like the preceding one, is a special case of the method of completing the plain component.

Let us see if the first key letter is A:

If it is A, the first letters of the plain text will be K, Q, W, and H, being left unchanged by the encipherment. The alphabet corresponding to the second letter of the key is that which gives the second letters of the messages: A, R, E, A. If this second key letter is A, the second clear letters are A, R, E, A. If it is B, the second clear letters are Z, Q, D, Z. (See Vigenère table, letters in key B, corresponding to the rows on which A, R, and E are found.) Let us draw up a table for each possible key, giving the equivalents to second letters of the ciphers, thus getting the second letters of the clear. We suppose, as we have said, that the first letters of the clear are K, Q, W, H.

### KEY A

| A B C D E F G H I J K L M N O P Q R S T U V W X Y Z |
| --- |

```
K   A Z Y X W V U T S R Q P O N M L K J I H G F E D C B
Q   R Q P O N M L K J I H G F E D C B A Z Y X W V U T S
W   E D C B A Z Y X W V U T S R Q P O N M L K J I H G F
H   A Z Y X W V U T S R Q P O N M L K J I H G F E D C B
```

If a clear message begins with Q, the second letter is U. So it is key X that should yield the second cipher letters. But the beginnings of our messages would be KD, QU, WH, HD. Of these four digraphs, three are out of the question at the beginning of a French message. Moreover, Q is hardly admissible as the first letter of one of our documents. The first key letter is not A.

Let us try B.

If the first letters have been enciphered with key B, and have given K, Q, W, H, the first clear letters were J, P, V, G. Let us form a table like the preceding one to look for the second key letter.

### KEY B

| A B C D E F G H I J K L M N O P Q R S T U V W X Y Z |
| --- |

```
J   A Z Y X W V U T S R Q P O N M L K J I H G F E D C B
P   R P       L       F       Z       V
V   E C       Y       S       M       I
G   A Y       U       O       I       E
```

At the beginning of a sentence, J can be followed only by a vowel—so all keys not corresponding to A, E, I, O, U, and Y are to be cast aside, and we leave the spaces for the corresponding letters vacant in our table. The digraphs PP, PF, PZ, PV, cannot begin a sentence.

Two solutions remain:

| KEY BA | KEY BG |
| --- | --- |
| JA | JU |
| PR | PL |
| VE | VY |
| GA | GU |

If we were sure that the key were clear, we would discard the second solution, but as we are not sure of this, we hesitate between the two which might both be acceptable if VY were the beginning of a proper name. Now we would have to go on to the third key letter, first trying out the key BA . . , then BG . . . But, in cases of this nature, we can direct our researches by means of the following procedure: In the table of digraphs, the frequency of every proposed digraph is considered, the sum of the frequencies of each of these combinations is gotten, and the chances are that the one with the highest total is the one to adopt, particularly when working with fairly numerous digraphs.

| | | | |
|---|---|---|---|
| JA_____ | 0 | JU_____ | 0 |
| PR_____ | 4 | PL_____ | 1 |
| VE_____ | 9 | VY_____ | 0 |
| GA_____ | 0 | GU_____ | 0 |
| Total_____ | 13 | Total_____ | 1 |

We will adopt key BA . . . as our solution.

Let us hunt the third key letter. The third letters of our messages are U, H, Q, U.

KEY BA

| | A | B | C | D | E | F | G | H | I | J | K | L | M | N | O | P | Q | R | S | T | U | V | W | X | Y | Z |
|---|---|---|---|---|---|---|---|---|---|---|---|---|---|---|---|---|---|---|---|---|---|---|---|---|---|---|
| JA | U | | R | | | N | L | | | | | H | | | | | | | | B | | | | | | V |
| PR | H | G | F | E | D | C | B | A | Z | Y | X | W | V | U | T | S | R | Q | P | O | N | M | L | K | J | I |
| VE | Q | | N | | | J | H | | | | | D | | | | | | | | X | | | | | | R |
| GA | U | | R | | | N | L | | | | | H | | | | | | | | B | | | | | | V |

PR must be followed by a vowel, so we will study only keys yielding the vowels. JAH causes us to discard key R; VEJ, key H; and VEH, key L. Keys D, T, and Z are left, and give three series of possible trigraphs.

We are going to treat the final digraphs of these trigraphs as we did those at the beginnings of our messages in the preceding trial, seeking the sum of the frequencies.

| KEY BAD | | KEY BAT | | KEY BAZ | |
|---|---|---|---|---|---|
| JAR_____ | 19 | JAB_____ | 3 | JAV_____ | 7 |
| PRE_____ | 25 | PRO_____ | 12 | PRI_____ | 11 |
| VEN_____ | 39 | VEX_____ | 0 | VER_____ | 19 |
| GAR_____ | 19 | GAB_____ | 3 | GAV_____ | 7 |
| Total_____ | 102 | Total_____ | 18 | Total_____ | 44 |

We will take the first solution, BAD, as our key.

Let us apply the same method for the fourth letters, V, W, I, H:

KEY BAD

| | A | B | C | D | E | F | G | H | I | J | K | L | M | N | O | P | Q | R | S | T | U | V | W | X | Y | Z |
|---|---|---|---|---|---|---|---|---|---|---|---|---|---|---|---|---|---|---|---|---|---|---|---|---|---|---|
| JAR | V | U | T | S | R | Q | P | O | N | M | L | K | J | I | H | G | F | E | D | C | B | A | Z | Y | X | W |
| PRE | W | V | U | T | S | R | Q | P | O | N | M | L | K | J | I | H | G | F | E | D | C | B | A | Z | Y | X |
| VEN | I | H | G | F | E | D | C | B | A | Z | Y | X | W | V | U | T | S | R | Q | P | O | N | M | L | K | J |
| GAR | H | G | F | E | D | C | B | A | Z | Y | X | W | V | U | T | S | R | Q | P | O | N | M | L | K | J | I |

Examining the tetragraphs which are formed by the letters in any one column with the trigraphs JAR, PRE, VEN, GAR, and underlining in each column the principal one which causes us to reject that column, we find only the column corresponding to key E to be admissible (presuming that our sentences do not open with such proper names as might begin with JARB, etc.). We then have:

KEY BADE

JARR

PRES

VENE

GARD

We could keep on in this fashion, but JARR strongly hints that we should try out the verb ARRIVER. The fifth letter of the first cryptogram is J, which would correspond to I in key B. This would yield the pentagraphs PRESS, VENEZ, GARDE. We could continue our decipherment in this way step by step with the key BADE which would soon be completely verified.

Theoretically, this system could be used with only two dispatches at hand, or even with just one if the key is known to be clear. But doubts and trials and errors are diminished in the same proportion as we have more messages.

At the beginning of the description of these procedures of solution, a condition restraining the use of them was clearly pointed out. This was the fact that we have square tables with known parallel alphabets to work on. In reality, polyalphabetic substitutions are composed with any sort of alphabets whatever. Before we abandon classic tables, we will mention a certain number of systems described and studied in the books already mentioned. We do this to complete the cryptographic equipment of our readers, by giving them a knowledge of the nomenclature devoted to cryptography, rather than for practical use in their work.

To encipher a clear letter by the Vigenère system, we have said that we take the letter found at the juncture of the key-letter column and the clear-letter row.

Beaufort.—In Beaufort's method, we use the same square table as in Vigenère's. However, we go down the column corresponding to the key letter until we reach the clear letter in this column; then we follow the row out to the column of the normal alphabet, and encipher the clear letter with the letter thus obtained.[1]

Thus, let the word ENNEMI be enciphered with the key BADE:

| Vigenère system | Beaufort system |
|---|---|
| B A D E B A | B A D E B A |
| E N N E M I | E N N E M I |
| F N Q I N I | D N K A L I |

The methods of solution already described, particularly the search for the key length, the division of the cryptogram into sets of this length, and the search for the successive alphabets, as well as the search for the probable word, apply in Beaufort's system. But, particularly in this last system, there is one thing to be noted. Let us pass on from the cipher DNKALI enciphered with a polyalphabetic-substitution system, supposedly unknown to us, to the clear ENNEMI. Let us seek the key that has been used. Applying Beaufort's method, we will hunt D, a cipher letter, in the left column; follow row D to clear E; and then go up the column to the top where we find our key letter to be B. However, ignorant of the fact that we are dealing with a Beaufort cipher, if we apply the Vigenère method, we will take the row of clear E; follow it to cipher D; and ascend the column to its first line. There, Z will be found for the key, and instead of BADE we will have ZAXW, which will appear to us as a random key, in nowise aiding our researches, whereas we might, perhaps, guess a letter of a clear key.

---

[1] Observe that this operation is identical with the process of deciphering in the Vigenère system. In other words, to decipher a Vigenère cryptogram is to encipher it with the original key by means of the Beaufort system.

But if we take the two complementary alphabets (reversed with the exception of A):

A B C D E F G H I J K L M N O P Q R S T U V W X Y Z

A Z Y X W V U T S R Q P O N M L K J I H G F E D C B

we see that Z=B, X=D, W=E.

So we call Beaufort's key the complement of that of Vigenère. When we find a random key in a polyalphabetic system, it is wise to make sure that the letters complementary to those found for the key do not yield a clear key.

**Gronsfeld.**—Gronsfeld's method consists of using a numerical key whose digits indicate the shift with respect to the normal alphabet of the alphabet to be used for the corresponding clear letter. Because of the simplicity of this method when the shift is only a few letters, it is quite widely used.

Let the key be 1034 to encipher ENNEMI.

```
1 0 3 4 1 0

E N N E M I

F N Q I N I
```

For E, we take the following letter, F; for the second, N, the third letter after it, Q; etc. It is evident that we thus return absolutely to Vigenère's method, and that our key would be transliterated by BADE. We must, however, remark that shifts from 0 to 9 only are used, and, therefore—our researches being limited to nine letters following a clear letter—the alphabets found one by one can be shifted not more than ten letters, one with respect to the other.

This observation will foster a special system of deciphering for the Gronsfeld type of cipher. Thanks to the cryptanalyst already cited for the ingeniousness of his observations on Vigenère's system, we will suppose in order to explain this system that 4 in the key has not been exceeded. In the general case in which the key digits may reach 9, the following table would have ten lines instead of five, but we would work in a similar way.

Let the cipher be: V Q E D W D N L F U D O F V U G . . .

Above each cipher letter, let us write out the four letters preceding it in the normal alphabet:

```
4   R M A Z S Z J H B Q Z K B R Q D
3   S N B A T A K I C R A L C S R E
2   T O C B U B L J D S B M D T S F
1   U P D C V C M K E T C N E U T G
0   V Q E D W D N L F U D O F V U H
```

Let us try to group the letters in the first few columns one to a column so as to form French words.

We see, for example:

S ' (line 3)
UN (lines 1–2)
UNE (lines 1–3–0), etc.

S ' would require the second word beginning in the second column to be a verb having a vowel as its initial letter. We have only vowel O from which we can form no verb here.

UNE must be followed by a feminine word, beginning with the fourth column. At this column we see the beginning of the word AVANIE (3–1–2–0–3–1), and the key would be 1–3–0–3–1–3–0–3–1, but we can go no further. Taking up UN, we find the word CAVALIER (2–3–1–3–2–3–1–3) from the third column on, and continuing with the key 1–3–2–3, we form the word BLESSÉ, which assures us of the correctness of this solution.

## CHAPTER V

## SLIDING-STRIP DEVICES AND DISKS

**Saint-Cyr.**—In practice we have not frequently met with the application of classic systems using tables as such. However, such systems are widely used in cipher machines; particularly in what is called the Saint-Cyr method. Inventors are always beguiled by this method which gave rise a short time before the war to many patents, fortunately S.G.D.G.[1]

As a matter of fact, we do not consider that there exists a Saint-Cyr method; it is nothing but an elegant mechanical application of the Vigenère method. The device, or Saint-Cyr "reglet", is composed of a rule and a slide. On the rule the alphabet is generally written twice in succession; on the slide the alphabet is such that when the two A's coincide, all the other letters coincide. If A on the slide is placed opposite B on the rule, the alphabet of the rule represents alphabet B of the Vigenère table with respect to the alphabet of the slide (shifted one letter). So, if we keep on shifting the clear letters of the slide, letter by letter, against the cipher letters of the rule, we get the 25 shifts of the Vigenère alphabets, the letter opposite A on the slide indicating the key letter.

To encipher the word ENNEMI with BADE as our key, we will successively place the rule as in the following figure:

```
A B C D E F G H I J K L M N O P Q . . .   Rule
  A B C D E F G H I J K L M N O   . . .   Slide for B
A B C D E F G H I J K L M N O P Q . . .   Slide for A
    A B C D E F G H I J K L M N . . .     Slide for D
```

Turning the figure clockwise through an angle of 90°, so that the A of the alphabet is on top, we quickly recognize the Vigenère alphabets.

Reading on the rule in its successive positions the letters of the word to be enciphered, and writing down the letters that correspond to them on the rule, we get F N Q . . .

Placing A on the slide opposite the key letter on the rule, and reading the letter on the slide opposite the clear letter on the rule, we get the Beaufort substitution. It is immediately understood why, in placing the alphabets vertically, we go down the key alphabet to the clear letter and use the letter of the corresponding alphabet A.

This device has been modified by the addition of numbers, punctuation marks, etc. It has been used with variants for each letter. Finally, to render the device more manageable and to avoid the necessity of repeating the alphabet twice to get coincidence, the two alphabets of the rule and of the slide have been written on two concentric disks. Of course, these disks can be used with a key word by successively turning A on the outer disk (let us call it the slide) to coincide with the key letters on the inner disk. Then on this inner disk we look for the cipher letter coinciding with the clear letter to be enciphered, which is found on the outer disk, and write it down. However, the use of disks and the ease of sliding one of them against the other

---

[1] S.G.D.G. means "Sans garantie du gouvernement" (without government guaranty). All patented French articles must be so marked.

indefinitely by keeping on turning has created rather special methods of encipherment which we will examine here. For these studies we will suppose that the alphabets that we will work with are normal.

**Disks.**—Disks are frequently used in the following fashion: Beginning with a starting point, defined by the coincidence of an exterior letter with an interior letter, the disk is turned in a prescribed direction after the encipherment of each letter, through a constant angle corresponding to 1, 2, etc., letters. Sometimes disks are used on which the fixed part bears 26 cells filled with the 25 letters of the alphabet (W omitted) and a marker, and the moveable part with 26 cells filled with the 26 letters. The clear letter is taken from the fixed part and the marker serves as a word separator.

Cryptograms so obtained are analogous to Vigenère ciphers using keys obtained either by taking the letters in order or else by taking them at intervals of 2, 3, . . . etc. The letter E will be shifted in each alphabet by 2, 3, . . . spaces with respect to the one preceding. Finally, we will recur to the first alphabet with the twenty-seventh letter enciphered; for if $n$ is the number of letters the disk has been turned, after the twenty-sixth letter has been enciphered we will have turned $n \times 26$ spaces—that is to say, $n$ complete revolutions—and we will recur to the first alphabet for the encipherment of the twenty-seventh letter. This is true for all the other letters as well as the first. We have the most general case by dividing the cipher up into sets of 26. If, however, we slide the disk by twos, we return to the initial alphabet at the fourteenth letter and sets of 13 will yield the solution.

There exists a practically mechanical system which, when displacements are equal, allows us to discover the translation of the cipher at the cost of several trials.

Let us first suppose that the disk has been turned through a constant angle. Let the cipher be QSWNJYSYO.

Under every cipher letter, let us write a normal alphabet, as if we were seeking the translation of a Julius Caesar type of cipher.

```
Q S W N J Y S Y O
R T X O K Z T Z P
S U Y P L A U A Q
T V Z Q M B V B R
U W A R N C W C S
V X B S O D X D T
W Y C T P E Y E U
X Z D U Q F Z F V
Y A E V R G A G W
Z B F W S H B H X
A C G X T I C I Y
```

Let us take the polygraphs formed with the first letter of the first column and the letters of the other columns slipped one interval per column, either by descending QTYQNDYFW, or by ascending QRUKFTMRG (all the while, we are supposing that the full table has been written out, the first line being written under the last, etc.). These two polygraphs are not French words. We will do the same with the second letter R and the third letter S, etc. This gives us nothing.

Let us take the first letter again, and consider the letters of the other columns slipped two intervals. We read: QUATRIÈME.

If we had obtained no results by a shift of two, we would have tried three, etc. This is a general method, and is rendered rapid by using a rule pivoted around the letter of the first column examined.

We may agree to turn the disk through variable angles after each letter, and some cipher machines perform this operation automatically. Let us, then, suppose that a numerical key has been applied, say, for example, 1, 2, 3, 4. In order to introduce equal shifts like those we have studied above, let us imagine that the movement proceeds by lengthy equal displacements of $1+2+3+4$ or 10 letters, these lengthy displacements comprising the short unequal interior displacements as subdivisions for extra study. As we have said, we recur to the first alphabet at the end of 26 equal displacements of shifts: if only the first letter were enciphered after each long shift, we would recur to the first alphabet at the twenty-sixth letter. But after this letter we have added to the cipher the three letters corresponding to the short shifts 2, 3, 4, before reaching the first letter of the second long shift. So then, we will have 26 times 4 letters before retrieving not the same alphabet but the same series. The period is, then, $26 \times 4 = 104$ letters. In totality, when the number of letters of the long shift is divisible by 2, the period is only half as long—52 letters.

It is very hard to apply the general method to these long periods. If the beginnings of the encipherments of several messages are definitely the same, the methods exposed above may be applied when the division is difficult. Otherwise, we will have to resort to the probable word.

The following method may also be tried. It is a part of Bassières' studies from which we have already borrowed. In order to abridge the description, we will not go into details about the operations in the example just ahead:

Let us take a cryptogram known to be enciphered with two concentric disks each bearing a normal alphabet. A trial of the sort just described yielded nothing; we, therefore, are led to suspect a key that turns the disks through unequal angles.

```
LDPNN   PHDQJ   EWBJI   EGDIZ   WUYVV   FPNYB   QFAZZ   BRRGJ
HFHRL   JQCVG   HJLRG   AMNKW   PBN.
```

To encipher with angles arranged in a series with such a key as 2–1–3 is to encipher with a series of connected square tables in which the alphabets of the uppermost rows progress in order (A of one following Z of the preceding). The key used is such as ACDGIJMOPS, etc., in which the intervals between the letters are 2–1–3–2–1–3–2–1–3, etc.

Now let us take a digraph enciphered with a square table by means of a series of key digraphs whose letters have a constant interval; for example, in the normal alphabet, the digraph EN enciphered by means of key digraphs of the same interval 2, AC, GI, MO. The encipherment, in the Beaufort system, gives us:

| Key_____ | AC | GI | MO |
|---|---|---|---|
| Clear_____ | EN | EN | EN |
| Cipher_____ | EL | YF | SZ |

The interval from E to L, Y to F, and S to Z, in the normal alphabet is 7. The resultant digraphs, therefore, have a constant interval, equal to the difference between the interval of the letters of the digraph to be enciphered (interval EN=9), and the interval of the key digraphs (interval A to C, G to I, M to O, =2). In Vigenère's system this would be the sum.

Again, let us encipher with a disk by constantly turning the movable disk clockwise through a given angle—say five letters. If we take the encipherment of a given letter on the fixed part in each of the positions of the disks, we get a series of letters read from the movable disk which have between them equal intervals of five letters in the ascending alphabet. Thus, the letter A, enciphered with a first alphabet A and constant angles of five (or with a table with alphabets A, F, K, P, etc.), will yield A, V, Q, L, etc. From the standpoint of the normal alphabet, the intervals of these letters are equal to 26—5, that is to say, 21. Conversely, to the intervals A, V, Q, L, counted as 21 in the direction of the normal alphabet, there correspond on the disk displacements in this same direction of interval 5 (26—21).

Having noted these things, we are first going to look for the number of terms in the numerical key, in other words, the number of short unequal shifts within one of the large equal shifts which we discussed in the description of the system.

If two clear digraphs with a given interval between their letters have been enciphered with key digraphs also having a given interval, we have just seen that they yield digraphs presenting this same peculiarity (the reverse is not true: We may have cipher digraphs of the same interval resulting from any clear or key digraphs). Now key digraphs separated by one or more key lengths, by the very definition of this system of enciphering, will have the above-mentioned quality; that is, of revealing the same interval between their letters. For example, if the key is 1–2–4, interval 1 in the series of key digraphs will occur at the end of three shifts of the disks, next of six, then of $3n$. Likewise, interval 2 will occur after every three shifts of the disks, etc. (The reverse is not true. Such a key as 1–2–1, 1–2–1 may be used, wherein intervals of one will occur without having been turned through a key length.) So, among the cipher digraphs yielding a given interval between these letters, a certain number (usually most of them) come from clear digraphs having the same interval and separated by one or more key lengths.[1] By studying the distribution of these digraphs of given intervals in the cipher and by seeking the interval that separates them in the cipher, the length of the key may be discovered.

Our successive cipher digraphs give intervals written below (for example, from L to D there are 18 letters of the normal alphabet).

| LD | DP | PN | NN | NP | PH | HD | DQ | QJ | JE | EW | WB |
|----|----|----|----|----|----|----|----|----|----|----|----|
| 18 | 12 | 24 | 0  | 2  | 18 | 22 | 13 | 19 | 21 | 18 | 5  |

| BJ | JI | IE | EG | GD | DI | IZ | ZW | WU | UY | YV | VV |
|----|----|----|----|----|----|----|----|----|----|----|----|
| 8  | 25 | 22 | 2  | 23 | 5  | 17 | 23 | 24 | 4  | 23 | 0  |

| VF | FP | PN | NY | YB | BQ | QF | FA | AZ | ZZ | ZB | . . . . . |
|----|----|----|----|----|----|----|----|----|----|----|------|
| 10 | 10 | 24 | 11 | 3  | 15 | 15 | 21 | 25 | 0  | 2  | . . . . . |

Let us take the number of letters that separate series of two digraphs yielding the same interval between letters. Among others, we find:

| | | | |
|---|---|---|---|
| LD — PH | (interval 18) | 5 letters |
| PH — EW | (interval 18) | 5 letters |
| PN — WU | (interval 24) | 18 letters |
| NP — EG | (interval 2) | 11 letters |
| NP — ZB | (interval 2) | 20 letters |
| | etc. . . . | |

If we do likewise with all the intervals, we find 5, 2, and 3 as the principal factors of the numbers of letters, the products in which the factor 5 enters being a little the most frequent.

---

[1] It can be proved by a statistical analysis that this statement is tenable only for short keys containing few repetitions. Even in such cases, the correct result is not necessarily the highest one. However, the idea can be extended so as to make the results obtained very reliable. (See note p. 41.)

We will say that our key has five elements—that its length is 5. In case the first result is not clear enough, the next-described trials should be made successively on several lengths.[1]

Next we will write out our cipher in five columns:

```
L D P N N
P H D Q J
E W B J I
E G D I Z
W U Y V V
F P N Y B
Q F A Z Z
B R R G J
H F H R L
J Q C V G
H J L R G
A M N V W
P B N
```

Now let us try to find how many places the disk has turned for a period comprising the sum of the short unequal shifts, or the total of the key digits (for example, if the key is 2–0–1–3–6, we seek the number 12). In due time, the purpose of this research will be seen.

The three digraphs LD, PH, and EW come, we suppose, from key digraphs having a given interval between their letters (the interval indicated by the first key digit). These three digraphs actually have the same interval between their letters (L to D; P to H; E to W; =18). Let us suppose that these digraphs, or at least two of them, equal the same clear digraphs. Then L and P would be equivalents for the same letter obtained by a shift of the disk equal to one whole key length. The disk would, then, have turned so as to give an interval of four between the two successive alphabetical equivalents (L and P) of a given letter. As we have seen, the disk would have turned 26—4=22 letters, and the period of the key would have 22 letters.

Let us make the same study of PH and EW: again a single key length, but the alphabetical interval from P to E is 15; this yields a different solution. Key length: (26—15)=11 letters. To tip the balance, let us try again. Let us, for example, take FH and JL on the ninth and eleventh rows, second and third columns. The common interval of F to H and of J to L is 2. Then let us take F and J. These letters are separated by two key lengths, and are only four letters apart in the alphabet. A shift of 24 letters (26—4/2) would be necessary for a key of five elements. This is possible. However, let us note that the result is not changed by supposing that the disk shifts are not four letters but 4+26 which brings about a recurrence to the same letter. Then the length of the key would be (26—30/2)=11, as we have already discovered.

We would keep on calculating by adding 26 as many times as necessary to make the division possible, when the distance which separates letters of the alphabet is not divisible by the number

---

[1] At this point it is possible to indicate an extension of the idea being developed, which is far-reaching in its applicability. Why consider only digraphs? Suppose the plain-text message contained two polygraphs or two whole words repeated in similar positions with respect to the key. These would yield two identical series of intervals, and would give a much more reliable indication of the key length than just one digraph. (For example, note the trigraphs NNP and ZZB in the text, which remove any doubt as to the correctness of the key length 5.) The value of this extended notion (which leads to what is known as similar formulae or *isomorphisms*) lies in the fact that it can be applied to cases where the alphabet is not known and also where the general system is not periodic.

of key lengths considered as separating digraphs of a given interval. By reviewing all the groups of digraphs having the same interval between their letters and placed similarly with respect to the key, that is to say, in the same columns, we would find that the key length is really 11. This means that the total shift for a given period is 11 letters. So each of the letters of the second set of five in our cipher has been enciphered by a position of the disk 11 letters removed in the reverse alphabet from the position in which the corresponding letter of the first set was enciphered. For example, if clear A was enciphered by A in the first set, it was enciphered by P in the second. By slipping all the letters of the second set back these 11 places in the alphabet, thus replacing P by A, our new letters would be those we would have obtained by enciphering the second set with the same disk positions as the first. Thus, slipping the successive sets back, we get a cryptogram enciphered by the Beaufort system and a key of limited length to which we can apply the general method.

To make the change, let us write the two alphabets below. The first is slid 11 letters with respect to the second:

L M N O P Q R S T U V W X Y Z A B C D E F G H I J K
A B C D E F G H I J K L M N O P Q R S T U V W X Y Z

Considering the letters of each set in the cryptogram as chosen from the lower alphabet, let us replace them by those corresponding to them in the upper alphabet, repeating the operation for each set as often as necessary to reduce it to the same alphabet as the first:

```
LDPNN   ASOBU   ASXFE   LNKPG
        PHDQJ   PHMUT   ACZEV
                EWBJI   PROTK
                        EGDIZ etc. . . .
```

We can then place the sets of the new cryptogram one under the other, to seek the frequencies:

```
L D P N N
A S O B U
A S X F E
L N K P G
.  .  .  .  .
```

One of the known methods will give us the key ABDDH and the translation:

Key _____ A B D D H A B D D H A B D D H A B D D H . . .
Cipher _____ L D P N N A S O B U A S X F E L N K P G . . .
Clear _____ L E S Q U A T R E B A T A I L L O N S
        N'ONT QUITTÉ LEUR QUARTIER QUE CE MATIN QUATRE HEURES.

If we then look for the shifts to print on the disk, or the numerical key, we determine that in the key ABDDH, the interval from A to B=1, from B to D=2, from D to D=0, from D to H=4. The first terms of the key are 1, 2, 0, 4, the total of which is 7. We have said that the total of the terms was 11, so that the last must be 4, and the key is 1–2–0–4–4.

These methods will be found applicable in the study of cryptograms obtained with certain cipher machines.

## Chapter VI

## AUTO-KEYS AND VARIOUS METHODS OF COMPLICATING THE VIGENÈRE SYSTEM

**Message keys.**—As we have seen, the analytical method of deciphering Vigenère ciphers rests on the discovery of the key length in order to retrieve the periodicity of the alphabets used. Now, if all periodicity is suppressed, the cryptanalyst will be considerably embarrassed. One of the procedures used with this in view consists of picking a very long key, even as long as the cipher itself. This can be accomplished by actually using a very long key, say a fable or a series of digits, etc. But there is another procedure called the "Auto-key". This means that, after taking a short key, easy to remember and spell (which is not always easy in the case of long keys), we encipher the beginning of the clear text; then the enciphering is continued by using this same text as the key.

**Auto-keys.**—To encipher L'ENNEMI ATTAQUE in auto-key with the key BADE, we arrange the encipherment as follows:

Key_____ BADELENNEMIATT

Clear_____ LENNEMIATTAQUE

On decipherment, the first letters deciphered by means of the prearranged key BADE will yield the key for what follows.

The classic method of deciphering an auto-key cryptogram as above defined is that of the probable word. Since the key is the clear message itself, the solution will be reached when the key letters, enabling us to pass from the text to the probable word, yield a series forming a word or a fragment of a word. But, for want of a word to choose, we may meet with no success. If we have several cryptograms, whose beginnings are enciphered with the same prearranged key, we may write them one under the other, and apply one of the already described methods to the first columns thus formed.

Major Bassières' studies extended to auto-keys, and he has pointed out the following considerations.

Let us first note that if the key has six letters in an auto-key system, the first clear letter will be the key for the seventh. So if we know the first, we know the seventh which will in turn serve for the thirteenth which we find without difficulty, and so on.

Moreover (and this note applies if a Vigenère table be used or else a table of the same type, having the property described below, while the preceding note only requires that the alphabet that served in enciphering be known), in the Vigenère system, we get the same letter by enciphering M with alphabet R as by enciphering R with alphabet M. If, in any clear text whatever, we take the intervals separating two successive appearances of a letter, this interval may take an endless number of values. Among these values, some will be found equal to the length of the key. If any one letter whatever is found both preceded and followed by another at an interval equal to the key length, the former will be enciphered by the first appearance of the latter, and will serve as the key for enciphering its second appearance. This phenomenon is made clear by the comparison of the two following lines:

C L E F x A m n p E q r s A

x A m n p E q r s A

E is enframed between two A's at intervals equal to the key. The first A serves as a key to encipher E, and E serves as a key to encipher the second A. These two encipherments of E

(43)

with key **A**, and **A** with key **E** will be represented by the same letter in the Vigenère system. The two like letters thus gotten in the cipher will be separated by an interval equal to the number of letters in the key. The reverse is not true, and like letters may be found at any intervals whatever. However, numerous selections among intervals separating repetitions of a given letter have, in our experience, given a definite majority to the one representing the key length.[1]

Let an auto-key cryptogram in Vigenère be as follows:

```
CEDHE  LCIUG  EWZDM  EMRVN  MEMHG  JEQRF  TICLR
PEDCP  RPEFI  V
```

If we pick out the intervals of the repetitions of a given letter between 5 and 10 (we will suppose that we are sure that the key has between 5 and 10 letters) such as EWZDME (5 letters), ELCIUGE (6 letters), CEDHELC (7 letters), we will find eleven intervals of 6 letters against two of 5, one of 7, and one of 9. So we will say that the length of the key is 6 letters.

(In the system of Beaufort, a research of the same kind can be made. However, it must be noted that instead of finding the same letter when S is enciphered by key M, or M by S (as is the case in the Vigenère system), we find the complementary letter in the reverse alphabets diminished by A.[2]

```
A B C D E F G H I J K L M
A Z Y X W V U T S R Q P O

N O P Q R S T U V W X Y Z
N M L K J I H G F E D C B
```

The cryptogram, given above, for example, enciphered in Beaufort becomes:

```
UWDHW  BGIOS  EKRNE  GELFX  WUWFG  ZWSJT  HACDR
REVYB  JJWHI  F
```

We will seek the interval between U and G, not U and U, and between W and E, etc., and we will reach the same result as above.)

Let us take up our Vigenère again, and try to reconstruct the key. With this in view, let us divide the cryptogram into sets of six letters.

```
C E D H E L        G J E Q R F
C I U G E W        T I C L R P
Z D M E M R        E D C P R P
V N M E M H        E F I V
```

Let us assume the first letter of the key—let us call it **A**. The first clear letter enciphered with key **A** will then be C. This first letter will be a key for the seventh, which is translated by C and which would therefore be A. The thirteenth letter given by Z in key A would be Z; the nineteenth given by V in key Z would be W; etc. By continuing, we would find that if the first letter of the key were A, the first clear letters of the sets of six would be

CAZWKJVJ

---

[1] This statement can be proved statistically correct. Given a sufficient number of tabulations, the most frequent interval is of necessity equal to the key length. The proof is based on an interesting property of the sum of the squares of the frequencies of the individual letters.

[2] This is equivalent to the statement that the sum of corresponding letters is 28 instead of 27.

By similar reasoning, if B were the initial letter of the key, we would get the following as first clear letters of the sets of six:

BBYXJKUK

We would keep on thus, and get a table for the 26 letters:

```
Key A,   C A Z W K J V J
    B,   B B Y X J K U K
    C,   A C X Y I L T L
    .    . . . . . . . .
    .    . . . . . . . .
    Y,   E Y B U M H X H
    Z,   D Z A V L I W I
```

As soon as we get one line of this table, the others may be deduced from it by writing the normal alphabet down the even columns and the reversed alphabet down the odd columns.

One of the resultant sets and one only is the right one—the one that corresponds to the first letter of the key. Its letters are clear, and the clear is subject to the law of frequencies. If we had enough elements, we would find one row on which E would have its maximum frequency, and that row corresponding to the maximum E would be the right one. However, though in the general case we cannot hope to apply the law of frequencies on this single letter, we can at least try to apply it to a group of frequent letters, for example, to ESARINTULO. We will next count up the total number of appearances of these letters for every row in the table, and consider the one giving the greatest total as correct. (If necessary, we will add the columns following if there are equal results after making trials).[1]

We will reproduce here only the columns giving the highest totals.

```
Key E,   Y E V A G N R N—(1 E, 1 A, 1 R, 2 N) = 5
    I,   U I R E C R N R                          6
    L,   R L O H Z U K U                          5
    R,   L R I N T A E A                          8
    V,   H V E R P E A E                          5
```

The first key letter will, therefore, be R.

To hunt for the second letter of the key, we will construct a similar table on the second column EIDNJIDF, supposing first that the letter is A, then B, etc.

We get:

```
Key A,   E E Z O V N Q P . . . . . . . . . . . .   4
    B,   D F Y P U O P Q . . . . . . . . . . . .   2

    E,   A I V S R R M T . . . . . . . . . . . .   6
    F,   Z J U T Q S L U . . . . . . . . . . . .   5
```

E gives us the maximum. The first two key letters will be R E, and the reconstructed cipher digraphs will be:

LA....RI....IV....NS....TR....AR....EM....AT..

---

[1] This type of calculation can be made much more accurate by weighting each letter with its individual frequency.

All these digraphs are perfectly acceptable. We will not carry our reconstruction any further. The key is RENNES and the text: LA QUATRIÈME DIVISION SE METTRA EN MARCHE DEMAIN MATIN.

We would work the same way with the rest of the key letters. However, we will remember to resort to the totals of the frequencies in case we at any time hesitate between two solutions. If we had hesitated here between the keys E and F (for example, because of a difference of only one letter in the ESARINTULO frequency), we would have considered the total of the digraphic frequencies by adding each of the possible solutions for the second letters next to the first letters of the sets.

| KEY R E | | | KEY R F | | |
|---|---|---|---|---|---|
| L | A | 12 | L | Z | 0 |
| R | I | 11 | R | J | 0 |
| I | V | 2 | I | U | 0 |
| N | S | 16 | N | T | 25 |
| T | R | 12 | T | Q | 1 |
| A | R | 19 | A | S | 3 |
| E | M | 20 | E | L | 16 |
| A | T | 10 | A | U | 8 |
| | Total | 102 | | Total | 53 |

The solution of the key R E would again be indicated by this process.

We will note that we did not assume that the key was clear. It must also be admitted that sometimes part of the operations in a brief document will not always give the right solution the first time. If the procedure that yields the key length leads us into error, we notice it, because repeated researches to find the key letters give us nothing valuable, and we will begin our trials again with another key length—the one that seems suitable after the first in the list of interval frequencies whence we deduced this length.

Vigenère or Beaufort auto-key ciphers may be attacked by utilizing the following data:

If we encipher the phrase: LA QUATRIÈME DIVISION... with the key RENNES and an autokey system with a Vigenère table, we get (see above):

CEDHE LCIUG EWZDM EMRV.....

We have just seen that we could determine the key length, which is 6 letters. Let us divide our text into sets of 6.

CEDHEL CIUGEW ZDMEMR V.....

Let us decipher the second set CIUGEW by taking as our key the first CEDHEL and by using the Vigenère table. We get

Key.......... CEDHEL
Cipher....... CIUGEW
Result....... AERZAL

Let us use this first result as the key for the decipherment of the third set in the same way, and then the new result to decipher the fourth, etc. As the enciphering method in Beaufort is the same as the deciphering method in Vigenère, from a practical point of view, we can say that having begun to encipher the second set in Beaufort with the key CEDHEL (first set), we encipher the other with an auto-key which, instead of being the clear of the text to be enciphered, is the cipher itself.

Thus we get:

```
CEDHEL   AERZAL   ZZVFMG   WORZAB   . . . . .
CIUGEW   ZDMEMR   VNMEMH   GJEQRF   . . . . .
AERZAL   ZZVFMG   WORZAB   KVNRRE   . . . . .
```

Now if we encipher the message directly: LA QUATRIÈME DIVISION... with a Vigenère table and a key formed by the juxtaposition of our key RENNES with the series of complementary letters already mentioned:

```
A B C D E F G H I J K L M
A Z Y X W V U T S R Q P O

N O P Q R S T U V W X Y Z
N M L K J I H G F E D C B
```

That is to say, with the key RENNESJWNNWI, we get:

```
R E N N E S J W N N W I
L A Q U A T R I E M E D
C E D H E L A E R Z A L

R E N N E S J W N N W I . . . . .
I V I S I O N S E M E T . . . . .
Z Z V F M G W O R Z A B . . . . .
```

This is the first line of our preceding encipherment.

It is explained in the following fashion:

To encipher in Vigenère is to shift the clear letter just as many spaces as alphabets have been passed.[1] Thus, we get the cipher letter by adding the order number of the key letters to that of the clear letter, the former being numbered in the alphabet where A=0, B=1, etc. Now let us consider how we got the two groups CEDHEL AERZAL...

The operations carried out in enciphering the first clear set LAQUAT with the key RENNES were the same in the two procedures (L+R, eleventh letter+seventeenth=twenty-eighth or second=C).

As for the second set AERZAL, it is on one hand the result of the deciphering of CIUGEW with the key CEDHEL.

CIUGEW is the encipherment of RIEMED with the key LAQUAT, thus, letter by letter RIEMED+LAQUAT (R+L=17+11=28 or 2=C).

CEDHEL is likewise LAQUAT+RENNES.

AERZAL=RIEMED+LAQUAT−LAQUAT−RENNES=RIEMED−RENNES.

On the other hand, AERZAL is the result of the enciphering of RIEMED by JWNNWI, that is to say RIEMED+JWNNWI.

Now, as we have noted, JWNNWI is the complement of RENNES. RENNES+JWNNWI=26 (the total of each group of letters of the same rank R+J, E+W, etc.). Therefore, JWNNWI=−RENNES.

---

[1] This observation permits us to study the Vigenère method of encipherment as a process of addition. Decipherment corresponds to subtraction.

It is quite natural, then, to find the same result.

Third set:
```
ZZFMG = ZDMEMR — AERZAL
      = IVISIO+RIEMED—RIEMED+RENNES
      = IVISIO+RENNES
```

that is to say, IVISIO enciphered with the key RENNES, and so on.

The cryptogram we got by enciphering the given auto-key message in Beaufort, starting out with the second group and using a key formed by the first group and then by an auto-key, has been transformed into a message obtained by a non-auto-key. The usual method of procedure in solving polyalphabetic problems is applicable. When other procedures have failed, or in order to get confirmation of assumptions, we can, therefore, make hypotheses on the length of the key, and thus try with sets of 4, 5, 6 letters, etc., to treat the results obtained a substitutions with a limited key.[1]

Here the 6-letter-key hypothesis and the division into groups of 12 letters would be confirmed by two repetitions of trigraphs.

```
C E D H E L A E R Z A L
Z Z V F M G W O R Z A B
K V N R R E J N P U A L
V Q N V R E J P V A
```

When a cryptogram has been enciphered by the Beaufort system, the operations are easier still.

The encipherment of the sentence: LA QUATRIÈME DIVISION... with the key RENNES and an autokey system in Beaufort gives us:

```
UWDHWB  GIOSEK  RNEGEL  FXWUWT  GZWSJT  HACDRR  EVYRJJ
WHIF
```

From the second group on let us encipher this cryptogram in Vigenère using as a key the first group followed by the result of the encipherment itself, we get

```
UWDHWB  AERZAL  RRVFEW  W...
GIOSEK  RNEGEL  FXWUWF  G...
AERZAL  RRVFEW  WORZAJ  C...
```

Now, the encipherment of the clear in Beaufort with the simple key RENNES gives us

```
RENNES  RENNES  RENNES  R...
LAQUAT  RIEMED  IVISIO  N...
UWDHWB  AERZAL  RRVFEW  W...
```

The first line of the preceding table yields us a transformation of our proposed auto-key cipher into a limited-key cipher. Suspecting different successive key lengths, we can try to find text in which repetitions will allow us to believe we have found the solution of the key length sought for and to work on the columns to find the alphabets.

---

[1] The reader should note that this method (and the following one) of transforming an auto-key message into a polyalphabet presupposes a knowledge of the alphabets being used.

In some cases, not the clear text but rather the cipher itself is used as a key. When the decrypter knows the table used in enciphering, there is not much difficulty in finding the text since he possesses both the cipher and the key that served to encipher it. He has only to locate this key, since the ignorance in which he finds himself regarding the prearranged key leaves him in the dark as to which cipher letter the auto-encipherment began with. This is accomplished with a few trials.

**Single-letter-keyed auto-keys.**—We must cite auto-key ciphers in which the prearranged key has only one letter, that is to say, in which any letter is enciphered by means of the one immediately preceding. Such ciphers, made up letter by letter, are easy to produce with such cryptographs as Saint-Cyr's rule without any effort of memory and without any researches in the text to determine which letters are to be enciphered in the same alphabet (transcription of the key above the text or placing it in a table). The procedures already mentioned make it possible to reduce auto-keys of this sort enciphered in Vigenère to a two-letter-key substitution, and those enciphered in Beaufort to a single substitution.

This method is also employed with the cryptogram taken as the key. Certain cipher machines operate thus. As we have already said, the solution of the problems of decipherment is simple when we know the cipher table and the key. If we were given: YYOII BSAEQ, we would write

```
Key_____ ? Y Y O I I B S A E Q
Cipher_____ Y Y O I I B S A E Q U
Clear_____ ? A Q U A T R I E M E
```

The trial will have to be made both in Vigenère and Beaufort. It will be noticed that since a letter enciphered in alphabet A is replaced by itself, the second letter of doublets are clear A's and the cipher letters following A remained unchanged upon encipherment.

**Broken keys.**—Besides long keys, auto-keys or not, the method of broken keys is a very effective means of breaking the periodicity of the key BOULOGNE—BOULOGNE—BOULOGNE; we encipher with the key BOULOGNE—BOUL—BOULO—BOULOGNE. Of course, if the key were interrupted at regular intervals, BOULOGNE—BOUL—BOULOGNE—BOUL—BOULOGNE, this simply gives us a cryptogram enciphered with the key BOULOGNE—BOUL, in which a certain number of repetitions would appear because of the recurrence of BOUL in the key, but in which the repetition somewhat further removed would indicate the period BOULOGNE—BOUL. The interesting thing is, then, to perplex the cryptanalyst, to break up the key at any time at the will of the encipherer. A classic method is to indicate this break and return to the first key letter by a special sign, usually the letter W. This letter is reserved for this purpose, and W in the clear is enciphered by double V.

The enciphering is then performed as follows:

```
Key_____ B O U L O G N E B O U L B O U L O G N E
Clear_____ L A Q U A T R I E M E W D I V I S I O N
Cipher_____ M O K F O Z E M F A Y H E W P T G O B R
```

```
Key_____ B O U L O G N B O U L O
Clear_____ S E M E T T W R A E N W
Cipher_____ T S G P H Z J S O Y Y K
```

In deciphering, which must be done letter by letter instead of writing the key BOULOGNE above the text from beginning to end and translating all the letters in key A, then in B, etc., as is often done, we have to go back to the beginning of the key every time we encounter a W.

For the cryptanalyst, the periodicity is broken. If there are not too many breaks and if there are close repetitions, we may sometimes guess the key length by working between two breaks (even without knowing it) and proceed to trials; however, all regularity is banished from the process. The studies that we have presented of the successive search for key letters when several ciphers are at hand (or even a single one with a clear key) or for working on the beginnings of certain ciphers written one under the other may be repeated even with the broken key. Account will be taken of the possibility of finding the break indicator in the cipher (all digraphs ending in W will do). With the probable-word method, we may try the word without modification; however, we must at the same time consider the result obtained in one position and in the position slid a place to the right.

Example: Cipher FRCGKJGCZB; probable word DIVISION.

Trials:

First:

| Cipher_____ | F R C G K J G C |
|---|---|
| Clear_____ | D I V I S I O N |
| Key_____ | C J H Y S B S P |

Second:

| Cipher_____ | R C G K J G C Z |
|---|---|
| Clear_____ | D I V I S I O N |
| Key_____ | O U L C R Y O M |

Third:

| Cipher_____ | C G K J G C Z B |
|---|---|
| Clear_____ | D I V I S I O N |
| Key_____ | Z Y P B O U L O |

We see in the third trial the letters OUL, which have already shown up in the second trial, and must belong to the key BOULO... (doubtless BOULOGNE).

We may also make a trial of interpolating a null between each of the digraphs of the probable word: DWIVISION, DIWVISION, etc. All these procedures have possibilities of success with a clear key; however, with a random key or one rather long the cryptanalyst will have a pretty hard time getting anywhere.

**Nulls.**—Again decrypting can be complicated by the introduction of null letters. If placed at the beginning, these nulls do not cause any serious trouble. The general periodicity is not affected. Only in cases where initial frequencies are being sought, or when a methodical search for key letters is being made will infrequent letters or letters forming infrequent digraphs cause any considerable confusion, whether left clear or enciphered.

If nulls are distributed throughout the text, surely they must be introduced only after the enciphering, otherwise they would not break into the periodicity. We can adopt certain letters not included in our cipher tables as nulls (see Porta's system further on). For example, J, K, and W are replaced by I, C, and V in the clear. Hence, the decipherer scratches out all the J's, K's, and W's from the cipher; the cryptanalyst no longer finds his repetitions at intervals corresponding to the length of the key. But this requires that the table be secret, otherwise the cryptanalyst will know readily that J, K, and W do not appear in it, and he will thence deduce that these letters are nulls. Now it is usually the case that, when the Vigenère table with normal alphabets is adopted, it is specifically in order to avoid the trouble of keeping the table secret. If this were not so, we might complicate this table to our advantage as we will see later on. Moreover, in case of telegraphic transmission, account must be taken of errors resulting from the erroneous change by the telegrapher of one letter for another. If we scratch out the letters before deciphering, and if a mistake has been made on one of the letters to be scratched out, the operations are complicated by the breaking of the coincidence of the key and of the text thus pruned. The same danger applies to the case where random nulls are arbitrarily introduced, indicated by nothing but the impossibility of translating the cipher thus modified by means of the key without shifting this key one space to the right where the nulls occur. This process is wearisome to the decipherer, obliged to work letter by letter. Every time an irregularity shows up in a prospective word, he asks himself if he is dealing with a null, with an error in enciphering, or with an error in transmission.

At all events, the use of nulls—very burdensome to the cryptanalyst when he has only one cryptogram—is less so, except at the beginning, when several are had with workable beginnings.

We treated extensively of polyalphabetic substitutions with normal alphabets. We did this because, as we have said, they have given rise to many ingenious works. Some people, like de Viaris, have even introduced algebraic notations in their theories. These refer to the relations between the rank of clear letters (A) in the normal alphabet, of the key (E), and of the cipher (Y): $A+E=Y$ (taking $A=0$, $B=1$, etc.: Vigenère system; $A+Y=E$: Beaufort system). These equations have been generalized, as a result of new systems. As a method of complicating work on normal alphabet tables, we will point out that of Rozier, who, in order to encipher a letter, goes down the tabular column corresponding to this letter until he reaches the key letter, then follows the row of this letter until he reaches the following key letter, and goes up the column to write into the cryptogram the letter at the top of the column.

Such systems, though hard, have given rise to studies proving the posssibility of solution. We will not dwell on them in this collection, since it is devoted to studies of a general nature.

CHAPTER VII

## POLYALPHABETIC SUBSTITUTIONS WITH RANDOM PARALLEL ALPHABETS

We have seen all the facilities afforded us in decrypting by the certainty that cryptograms had been enciphered by means of systems using normally ordered alphabets.

Now, frequent use is made of random alphabets whether they be a single alphabet, slid parallel to itself, yielding a table like Vigenère's and capable of being used with Saint-Cyr sliding strips or disks, or whether they be alphabets totally different one from another.

The problem, then, generally comprises the discovery not only of the key indicating the order of the alphabets but also of the alphabet or alphabets themselves. Still, there are certain cases where the cryptanalyst from some source or other knows the alphabet used, and all he has to look for is the key. This is done by the methods already described; looking for the key length by means of repetitions, dividing the cipher into sets of this length, looking for E or any other letter in each column formed by the superimposition of these sets. The identification of letters brings about the recognition of the alphabets used, supposedly known, and the correct placing of all the letters.

**Porta.**—As classic alphabets, we will cite those of Porta's system. We will describe them under the form in which they are met with in old works, with 22 letters only (J is enciphered by I, K by Q, and V and W by U); however, similar tables can be made with 26 letters.

The table is composed of 11 reciprocal alphabets. Each one is used with two key letters (the same alphabet for the key letters A and B, for example). Any letter on one of the alphabet rows is enciphered by the corresponding letter on the other row.

PORTA'S TABLE

```
A.B  { A B C D E F G H I L M
       N O P Q R S T U X Y Z

C.D  { A B C D E F G H I L M
       Z N O P Q R S T U X Y

E.F  { A B C D E F G H I L M
       Y Z N O P Q R S T U X

G.H    . . . . . . . . . .
```

etc. . . .

*Example of encipherment*

Key_____ B A D E B A D E B A

Message_____ L A D I V I S I O N
Cipher_____ Y N P T H X G T B A

Porta has thus indicated a convenient means of reconstructing a series of different alphabets from memory. We have seen how such alphabets can be reconstructed by means of keywords.

(52)

**Analysis of the method of solution.**—So that we can present a number of observations on the deciphering of polyalphabetic substitutions with random alphabets, we will take an example of this kind of cipher and effect a study of it, passing rapidly over the operations already described and explained in connection with normal alphabets.

Let us take the cryptogram below, supposedly received in sets of five letters, but written by us in sets of seven in order to avoid rewriting it.

A study of repetitions, in fact, leads us to this conclusion; for though the repetition of OX (sets 23 and 27) is at interval of $24=2^3\times3$, that of ZW (15–28) at an interval of $95=5\times19$, that of WX (4–26) at an interval of $147=7^2\times3$, and that of FX (2–4) at an interval of $18=2\times3^2$, etc., the majority of the other repetitions, especially those of polygraphs, place the factor 7 to the fore [QDIH (1–5), interval $28=2^2\times7$; QDIH (5–24), $133=7\times19$; PZ (2–3)$=7$; LX (3–11), $63=7\times3^2$; LX(11–16), $35=5\times7$; RQ (1–17), $112=7\times2^4$; DCHQS (10–20), $70=7\times2\times5$; MVMDC (20–25), $35=7\times5$, etc.]. The key, then, must have seven letters.

| 1 | 2 | 3 | 4 | 5 | 6 | 7 | 8 |
|---|---|---|---|---|---|---|---|
| YRQDIHP | MFXKPZR | DLXCPZB | MZWXSFX | TSQDIHL | MMXIJZH | CRFPSLC | MLQTEZQ |

| 9 | 10 | 11 | 12 | 13 | 14 | 15 | 16 |
|---|---|---|---|---|---|---|---|
| GRMASLR | ITIDCHQ | SLXRSWH | JRIACQH | ZRRDYHB | MBIXEKM | ZWWPZTM | MLXQOEP |

| 17 | 18 | 19 | 20 | 21 | 22 | 23 | 24 |
|---|---|---|---|---|---|---|---|
| PRQFZSB | MVUVSSJ | MZQTURU | MVMDCHQ | SMGTRRT | ZVMDSSR | YESDYOX | WHQDIHU |

| 25 | 26 | 27 | 28 | 29 | 30 | 31 | 32 |
|---|---|---|---|---|---|---|---|
| MVMDCLY | XWXZEKM | ZOXDVWQ | WTXNZWE | MLREIWH | SKQASQH | EKPIYSL | MFXGMLH |

| 33 | 34 | 35 | 36 | 37 | 38 | 39 | 40 |
|---|---|---|---|---|---|---|---|
| XEWQPCH | XHXRIEO | WRUDXRM | MZWPECT | MSKQYRM | SRMRPSM | MEACERN | CVZDURT |

| 41 | 42 | 43 | 44 | 45 | 46 | 47 | 48 |
|---|---|---|---|---|---|---|---|
| IWSEOFX | WQWGMWH | CRAYERC | MMGQILX | YESEMRL | MVBKSSB | ZZYGMRX | YEQEEHP |

| 49 | 50 | 51 | 52 | 53 | 54 | 55 | 56 |
|---|---|---|---|---|---|---|---|
| MLAXFRJ | MRUMRKR | IVDTERB | IFXRQZH | CRUDQZX | XZHNSRL | ISQPYOX | YWXDFRE |

| 57 | 58 | 59 | 60 | 61 | 62 | 63 | 64 |
|---|---|---|---|---|---|---|---|
| ILWTVPE | MLRQPVR | MLQDORB | ZZGGMEY | XREECRM | IHRDUQX | WHKDCKT | CZXR |

Let us make the frequency table for each column. To accelerate the description, we will not reproduce it here, as this first operation would give it to us. It will be found below with additions. We find that a comparison of various columns does not show us the parallelism which an experiment with a Vigenère table with normal alphabets usually shows; so the alphabets are probably not normally ordered. The most frequent among the 63 or 64 letters per column are in each column as follows: M=21; R=12; X=14; D=17; S=9; R=16; H=9. We will take them for E. Having replaced these letters by E in their respective columns, we will count the digraphs formed by the other letters with E, and then we get the frequency table which follows, to which has been added digraphs with E.

| 1 | 2 | 3 | 4 | 5 | 6 | 7 |
|---|---|---|---|---|---|---|
| M 0/21/1 | R 1/12/0 | X 0/14/2 | D 2/17/1 | S 1/9/1 | R 1/16/0 | H 0/9/0 |
| I 0/7/0 | L 6/9/3 | Q 2/10/4 | R 4/6/1 | C 4/7/2 | H 0/7/0 | X 1/8/0 |
| Z 1/6/1 | V 4/7/0 | W 0/6/0 | T 0/5/0 | E 0/7/3 | S 3/6/0 | M 3/7/3 |
| W 0/5/1 | Z 3/7/2 | M 2/5/3 | Q 1/5/0 | I 3/6/0 | Z 0/6/2 | B 2/6/3 |
| X 2/5/1 | E 1/5/0 | R 1/4/2 | E 0/5/0 | M 0/6/2 | W 1/5/3 | R 0/5/1 |
| Y 0/5/1 | W 0/4/2 | U 3/4/2 | G 2/4/0 | Y 2/5/1 | L 2/5/1 | Q 0/4/0 |
| C 3/5/3 | H 0/4/1 | S 0/3/1 | P 0/4/1 | P 0/5/0 | K 0/4/0 | L 2/4/3 |
| S 1/4/1 | M 2/3/1 | G 0/3/0 | A 0/3/2 | O 1/3/1 | E 0/3/0 | T 3/4/1 |
| G 0/1/1 | S 1/3/0 | A 1/3/0 | X 0/3/1 | U 2/3/2 | Q 1/3/2 | P 0/3/2 |
| E 1/1/0 | F 2/3/3 | I 1/3/1 | I 1/2/0 | Z 0/3/0 | F 1/2/0 | E 1/3/2 |
| J 1/1/1 | P 0/2/1 | K 0/2/1 | C 1/2/0 | F 1/2/2 | O 0/2/0 | U 1/2/2 |
| D 0/1/0 | K 0/2/0 | F 1/1/0 | N 1/2/1 | Q 1/2/0 | C 0/1/1 | C 1/2/2 |
| P 0/1/1 | B 1/1/0 | I 0/1/0 | K 1/2/1 | V 1/2/0 | T 0/1/0 | Y 0/2/0 |
| T 0/1/0 | O 0/1/1 | D 0/1/0 | Z 1/1/0 | J 0/1/0 | V 0/1/0 | J 1/2/2 |
|  | Q 0/1/0 | Z 0/1/1 | F 0/1/0 | R 0/1/1 | P 0/1/0 | O 0/1/0 |
|  |  | H 0/1/0 | V 0/1/1 | X 1/1/1 |  | U 1/1/0 |
|  |  | E 0/1/0 | Y 0/1/0 |  |  |  |
|  |  | B 0/1/0 |  |  |  |  |

A preliminary observation: Suppose we had found very many digraphs EE formed by letters which had been obtained merely on the basis of being the most frequent in their respective columns. Then we would have had to assume that at least one of them was not E, since EE is an infrequent digraph. In the two columns producing these sequences, we would have had to try to see if another frequent letter, though not the most frequent, did not seem rather to be E, giving few digraphs with the neighboring E's.

According to the count of digraphs, we can make assumptions on certain letters by classifying them as vowels or consonants.

We will suspend consideration of the identification of letters appearing only once, and also that of frequent letters giving but few digraphs with E, or giving no digraphs beginning with E although forming some ending with E.

We will, then, consider as probable vowels, other than E

| 1 | 2 | 3 | 4 | 5 | 6 | 7 |
|---|---|---|---|---|---|---|
| I | K | W | T | P | H | X |
|   | G | E | Z | K | Q |   |
|   |   |   | E |   | Y |   |

NOTE.—We have taken X₇ (which might be open to question since it has one digraph) to be a probable vowel, because it has but one digraph in eight occurrences. However, we will be ready to drop this assumption at any moment.

As almost certain consonants, we take

| 1 | 2 | 3 | 4 | 5 | 6 | 7 |
|---|---|---|---|---|---|---|
| Z | L | Q | R | C | W | M |
| X | Z | M | N | Y | L | B |
| C | M | R | K | O | Q | L |
| S | F | U | I | U |   | T |
|   |   | I |   | F |   | E |
|   |   |   |   |   |   | U |
|   |   |   |   |   |   | C |
|   |   |   |   |   |   | J |

We have no means of actually determining the exact value of these letters. Let us rewrite our cipher, indicating under the letters the hypotheses we have formed relative to them.

We will not reproduce this table here. It will be found later on increased by some additions. We examine it, but our eyes meet no important result, except the possibility that the first letter of the telegram might be L, beginning the article LE. We enter this value in the cipher, and immediately examine the digraphs with L: Three out of four times L is followed by cipher E in the second column (we will write $E_2$). Now $E_2$ is frequent, and gives only one digraph with E; according to the digraph table, there is a likelihood of having LA; frequency peculiarities do not contradict this. So we will assume $E_2 = A$.

In spite of these assumptions, we cannot get any further. We are going to try to determine some vowels by means of diphthongs, but first let us try to find some more by means of long sequences. In the fifty-fifth group, we find a sequence of five consonants SQPYO between two vowels. Such is possible if the third letter $P_4 = S$. Now, $P_4$ is not very frequent, and only gives one digraph out of four with E; it would not give ES, and it is, hence, probable that it is not S. As we lack vowels, let us try to find which of the five letters stands the best chance of being a vowel. To do this, let us consider for each of the repetitions of each of the letters the interval separating it from the nearest known vowel. Let us get the mean of these intervals (the total of the number of intervals 1 added to twice the total of intervals 2, etc., and the sum of the whole divided by the frequency of the letter). We get:

$$S_2 \text{------} \quad (2 \times 1) + (1 \times 2) = 4 \qquad \text{mean interval} = 4/3$$
$$Q_3 \text{------} \quad (9 \times 1) + (1 \times 2) = 11 \qquad \text{``} \qquad \text{``} \quad = 11/10$$
$$P_4 \text{------} \quad (3 \times 1) + (1 \times 3) = 6 \qquad \text{``} \qquad \text{``} \quad = 6/4$$
$$Y_5 \text{------} \quad (3 \times 1) + (1 \times 2) + (1 \times 3) = 8 \qquad \text{``} \qquad \text{``} \quad = 8/5$$
$$O_6 \text{------} \quad (2 \times 1) = 2 \qquad \text{``} \qquad \text{``} \quad = 2/2$$

The greatest mean interval is that of $Y_5$. However, according to the table of digraphs, we had formed the hypothesis that $Y_5$ was a consonant. We find two contradictory hypotheses on our hands, and will leave $Y_5$ as doubtful with a preponderance in favor of a vowel. We have no more long sequences between vowels.

Let us go back to our consideration of diphthongs. We know that, normally, second letters are likely to be U's or I's, that the most frequent diphthong is OU, and that I fairly often precedes E and O, while it is itself preceded by A. Placing the letters in their columns, we get the following diphthongs:

| 1 | 2 | 3 | 4 | 5 | 6 | 7 | |
|---|---|---|---|---|---|---|---|
| | | | | | H | Q | (group 10–20) |
| | | G | T | | | | (21) |
| | A | W | | | | | (33) |
| | | W | T | | | | (56) |
| | | | | | E | Y | (60) |

We really have very little information here. We will keep as a possible U, $T_4$, $Y_7$, or $Q_7$; the diphthong of group 33 is perplexing (A would suggest U but then T could not possibly be U). As we have to take account of vowel digraphs resulting from the end of one word and the beginning of the following word, if we assume $A_2W_3$ to be a digraph of this sort, we can try the values A and O for $G_3$ and $W_3$.

Seeing the delicacy of the basis on which these assumptions rest, and lacking a sufficiently long message to furnish us with more information, we are going back to our frequency table, where, on the basis of the frequency of $L_2$, $Q_3$, $R_4$, and $C_5$, and their digraphs with $E_p$, we are going to assume that these letters equal $S_p$. We transfer these values to the cipher, and get the table which follows, in which no apparent error weakens our assumptions (From the hypothesis on diphthongs, we have written only $T_4=U_p$ in the table).

```
 1 2 3 4 5 6 7     1 2 3 4 5 6 7     1 2 3 4 5 6 7     1 2 3 4 5 6 7
 Y R Q D I H P     M F X K P Z R     D L X C P Z B     M Z W X S F X
 L E S E . v .     E . E c v . .     . S E . v . c     E c v . E . v

 T S Q D I H L     M M X I J Z H     C R F P S L C     M L Q T E Z Q
 . . S E . v c     E c E . . . E     . E . E c c       E S S v . . v

                              10(Q)
 G R M A S L R     I T I D C H Q     S L X R S W H     J R I A C Q H
 . E c . E c .     v . c E S v v     c S E S E c E     . E c . S c E

 Z R R D Y H B     M B I X E K M     Z W W P Z T M     M L X Q O E P
 c E c E . v c     E . c . . v c     c . v . v . c     E S E . c v .
                                                                  20(Q)
 P R Q F Z S B     M V U V S S J     M Z Q T U R U     M V M D C H Q
 . E S . v . c     E . . . E . c     E c S U c E c     E . c E . v v

 S M G T R R T     Z V M D S S R     Y E S D Y O X     W H Q D I H U
 c . v U . E c     c . c E E . .     L A . E c . v     . . S E . v c

 M V M D C L Y     X W X Z E K M     Z O X D V W Q     W T X N Z W E
 E . c E S c v     c . E . . v c     c . E E . c v     . . E c v c c

                              30(H)
 M L R E I W H     S K Q A S Q H     E K P I Y S L     M F X G M L H
 E S c v . c E     c v S . E . E     . v . . c . c     E c E . . c E

 X E W Q P C H     X H X R I E O     W R U D X R M     M Z W P C R T
 c A v . v . E     c . E S . v .     . E . E . E c     E c v . S E c

                                                                  40(T)
 M S K Q Y R M     S R M R P S M     M E A C E R N     C V Z D U R T
 E . . . . E c     . E c S . . c     E A . . . E .     c . . E c E c

 I W S E O F X     W Q W G M W H     C R A Y E R C     M M G Q I L X
 v . . v c . v     . . v . . c E     c E . . . E c     E c v . . c v

 Y E S E M R L     M V B K S S B     Z Z X G M R X     Y E Q E E H P
 L A . v . E c     E . c E . c       c c E . . E v     L A S v . v .

                        50(R)
 M L A X F R J     M R U R M K R     I V D T E R L     I F X R Q Z H
 E S . . . E c     E E c S . v .     v . . U . E c     v c E S . . E

 C R U D Q Z X     X Z H N S R L     I S Q P Y O X     Y W X D F R E
 c E c E . . v     c c . c E E c     v . S . c . v     L . E E . E c

                                                                  60(Y)
 I L W T V P E     M L R Q P V R     M L Q D O R B     Z Z G G M E Y
 v S v U . . c     E S c . v . .     E S S E c E c     c c v . . v v

 X R E E C R M     I H R D U Q X     W H K D C K T     C Z X R
 c E . v S E c     v . c E c c v     . . c E S v c     c c E S
```

Unfortunately an examination of this table again yields us no new information toward solution.

However, let us transfer our values obtained to a correspondence table:

| Plain | A | B | C | D | E | F | G | H | I | J | K | L | M | N | O | P | Q | R | S | T | U | V | W | X | Y | Z |
|---|---|---|---|---|---|---|---|---|---|---|---|---|---|---|---|---|---|---|---|---|---|---|---|---|---|---|---|
| Cipher 1 | | | | | | | M | | | | | | | | Y | | | | | | | | | | | |
| 2 | | E | | | | | R | | | | | | | | | | | | | | L | | | | | |
| 3 | | G? | | | | | X | | | | | | | | | W? | | | | | Q | | | | | |
| 4 | | | | | | | D | | | | | | | | | | | | | | R | | T | | | |
| 5 | | | | | | | S | | | | | | | | | | | | | | C | | | | | |
| 6 | | | | | | | R | | | | | | | | | | | | | | | | | | | |
| 7 | | | | | | | H | | | | | | | | | | | | | | | | | | | |

**Symmetry of position.**—Let us form a new hypothesis—a very important one. Let us imagine that the substitution table actually comprised random alphabets, but that these alphabets were parallel like those of the Vigenère table. That is to say, let us imagine that the same alphabet is repeatedly shifted parallel to itself, all the letters being slid through the same interval in each successive alphabet. Then we would have the same arrangement as with a pair of sliding strips like Saint-Cyr's. One would bear the normal alphabet, and the other the random substitution alphabet. If we knew the position of one of the letters on the second strip for one of the seven alphabets, we could thence deduce the translation of all the other letters whose intervals with the former remain constant. If E is four places from R in alphabet 2, it will still be four from it in alphabet 4, and from the position of $R_4 = S_p$, we deduce $E_4 = O_p$. It is this principle of the invariance of intervals when the alphabets are parallel that Kerckhoffs has advanced under the name of *symmetry of position*. When the equivalents of several letters are known in the different alphabets, this principle makes it possible thence to deduce the equivalency of certain others by simply inscribing the letters into a table at their proper interval with respect to the letters already known.

$E_4$, according to the frequency table, is a vowel, and calling it $O_p$ in nowise contradicts our previous assumptions.

However, if we grant the assumption of parallel alphabets, alphabet 6, having the same $E_p$ as alphabet 2, will be the same as the latter. An examination of the frequency of the different letters, in spite of the difference of their percentage, does not contradict this assumption. The order of the letters, rated by frequencies, is not the same; yet there is no contradiction either in the frequencies or in the digraphs with $E_p$. Thus we can finish column 6 of the correspondence table and of the cipher.

As we have letters common to alphabets 2 and 4, which give us a starting point for the juxtaposition of these two alphabets with their proper shifts, we write in all the letters appearing in each of them. We have $T_2 = G_p$; $D_2 = Q_p$; $I_4 = C_p$, and we can write these values into the cipher.

But still we do not see any words appearing in it.

Let us try our hand with symmetry of position. We have to find at least one letter in each alphabet figuring in another, so as to find a limit as to their relative shift. Supposing them vowels, we have made an hypothesis on $X_7$ and $Q_7$ permitting studies of X and Q, the interval between which we know to be $X_3 - Q_3$, equal to 14 letters of the normal alphabet. We are going to study the vowels the interval of which is 14. AO and UI have this interval. Let us first try $X_7 = A_p$, and $Q_7 = O_p$; by symmetry of position, it turns out that $H_3 = I_p$. $H_3$ is not very frequent, but besides that, there is no objection. Its position in group 54 corresponds quite well to a probable vowel. Next, let us try $X_7 = U_p$ and $Q_7 = I_p$; this would cause $H_3$ to equal $O_p$; however, this place is already taken, though very doubtfully, by either $G_3$ or $W_3$. The trial is not so convincing. We can complete it by carrying G and W over into alphabet 7, which might also have decided us on the value of $G_3$ and $W_3$ (trials to be made: $G_3 = A_p$ and $W_3 = O_p$ with $X_7 = A_p$ and $Q_7 = O_p$, next $G_3 = O_p$ and $W_3 = A_p$ with the same values for $X_7$ and $Q_7$). $G_3 = A_p$ and $W_3 = O_p$ give $W_7 = K_p$, $G_7 = W_p$. These are both infrequent letters and in fact, $G_7$ and $W_7$ do not occur at all. However, as we would get a result of the same sort with $G_3 = O_p$, and $W_3 = A_p$, we have not drawn much information from this experiment. We get nothing that weakens our assumptions—we get nothing that strongly supports them.

So our correspondence table is:

| | A | B | C | D | E | F | G | H | I | J | K | L | M | N | O | P | Q | R | S | T | U | V | W | X | Y | Z |
|---|---|---|---|---|---|---|---|---|---|---|---|---|---|---|---|---|---|---|---|---|---|---|---|---|---|---|---|
| 1 | | | | M | | | | | | Y | | | | | | | | | | | | | | | | |
| 2 | E | | | | | | R | | T | | | | | | | | D | | L | | | | | | | |
| 3 | G? | | | | | | X | | H | | | | | | W? | | | Q | | | | | | | | |
| 4 | | | | D | | | | | | | | | E | | | | | R | | T | | | | | | |
| 5 | | | | | | | S | | | | | | | | | | | C | | | | | | | | |
| 6 | E | | | | | | R | | T | | | | | | | | D | | L | | | | | | | |
| 7 | X | | | | | | H | | | | W? | | | | | Q | | | | | | G? | | | | |

Of course, we will carry these assumed values over into our cipher, but we are still obliged to hunt new elements.

Let us keep on striving to introduce into one of the alphabets a letter already occurring in another, in order to get a limit on how to evaluate the shifting. We have seen that $Y_5$, which we had considered a consonant, was probably a vowel. Let us test $Y_5$ in the vowel places and estimate the results by means of interval YM taken from alphabet 1. If $Y_5 = O_p$, $M_5 = H_p$; now $M_5$ is frequent and $H_p$ infrequent. If $Y_5 = I_p$, $M_5 = B_p$ and the same observation is true. If $Y_5 = A_p$, $M_5 = T_p$, which is entirely plausible. $Y_5 = U_p$ would be another plausible solution, $M_5 = N_p$. However, if we transfer the intervals YS and YC taken from alphabet 5 to alphabet 1, we find with $Y_5 = A_p$, we get $S_1 = P_p$, $C_1 = D_p$, which agree well with the frequencies ($S_1 = 4_p$, $C_1 = 5_p$) and for $Y_5 = U_p$, $S_1 = V_p$, $C_1 = J_p$, which is not satisfying on account of the infrequency of J. So, $Y_5 = A_p$.

While we are in alphabet 5, let us keep on studying its vowels. $P_5 = I_p$, $Z_5 = O_p$ would give $P_1 = T_p$, $Z_1 = Z_p$ which will not do because the frequency of $Z_1 = 6$ and that of $P_1 = 1$. On the other hand, $P_5 = O_p$ and $Z_5 = I_p$ give $P_1 = Z_p$, $Z_1 = T_p$ which is quite acceptable. Now, we will take these values as correct.

Granting the foregoing assumptions, our cryptogram has developed as follows (the capitals are identified letters, the little letter " c " means a consonant, and " v ", a vowel):

```
1 2 3 4 5 6 7      1 2 3 4 5 6 7      1 2 3 4 5 6 7      1 2 3 4 5 6 7

Y R Q D I H P      M F X K P Z R      D L X C P Z B      M Z W X S F X
L E S E . v .      E . E c O . .      . S E . O . c      E c O . E . A

                              5
T S Q D I H L      M M X I J Z H      C R F P S L C      M L Q T E Z Q
. . S E . v c      E c E . . . E      D E . . E S c      E S S u . . O

                          10
G R M A S L R      I T I D C H Q      S L X R S W H      J R I A C Q H
. E c . E S .      v G c E S v O      P S E S E c E      . E c . S c E

                                                15
Z R R D Y H B      M B I X E K M      Z W W P Z T M      M L X Q O E P
T E c E A v c      E . c . . v c      T . O . I G c      E S E . c A .

                                                            20
P R Q F Z S B      M V U V S S J      M Z Q T U R U      M V M D C H Q
Z E S . I . c      E . . . E . c      E c S U C E c      E . c E S v O

S M G T R R T      Z V M D S S R      Y E S D Y O X      W H Q D I H U
P . v U . E c      T . c E E . .      L A . E A . A      . . S E . v c

                25
M V M D C L Y      X W X Z E K M      Z O X D V W Q      W T X N Z W E
E . c E S S v      c . E . . v c      T . E E . c O      . G E c I c c

                              30
M L R E I W H      S K Q A S Q H      E K P I Y S L      M F X G M L H
E S c O . c E      P v S . E . E      . v . . A . c      E c E . T S E

                                          35
X E W Q P C H      Z H X R I E O      W R U D X R M      M Z W P C R T
c A O . O . E      T . E S . A .      . E . E . E c      E c O . S E c

                                                            40
M S K Q Y R M      S R M R P S M      M E A C E R N      C V Z D U R T
E . . . A E c      P E c S O . c      E A . . . E .      D . . E c E c

I W S E O F X      W Q W G M W H      C R A Y E R C      M M G Q I L X
v . . O c . A      . . O . T c E      D E . . . E c      E c A . . S A

                45
Y E S E M R L      M V B K S S B      Z Z X G M R X      Y E Q E E H P
L A . O T E c      E . . c E . c      T c E . T E A      L A S O . v .

                              50
M L A X F R J      M R U R M K R      I V D T E R B      I F X R Q Z H
E S . . . E c      E E c S T v .      v . . U . E c      v c E S . . E

                                          55
C R U D Q Z X      X Z H N S R L      I S Q P Y O X      Y W X D F R E
D E c E . . A      c c I c E E c      v . S . A . A      L . E E . E c

                                                            60
I L W T V P E      M L R Q P V R      M L Q D O R B      Z Z G G M E Y
v S O U . . c      E S c . O . .      E S S E c E c      T c A . T A v

X R E E C R M      I H R D U Q X      W H K D C K T      C Z X R
c E O S E c .      v . c E c c A      . . . c E . S . v . c      D c E S
```

with the correspondence table:

| | A | B | C | D | E | F | G | H | I | J | K | L | M | N | O | P | Q | R | S | T | U | V | W | X | Y | Z |
|---|---|---|---|---|---|---|---|---|---|---|---|---|---|---|---|---|---|---|---|---|---|---|---|---|---|---|---|
| 1 | | | C | M | | | | | | | Y | | | | S | | | | Z | | | | | | P | |
| 2 | E | | | | R | | T | | | | | | | | | | | | D | | L | | | | | |
| 3 | G? | | | | X | | | H | | | | | | | W? | | | Q | | | | | | | | |
| 4 | | | | | D | | L | | | | | | E | | | | R | | T | | | | | | | |
| 5 | Y | | | | S | | | | Z | | | | | | P | | | | C | M | | | | | | |
| 6 | E | | | | R | | T | | | | | | | | | | | | D | | L | | | | | |
| 7 | X | | | | H | | | | | | W? | | | Q | | | | | | | | G? | | | | |

We might begin to hunt for probable words in the cryptogram. The last words, with their known letters and consonant-vowel assumptions, might be DES ORDRES. Nevertheless, we shall continue the analytical method with the symmetry-of-position idea and the study of frequencies.

An examination of the tables would suggest seeking the value of $H_6$ (frequency 7, digraphs 0) as an interesting study. Here we will not go into all the trials involved in this. The trigraph SHO of groups nos. 10 and 20 would encourage trying $H_6$ for $I_p$, an assumption which would block the accepted results in alphabet 3 (if they had a common letter, the others would also have to be so). The other trials—$H_6 = O_p$, for example, which results in $T_3 = A_p$—block previous assumptions, or else are unconvincing. We wind up by vaguely suspecting that $H_6$ is not a vowel.

The pairs of alphabets now have as common letters: 1–5 = C, M, Y, S, Z, P; 3–7 = G?, X, H, W?, Q; 2–4 = E, R, T, D, L; but we have no means of combining these three series. Let us try to find a letter of one series still unidentified but appearing in another series; for example, $M_7$ which is frequent (7 times) and resembles a consonant (six digraphs with $E_p$). Following the ESARINTULO [1] order, let us first call $M_7 = S$. According to the intervals between this assumed $M_7$ and the letters $Q_7$ and $X_7$, it would result that $Q_1$ would represent $A_p$ and $X_1$, $M_p$; the frequencies of $X_1$ (5 times) and of $Q_1$ (0 times) make this assumption scarcely reasonable.

Next, let us try $M_7 = R_p$. The result would be that $H_1 = R_p$. But $H_1$ does not appear at all. Thus, it would also result that $W_1$ whose frequency is 5 would equal $X_p$ or $J_p$, depending on whether $W_3$ is in its correct position or should be interchanged with $G_3$ (likewise with $W_7$ and $G_7$). Let us reject this theory too.

Let us test $M_7 = N_p$. Then, $Y_7 = U_p$, and $Y_7$ ought to be a vowel. $Z_7 = B_p$, $P_7 = I_p$, $C_7 = M_p$ reveal nothing contradictory.

In alphabet 1, $X_1 = R_p$ agrees with the frequency 5 with three digraphs. However, $W_1 = B_p$, $G_1 = N_p$ do not fit with the frequencies $W_1 = 5$, $G_1 = 1$. We have always hesitated up to the present upon the allocation of W and G between the two places attributed to them. By inverting them and writing $W_1 = N_p$ and $G_1 = B_p$, we will get normal frequencies.

Now we have two series of random-alphabet letters arranged in their order and at their proper interval:

```
G . C M Q . . . . . Y . W . S . X . Z . H . . . P .
E . . . R . T . . . . . . . . . . . D . L . . . . . .
```

[1] The author is not consistent in his use of the series of relative frequencies—he some times uses ERASINTULO and at other times ESARINTULO.

Unhappily, the two series can be dovetailed into one another in several different positions with no superimposition of letters.

In transferring the new values to the cipher, particularly $P_7 = I$, and considering $H_6$ (which is second in frequency in 6, which we first supposed to be a vowel because it gave no digraphs with E, and which we could not identify as a vowel), we find sequences for it with vowels which confirm that it is probably a consonant.

| | | |
|---|---|---|
| Group | 1 | LESE.H$_c$IE |
| | 10 | ESH$_c$OPSESE |
| | 13 | EAH$_c$.E |
| | 20 | ESH$_c$OP |
| | 48 | LASOH$_c$IES |

Trying various translations, we are led to fancy that $H_6 = T_p$. As $L_6 = S_p$, H would then be placed immediately to the right of L in the random alphabet which would become:

$$\text{G E C M Q R . T . . Y . W . S . X D Z L H . . . P .}$$

The table of alphabets is now:

| | A | B | C | D | E | F | G | H | I | J | K | L | M | N | O | P | Q | R | S | T | U | V | W | X | Y | Z |
|---|---|---|---|---|---|---|---|---|---|---|---|---|---|---|---|---|---|---|---|---|---|---|---|---|---|---|---|
| 1 | . | G | E | C | M | Q | R | . | T | . | . | Y | . | W | . | S | . | X | D | Z | L | H | . | . | . | P |
| 2-6 | E | C | M | Q | R | . | T | . | . | Y | . | W | . | S | . | X | D | Z | L | H | . | . | . | P | . | G |
| 3 | W | . | S | . | X | D | Z | L | H | . | . | . | P | . | G | E | C | M | Q | R | . | T | . | . | Y | . |
| 4 | . | S | . | X | D | Z | L | H | . | . | . | P | . | G | E | C | M | Q | R | . | T | . | . | Y | . | W |
| 5 | Y | . | W | . | S | . | X | D | Z | L | H | . | . | . | P | . | G | E | C | M | Q | R | . | T | . | . |
| 7 | X | D | Z | L | H | . | . | . | P | . | G | E | C | M | Q | R | . | T | . | . | Y | . | W | . | S | . |

and the beginning of the cipher yields:

```
Y R Q D I H P    M F X K P Z R    D L X C P Z B    M Z W X S F X
L E S E . T I    E . E . O R P    S S E P O . .    E R A D E . A
T S Q D I H L    M M X I J Z H    C R F P S L C    M L Q T E Z Q
I N S E . T D    E C E . . R E    D E . L E S M    E S S U R R O
G R M A S L R    I T I D C H Q
B E R . E S P    . G . E S T O
```

This time words are easily guessed, "LE SEPTIÈME CORPS SE PORTERA DEMAIN SEPT DÉCEMBRE DE BLESMES SUR ROBERT-ESPAGNE STOP", and the alphabet will fill up more and more. We give it fully here:

$$\text{A T N B Y J W F S K X D Z L H V O U P I G E C M Q R}$$

After the above sentence, already translated, the text of the cryptogram continues

". . . STOP SES ÉLÉMENTS DE TÊTE ATTEINDRONT LA LIGNE SERMAIZE-ST. EULIEN VERS UNE HEURE STOP COUVERTURE EN PLACE AVANT SEPT HEURES SUR LE FRONT VEEL-LONGEVILLE STOP LE POST DE COMMANDEMENT SERA À ROBERT-ESPAGNE LE GÉNÉRAL SE RENDRA EN PERSONNE AUPRÈS DU GÉNÉRAL COMMANDANT LE 2e CORPS À LA COTE 230 A LA SORTIE SUD DE VEEL STOP AU FUR ET À MESURE DE LEUR ARRIVÉE DANS LA VALLÉE DE LA SAULX LES TROUPES SE METTRONT AU REPOS EN ATTENDANT DES ORDRES."

We might be interested in trying to find out if the key is clear and what it turns out to be.

Let us note, with respect to this, that, although we do not know the letter which begins the random alphabet and which constitutes an indicator (or, although we are ignorant of the indicator if it is outside the alphabet), the whole alphabet will have undergone shifts parallel to this letter. If, in passing from the first to the second columns, the indicator letter has been slid two places, all the letters of the alphabet will have been slid two places. The succession of key letters may, then, be indicated not solely by the letters which are located successively opposite the indicator (and which will yield a meaning if the key is clear) but also by the letters located successively opposite any given letter of the alphabet. So let us establish the series of these keys and, if they from a clear one, we will see it appear.

Suppose that the indicator letter was P. It was set successively opposite ZXMLOXI.[1] That does not give anything. Next suppose that it was the letter next to P. This letter was slipped successively opposite the letters next to the preceding AYNMPYJ. In order to continue looking for the indicator letter by considering the letters with which it has coincided, we see that after having written the first series of these letters on a row we only have to keep on writing the normal alphabet under each of them:

```
Z X M L O X I
A Y N M P Y J
B Z O N Q Z K
C A P O R A L
```

and we find the clear key CAPORAL. By performing this operation as soon as we have the translation of the same letter in several columns we can sometimes guess the key and fix the position of the columns still unknown by means of their relation to the others.

For this study, we had rather favorable conditions. The cipher was long—445 letters. The E's had the highest frequency in every column. The digraphs with E gave good information, save for $H_6$. Then, too, in this example, we tried to call attention to a series of notes valuable as the case brought them up rather than to arrive at the speediest possible translation. Finally, the table was formed with parallel alphabets.

Even in this last case, there are ciphers in which the analytical method encounters very grave difficulties, and in which the matter of the probable word must be resorted to.

**Example of the application of the method of the probable word.**—Let us take the following cipher of 188 letters. We will say that it was intercepted on May 5 by a wireless station during military operations and that we know the enemy to be using a Saint-Cyr-type rule with a frequently changed random alphabet.

The radiogram was dispatched by an army corps station. In order to study it, we forthwith write the cipher out in sets of seven letters; the repetitions, indeed, lead us to believe that the key has seven letters (QVT, first and sixth groups; interval 35—EHLUI, ninth and twenty-fifth; interval 112—ZKE, tenth and twentieth; interval 70—YE, fourteenth and fifteenth; interval 7, etc.).

| | | | | 5 | | | |
|---|---|---|---|---|---|---|---|
| YEQVTBH | JRKVRBN | TKIRSXQ | XHXQYQH | JEHGOEB | TSQVTFX | TQXRSXB | DEAPTLY |
| XEHLUIN | ZKERSLX (10) | HEIAXET | CRQFMHH | TSKQPSB | YEMEQHH | YETDQOH (15) | GRWTOKM |
| ZLAQRRN | YRWRSXB | ARAQSLN | ZKEKYSB (20) | FSIDORM | ZQWGCWX | PKIDYVE | WEYFMNP |
| DEHLUIB (25) | AKAQCLY | XFWQUR. | | | | | |

[1] It is more usual to pick the indicator letter from the line above the box so that the key actually appears in one of the columns.

The frequency arrangement for each column gives us:

| 1 | | 2 | | 3 | | 4 | | 5 | | 6 | | 7 | |
|---|---|---|---|---|---|---|---|---|---|---|---|---|---|
| T | 4 | E | 9 | A | 4 | Q | 6 | S | 4 | L | 4 | B | 6 |
| Y | 4 | K | 5 | I | 4 | R | 4 | O | 3 | R | 3 | H | 5 |
| Z | 4 | R | 5 | W | 4 | D | 3 | R | 3 | X | 3 | N | 4 |
| X | 3 | S | 3 | H | 3 | V | 3 | T | 3 | B | 2 | X | 3 |
| A | 2 | Q | 2 | Q | 3 | F | 2 | U | 3 | E | 2 | M | 2 |
| D | 2 | F | 1 | E | 2 | G | 2 | Y | 3 | H | 2 | E | 1 |
| J | 2 | H | 1 | K | 2 | E | 2 | C | 2 | I | 2 | P | 1 |
| C | 1 | L | 1 | X | 2 | A | 1 | Q | 2 | S | 2 | Q | 1 |
| F | 1 | | | M | 1 | X | 1 | M | 1 | F | 1 | T | 1 |
| G | 1 | | | T | 1 | K | 1 | N | 1 | K | 1 | Y | 1 |
| H | 1 | | | Y | 1 | P | 1 | P | 1 | N | 1 | Z | 1 |
| P | 1 | | | | | T | 1 | X | 1 | O | 1 | | |
| W | 1 | | | | | | | | | Q | 1 | | |
| | | | | | | | | | | V | 1 | | |
| | | | | | | | | | | W | 1 | | |

E is uncertain in columns 1 and 3. By assuming that $E_2$ and $Q_4$ equal $E_p$, we may determine that $Y_1$, $A_3$, and $I_3$ give digraphs with $E_2$ and $Q_4$ and should not be $E_p$, but the sequences $S_5L_6$ and $Q_4S_5L_6$ (groups 10 and 19) inspire us with doubts as to the value of the first letters of the first row in our table insofar as $E_p$ is concerned. These doubts would be increased by a further study of the digraphs, which we have not reproduced here. The segregation of the vowels appears to us as almost impossible.

In such cases, there is occasion for drawing on the method based upon the assumption that a given word occurs in the cipher and upon the identification of this word. Not knowing the alphabets, the cryptanalyst cannot just slip the probable word along under the text, as he can in the Vigenère table with normal alphabets, and in each position look for the key letter that would give the alphabet in which the clear letter corresponds to the cipher letter. The intuitive faculties and ingeniousness of the cryptanalyst must be depended upon.

The cipher in question having been offered as an exercise, here is how the problem was solved by one of those who tried it.

Among known data, he noted that it was definitely known that the document had been radiotelegraphed by an army corps. He had worked on problems of this kind before, with similar auxiliary information, and he had seen how often they related to information or orders, and that the formal beginning was usually "LE CORPS D'ARMÉE..." or "LA DIVISION" with verbs in the future, numbers of units, and dates. For example "DEMAIN LE CORPS D'ARMÉE ATTAQUERA..." or "LA DEUXIÈME DIVISION PARTIRA DEMAIN À n HEURES ...", etc.

His attention was attracted by certain similarities between the first two groups:

```
Y E Q V T B H
J R K V R B N
```

two V's and two B's at a seven-letter interval and, after a few trials, the aim of which was to reconstruct the beginnings of sentences presenting this peculiarity, that is to say, of the type:

. . . V . B . . . . V . B .

he came to adopt the words "LA SIXIÈME DIVISION", which as we see:

```
L A S I X I E
M E D I V I S
I O N
```

constitutes a solution of the problem, which is in no wise contrary to the frequency list ($X_p$ appears 3 times in 26, but we have to assume irregularities like this in such short ciphers).

So, from this assumption, he wrote the values found into the correspondence table:

| | A | B | C | D | E | F | G | H | I | J | K | L | M | N | O | P | Q | R | S | T | U | V | W | X | Y | Z |
|---|---|---|---|---|---|---|---|---|---|---|---|---|---|---|---|---|---|---|---|---|---|---|---|---|---|---|---|
| 1 | | | | | | | | | T | | Y | J | | | | | | | | | | | | | | |
| 2 | E | | | | R | | | | | | | | K | | | | | | | | | | | | | |
| 3 | | | K | | | | | | | | | I | | | | | Q | | | | | | | | | |
| 4 | | | | | | | | V | | | | | | | | | | | | | | | | | | |
| 5 | | | | | | | | | | | | | | | | | | | | R | | T | | | | |
| 6 | | | | | | | | B | | | | | | | | | | | | | | | | | | |
| 7 | | | | | H | | | | | | | | | | | | | | N | | | | | | | |

Knowing that the cipher had been composed with a movable alphabet, he applied symmetry of position which gave him:

| | A | B | C | D | E | F | G | H | I | J | K | L | M | N | O | P | Q | R | S | T | U | V | W | X | Y | Z |
|---|---|---|---|---|---|---|---|---|---|---|---|---|---|---|---|---|---|---|---|---|---|---|---|---|---|---|---|
| 1 | I | | E | | | | Q | R | T | | Y | J | | | | K | | | | | | | | | | |
| 2 | E | | | Q | R | | T | | Y | J | | | K | | | | | | | | | | | | I | |
| 3 | | | K | | | | | | | | | I | | E | | | Q | R | | T | | | Y | J | | |
| 4 | | | | | | | | V | | | | | | | | | | | | | | | | | | |
| 5 | Y | J | | | K | | | | | | | | | | I | | E | | Q | R | | T | | | | |
| 6 | | | | | | | | B | | | | | | | | | | | | | | | | | | |
| 7 | | | | | H | | | | | | | | | | | | | | N | | | | | | | |

putting these values through the cryptogram, he got:

```
Y E Q V T B H    J R K V R B N    T K I R S Q X    X H X Q Y Q H
L A S I X I E    M E D I V I S    I O N . . . .    . . . . A . E

        5
J E H G O E B    T S Q V T F X    T Q X R S X B    D E A P T L Y
M A . . . . .    I . S I X . .    I D . . . . .    . A . . X . .

                              10
X E H L U I N    Z K E R S L X    H E I A X E T    C R Q F M H H
. A . . . . S    . O P . . . .    . A N . . . .    . E S . . . E

                                            15
T S K Q P S B    Y E M E Q H H    Y E T D Q O H    G R W T O K M
I . D . . . .    L A . . U . E    L A V . U . E    . E . . . . .

                                                          20
Z L A Q R R N    Y R W R S X B    A R A Q S L N    Z K E K Y S B
. . . . V . S    L E . . . . .    . E . . . S .    . O P . A . .

F S I D O R M    Z Q W G C W X    P K I D Y V E    W E Y F M N P
. . N . . . .    . D . . . . .    . O N . A . .    . . Y . . . .

              25
D E H L U I B    A K A Q C L Y    X F W Q U R
. A . . . . .    . O . . . . .    . . . . . .
```

There is nothing contradictory in the sequences thus obtained. We said that we might reasonably expect a verb in the future close to the beginning of the document. Such a verb might give us the A in the fourth group, in which case $Q_4$ would be $R_p$, and this assumption permitted him to add to the table the values $V_1=W_p, V_2=U_p, V_3=J_p, V_5=L_p, K_4=C_p, I_4=M_p, E_4=O_p$, etc. As the values arrived at are not in contradiction to the frequencies, the initial assumption is strengthened. But it is not possible to read the document yet.

Then he turned to the date of the dispatch: 5 Mai. In the sixth group occurs the word SIX followed by two unknown letters and an $I_p$; he reads:

LA SIXIÈME DIVISION . . . . . . RADEMAIN . . . . . SIXMAI . . . .

andt he identifications $Q_6=D_p, H_3=I_p, G_4=N_p, F_6=M_p, X_7=A_p$ enabled him to piece together all the alphabet fragments of the seven columns and get the following letters of the alphabet on the strips placed in the position of alphabet 1:

```
A B C D E F G H I J K L M N O P Q R S T U V W X Y Z
I . E . . Q R . T N B Y J . F . K X . . . H V . . .
```

The first words of the cipher then became

```
Y E Q V T B H    J R K V R B N    T K I R S X Q    X H X Q Y Q H
L A S I X I E    M E D I V I S    I O N S . P O    R T E R A D E

J E H G O E B    T S Q V T F X    T
M A I N . A T    I . S I X M A    I . . . . . .
```

The position of S and O in the alphabet are immediately deduced.   Now we can read the text:

"LA SIXIEME DIVISION SE PORTERA DEMAIN MATIN SIX MAI DE SEPT—SAULX SUR AIGNY STOP SES AVANT—GARDES ATTEINDRONT LA ROUTE LA VEUVE BEAUMONT SUR VESLE À SEPT HEURES STOP CANTONNEMENT DANS LA ZONE AULNAY ATHIS AIGNY THOURS SUR MARNE"

The alphabet used to prepare the exercise is the following:

I G E C M Q R A T N B Y J W F S K X D Z L H V O U P

The above remarks on the form, the possible destination, the date, etc., are such as we have to use constantly to solve problems unsolvable by the analytical methods.   These analytical methods usually have the advantage of requiring almost mechanical actions only, much of the drudgery of which can be intrusted to clerks.   Great centers for the study of cryptography, which recognize by some means (often by a description published by the author) systems susceptible to use for the ends of warfare or diplomacy, endeavor to find means for the solution of such systems based on operations requiring routine labor only (making frequency tables, addition, symmetry of position, etc.)[1].   However, experienced cryptanalysts often avail themselves of such details as we noted above, and the experience of the years from 1914 to 1918, to cite only those, prove that in practice elements of this nature are at his disposal, permitting assumptions much more audacious than those that answered for the solution of the last example.   So the reader would be wrong in fancying that such fortuitous elements are found only in cryptographic works in which the author deciphers a document that he himself has enciphered.   Cryptographic correspondence, on the condition that it is intense and that numerous workable elements are at hand, often furnishes elements for study so complete that an author would not dare use them all to solve a problem for fear of being accused of outright exaggeration.

[1] See for example the work entitled *L'Indice de coincidence et ses applications en Cryptographie*, by Fournier, 1921, a translation of a work in the English language.   Note; This is a translation from the manuscript of *The Index of Coincidence and its Applications in Cryptography* by William F. Friedman, Riverbank Publication No. 22, 1922.

CHAPTER VIII

## POLYALPHABETIC SUBSTITUTIONS WITH ALPHABETS SUPPOSEDLY NON-PARALLEL WITH SINGLE OR VARIANT NUMERICAL VALUES, ETC.

When we are dealing with ciphers obtained from random alphabets differing from each other, and when we do not know these alphabets, the problem gets harder and harder.

If the key is short enough and the cipher long enough for the frequencies to yield sufficient information in each column, we determine the E's; we seek to recognize the vowels and study each alphabet separately, just as we had begun to do in the foregoing example, where, for want of data, we had to resort to symmetry of position in order to profit in each of the alphabets by discoveries already made in the others, which were parallel. If we have several ciphers presumably made with the same key, we can work on the beginnings.

But we take it that systems of this kind, with long, frequently changing keys, care having been taken not to encipher long cryptograms, may constitute one of the finest modes of secret communication at the present time, particularly if we take the precaution to prevent the key from revealing itself as clear to a cryptanalyst who may have gotten the alphabets and the probable word. Now, we can avoid divulging the clear key by enciphering, for example, not in the alphabet indicated by the key letter, but in the next alphabet to the left or right.

**Polyalphabetic substitutions with numerical variants.**—Everything that we have said about polyalphabetic systems in letters would apply to systems in which one letter is represented by a group of digits or of letters. We can make tables, or better still, sliding strips or disks in which the letters are replaced by groups, and then have all the data mentioned above. In Vigenère's system, with numerically ordered groups like those of the first column, let the translation of the letters of the normal alphabet be written to the left of the table, random parallel alphabets, with symmetry of position, and any random alphabet whatever. The use of groups even permits the introduction of a new element, variant values. The movable-strip device described at the end of chapter III enables us to use variant values and random alphabets in polyalphabetic substitution. It is again in the study of repeated words of the clear text, similarly located with respect to the key, that we may hope to find a means of undertaking the decrypting of this kind of system, which—we must not hide the fact—appears extremely secure, indeed.[1] Those that, together with variant-value devices, come into the scope of the applications of the following paragraph are equally so, and it has been only because of the indiscretion of the encipherer—for example, in the inscription, at the beginning of equal sets of indicator groups designating the successive translations of A and, hence, the order of groups—that we have been able to find data giving satisfying results.

**Polyalphabetic substitution by sets.**—Up to the present, we have alluded to systems in which the principle was that the alphabets used changed at each letter, except for doublets in the key.

These continual shifts, especially when we encipher with instruments like Saint-Cyr's sliding strips or Carmona's device, have sometimes proven wearisome. Thus, in certain ciphers, it is recognized that the encipherer enciphers several successive letters with the same key; for

---

[1] This statement applies only when there is a limited amount of text for study.

example, the five letters of the same group of the telegram. In documents written and not telegraphed, we may also find substitutions with keys changing with each word, but in which a whole word is enciphered with the same key. As the words thus keep their formulae, the probable-word method is applicable; and often it is seen that the number of substitution alphabets is limited, that the $n^{th}$, $N+n^{th}$, $2N+n^{th}$, etc., words are enciphered with the same alphabet, so that, when the system is thus determined, we may, even without discovering a suitable probable word, study the documents in the analytical way, grouping together the words enciphered in the same alphabet in order to examine them as a simple substitution.

In this order of ideas, it is sometimes interesting, when we have a cryptogram enciphered in word lengths but which is not a simple substitution, to write the words one under the other, placing letters having corresponding positions in the words in columns. By their similarity, sometimes the ends of words of equal length reveal that the system used was a polyalphabetic substitution in which the key was broken at the end of each word, and recommenced at the beginning of the following word. Taking the alphabets next to the clear alphabet, with a Gronsfeld-type key indicating the shifts to be undergone at each letter to encipher it, we get a system that may be employed without auxiliary data, the operations taking place in our heads. Moreover, systems with "keys broken at each word" may be applied to telegraphic transmissions provided such key interruptions are pointed out, or else the words must be separated as we saw earlier by the interpolation of W after each word.

**Alphabet changes.**—This sort of system may, again, apply under the following circumstances: After having enciphered part of a telegram with a random alphabet sliding parallel to itself (for example, as in the case of sliding strips or a disk), which enables the correspondents to work quite simply, and enables the cryptanalyst, if he knows the system, to bring symmetry of position into play, the alphabet is changed without changing the key. This requires, for example, only the replacing of the upper face of the slide of a Saint-Cyr rule by the lower face bearing another alphabet. This does not complicate the work of the correspondents very much. For the cryptanalyst it does not change the length of the key. If he does not then perceive that the repetitions are localized in the two parts of the telegram without overlapping (and, again, by choosing alphabets, we can place frequent letters in the same places even when we change), he is completely bewildered in the frequency counts.

We cite this system because disk devices have been brought to apply to it. By dividing the inner disk up into a certain number of superimposable sectors, and by making these sectors, say in the form of thin cardboard, movable with respect to one another, we break the alphabet up into series of four or five letters whose relative order is readily changeable (Mr. Pasanisi is the inventor of an apparatus of a similar type).

It has been through a study of repetitions, due to the slips of the encipherer, that we have seen translations obtained of documents enciphered by this method. Or else, indicators, meant to show the order of sectors (enumerated), the starting position on the movable strip with respect to the fixed one, and the regular shifting performed on the disk formed an ensemble of some special aspect drawing atzntion and enabling people to try to group certain cryptograms so as to study them together. The subject would be too long to go into in detail here, and would, moreover, have no interest as an example of general order. So we shall not dwell on it.

## Chapter IX

## RECONSTRUCTION OF ALPHABETS

In the study of polyalphabetic substitutions, we first examined the use of Vigenère alphabets. Then we took up tables with a random alphabet as their basis, but still of the Vigenère type, with a slip of one letter from alphabet to alphabet. Lastly we spoke of non-parallel random alphabets. Quite often we do not know beforehand what type we are concerned with; we reconstruct the identities of the letters of several alphabets, sometimes by regular means, sometimes by a fortunate coincidence (for example, work on the beginnings of long-key telegrams, possession of a fragment of the plain text of a cryptogram, etc.), and as the correspondence tables are often written by the cryptanalyst as deciphering tables, the alphabetical order being that of the cipher alphabet, while in Vigenère squares the alphabetical order is that of the clear letters, nothing indicates at first sight that the various alphabets issue from one single table. At this stage, we should try to find out whether the alphabets are parallel or not.

**Normal basic alphabets.**—If the basic alphabet of the table (or strip) is normally arranged, the reconstruction is easy.

Let us take, for example, the following results wherein I is the cipher alphabet, and II and III, two clear alphabets yielding letters in the clear for two periods of the decipherment.

```
  I.  A B C D E F G H I J K L M N O P Q R S T U V W X Y Z

 II.  E A D N W L O K C M T B Q S P Y R V X H Z G J U I F
III.  L H K U D S V R J T A I X Z W F Y C E O G N Q B P M
```

By taking the trouble to reconstruct the deciphering tables

```
A B C D E F G H I J K L M N O P Q R S T U V W X Y Z
B L I C A Z V T Y W H F J D G O M Q N K X R E S P U
```

and

```
A B C D E F G H I J K L M N O P Q R S T U V W X Y Z
K X R E S P U B L I C A Z V T Y W H F J D G O M Q N
```

we see that there is only one cipher alphabet and that it is simply slid along.

**Random basic alphabets.**—But if, though a square table was used (or a similar system producing an alphabetic shift without changing the letters), a basic alphabet in normal order has not been taken, the experiment that we have just performed here will not work. However, it is interesting to find, when it exists, the arrangement which yields the whole series of alphabets; for example, the single table.

We are going to study the problem proposed as follows: To reestablish in the alphabets an order which enables us (when it is possible) to reduce a series of secondary alphabets reconstructed in the course of decipherment to a square table, a Saint-Cyr rule, or a disk.

This problem is worked out by realizing that the linear or angular intervals between letters of the basic alphabet in the square table (or on the disk) should make possible their coincidence, in all the positions that this alphabet takes as it is slid along, with the clear alphabet which

(69)

serves as a key. The distance between two letters of a given alphabet in one of the positions cannot vary when the alphabet passes to a second position. Hence, we conclude that if, in the alphabet, a certain number of letters separate the characters placed in one of the positions opposite two key letters of the clear, it is this same number of letters which will separate the characters placed opposite these same key letters in another position. In other words, if we have the equivalents in two positions of the alphabet:

| CLEAR | POSITION I | POSITION II |
|:---:|:---:|:---:|
| A | Q | E |
| B | P | S |
| C | E | F |

we will get in the basic alphabet of the table the same number of letters between Q and P as between E and S; between P and E as between S and F, etc.[1]

Then let the results of the decipherment be:

I.   A B C D E F G H I J K L M N O P Q R S T U V X Y Z

II.   D E C K U P X Y G Q R H I A J L B N M T O F Z S V
III.   J S V L K B T O Y F Z Q R P I D M X C U A N G H E

Let us pick at random a digraph in I, say AE. The corresponding letters in II are DU. The interval of DU in III will correspond equally with that of DU in II and of PT in I, or of LT in II, etc.; that of PT in I, is, therefore, equal to that of LT in II. That of LT in III is equal to the latter, but equal also to that of DG in I and KX in II. So we shall write these intervals, all equal, under the form given below, and, when we have considered a certain number of equal intervals, a division of the number of letters of the alphabet and at most equal to it, we will discover our first interval. The problem of placing all the letters will be solved only if our first interval is chosen so as not to retrieve the first digraph before using all the intervals. If it is otherwise, if the cycle is closed too soon, we will try a different interval with another digraph.

| AE, | PT, | DG, | ER, | TV, | GJ, | RL, | VY, | JB, | LZ, | YC, | BS, | ZQ, |
|:---:|:---:|:---:|:---:|:---:|:---:|:---:|:---:|:---:|:---:|:---:|:---:|:---:|
| DU, | LT, | KX, | UN, | TF, | XQ, | NH, | FS, | QE, | HV, | SC, | EM, | VB, |
| CF, | SN, | QU, | FH, | NI, | UX, | HK, | IM, | XO, | KA, | MP, | OD, | AE, |
| CP, | MA, | BO, | PY, | AG, | OZ, | YR, | GI, | ZJ, | RD, | IL, | JK, | DU, |

To get the alphabet, let us place the digraphs following each other in such an order that the first letter of one is the same as the second letter of the one that precedes, AE, ER, RL, etc., and let us consider the first letter of each digraph.

A E R L Z Q U X O D G J B S N I M P T V Y C F H K

D U N H V B O Z J K X Q E M A G I L T F S C P Y R

Considering I, II, and III, we see that the letters A E R L will represent two sequences in the same order D U N H and J K X Q, etc.

Thus, among many solutions, we have gotten one enabling us to perform the same operations as we could have performed on the actual alphabets of the encipherer, when we are, generally speaking, ignorant of them.

---

[1] Here we see the beginning of the idea of indirect symmetry.

When, instead of being different from the basic alphabet of the table, the key alphabet is the same, and when there is a square table with a random alphabet such as

```
M B O K L A C . . .

M   M B O K L A C
B   B O K L A C F
O   O K L A C F H
K   K L A C F H W
L   L A C F H W X etc.
```

the two lines of digraphs present the same succession of letters with a shift.

Let the results of deciphering be:

```
  I.   A B C D E F G H I J K L M N O P Q R S T U V X Y Z

 II.   Q P E N U R I L Y M Z O C V S F G X T H J K B A D
III.   E S F G R H J K M B A Z P I D T U L N V X Y O C Q
```

The digraphic sequences of the same interval are formed

| AP, | ZC, | OA, | BZ, | MO, | YB, | KM, | LY, | XK, | JL, | IX, | VJ, | HI, |
|-----|-----|-----|-----|-----|-----|-----|-----|-----|-----|-----|-----|-----|
| QF, | DE, | SQ, | PD, | CS, | AP, | ZC, | OA, | BZ, | MO, | YB, | KM, | LY, |

| RV, | UH, | GR, | NU, | TG, | FN, | ET, | QF, | DE, | SQ, | PD, | CS, | AP, |
|-----|-----|-----|-----|-----|-----|-----|-----|-----|-----|-----|-----|-----|
| XK, | JL, | IX, | VJ, | HI, | RV, | UH, | GR, | NU, | TG, | FN, | ET, | QF, |

and we draw from it the alphabet, as much from the table as from the column which borders on it on the left where the clear letter is taken.

```
A P D E T G R V J L Y B Z C S Q F N U H I X K M O
Q F N U H I . . . .
E T G R V . . . . .
```

It should be noted that this is not necessarily the alphabet of the encipherer.[1]

**Reconstruction of the keyword of an alphabet.**—When we are sure *a priori* that the alphabet of the table is the same as the alphabet of the left-hand column (clear letters), we can be satisfied with a single correspondence table to reestablish the alphabet.

Let the deciphering table be:

```
 I.   A B C D E F G H I J K L M N O P Q R S T U V X Y Z
II.   F K L H G M N P Q S T V Y Z J X U I A E C D B R O
```

Sequences like MNPQ suggest the idea of an alphabet derived from a keyword. In this case, in reconstructing the sequences of letters of the alphabet, it is likely that we will reconstruct an order of letters wherein the keyword will appear again, followed by the succession of the letters not used. Let us start, then, with PQ which corresponds to HI; HI gives as an interval equivalent to that of HI, DR, etc.

| PQ, | HI, | DR, | VY, | LM, | CF, | UA, | QS, | IJ, | RO, | YZ, | MN, | FG, |
|-----|-----|-----|-----|-----|-----|-----|-----|-----|-----|-----|-----|-----|
| AE, | ST, | JK, | OB, | ZX, | NP, | GH, | ED, | TV, | KL, | BC, | XU, | PQ, |

---

[1] It is obtained from the original alphabet by decimation.

whence the alphabet (PQ, QS, ST)—

P Q S T V Y Z X U A E D R O B C F G H I J K L M N

or by reversing it.

B O R D E A U X Z Y V T S Q P N M L K J I H G F C

**Another way of finding the basic alphabet.**—These methods are particularly interesting when we come across polyalphabetic substitutions in which the alphabets at first seem random. In fact, such substitutions have been used with tables which were modified little by little with time or with the number of telegrams. So then, it is good to seek to approximate as closely as possible the conditions in which the correspondents are placed, and to be not all all satisfied with correspondence tables obtained for each alphabet which enable us to translate the first cryptograms, but in which no law appears, which necessitates an entirely new effort for each message. Still we do not always arrive at a result; for the alphabets may really be different and irreducible.

The difficulty of the method's application rests almost always on this fact, that a certain number of infrequent letters are missing in the correspondence table drawn up in the course of encipherment, and do not permit the continuance of the chain of digraphs. Nevertheless, in certain cases, we can take into account observations on the construction of alphabets in order to get solutions.

Let the correspondence, for example, be:

I.  Z D R U X O B C F G H I J K E L M A N P Y Q V S T
II. A B C D E F G H I J K L M N O P Q R S T U V X Y Z

in which the normal alphabet is the clear and the other the cipher. In the relative position in which we have placed them, and by turning the page clockwise 90° so as to put A on top, we may consider them as written in a square table, II forming the reference alphabet, that is to say the left-hand column placed opposite the table and I playing the role of a column of the table.

By hypothesis, we know from the encipherer's habits that the single alphabet of the square table is based on a keyword, followed by the letters not used, placed in direct or reverse order. As a consequence, outside the keyword, we may find sequences such as MNP (direct order) or PNM (reverse order), but we would not find either MPN or NPM.

Of course, the method set forth above is applicable if we have the complete correspondence table as we have inscribed it above. However, in order to succeed in filling the gaps, we are going to proceed to the developments hereinafter.

A square table is involved. If alphabet I were the first to the left of the table, its letters would be the same as those of the column of reference letters (where we read the clear letters). That is not the case here.

If alphabet I were the second one of the table, it would be shifted with respect to the clear as we see in the following scheme:

|   | 1 | 2 | 3 | 4 | 5 |   |
|---|---|---|---|---|---|---|
| M | M | P | R | V | T |   |
| P | P | R | V | T | Z |   |
| R | R | V | T | Z | A |   |
| V | V | T | Z | A | M |   |
| T | T | Z | A | M | X | etc. |

Then the letter which corresponded to **A**, that is to say **Z**, would fall under **A** in the alphabet (like **P**, which in alphabet 2 corresponds to **M**, is written under **M** in the alphabet MPRV); under **Z** we would get **T** (which translates **Z**), etc., and the alphabet would be

A Z T P L I F O E X V Q M J G B D U Y S N K H C R A

In this we do not see any keyword appearing in the clear; sequences like **FUE**, **MJG**, are contrary to what we know about the formation of the alphabet: an hypothesis to cast aside.

If I were the third alphabet,[1] **Z** would occur two places below **A** (like or with respect to **M** in the scheme). After having written the first 13 letters at intervals of two letters

A . Z . T . P . . . ,

we would then have to fill in the intervals with the last letters, always at intervals of 2. The alphabet would be:

A J Z G T B P D L U I Y F S O N E K X H V C Q R M A

This too is to be rejected (BPD, XHV, ...).
Let us place the letters at intervals of 3:

| 1 | 2 | 3 | 4 | 5 | 6 | 7 | 8 | 9 | 10 | 11 | 12 | 13 | 14 | 15 | 16 | 17 | 18 | 19 | 20 | 21 | 22 | 23 | 24 | 25 |
|---|---|---|---|---|---|---|---|---|----|----|----|----|----|----|----|----|----|----|----|----|----|----|----|----|
| A | U | X | Z | Y | V | T | S | Q | P | N | M | L | K | J | I | H | G | F | C | B | O | R | D | E |

This time we have the right alphabet. If we hadn't gotten it, we would have kept on making our trials.

Now, this method is applicable even when there are gaps, provided some hypothesis or other is made on the position of the different heads of sequences, hypothesis based on the construction of the alphabet.

Let the correspondence be:

I. G . K M F P Q . U . . D Y H B Z . C I R L E . . S
II. A B C D E F G H I J K L M N O P Q R S T U V X Y Z

The letters **A J N O T V X** are lacking in the cipher alphabet. Let us operate as if to form the alphabet with letters juxtaposed; we get suddenly interrupted sequences:

A G Q . . . T R C K . . . V E F P Z S I U L D M Y . . . N H . . . O B

They suffice to show us that the alphabet by juxtaposition does not give the clear keyword, and has sequences (SIU, RCK, ...) which are inadmissible.

Let us next try the alphabets shifted in increasing order, beginning with the largest sequence.

| 1 | 2 | 3 | 4 | 5 | 6 | 7 | 8 | 9 | 10 | 11 | 12 | 13 | 14 | 15 | 16 | 17 | 18 | 19 | 20 | 21 | 22 | 23 | 24 | 25 |
|---|---|---|---|---|---|---|---|---|----|----|----|----|----|----|----|----|----|----|----|----|----|----|----|----|
| V |   | E |   | F |   | P |   | Z |   | S |   | I |   | U |   | L |   | D |   | M |   | Y |   |   |

Let us seek to interpolate **T R C K**, for example. In order to manage to get an alphabetic sequence between **T** and **R**, we have to place **S** in it, which will yield ZTSRICUKL. This will not do (ICUK), and the solution is not right.

---

[1] The further results can be very readily obtained by decimating the sequence corresponding to alphabet 2. It should be noted at this point that the author leaves out of consideration those intervals which do not yield complete sequences.

We will relieve the reader of the monotony of trials on intervals 3, 4, and 5.
Interval 6 gives:

| 1 | 2 | 3 | 4 | 5 | 6 | 7 | 8 | 9 | 10 | 11 | 12 | 13 | 14 | 15 | 16 | 17 | 18 | 19 | 20 | 21 | 22 | 23 | 24 | 25 |
|---|---|---|---|---|---|---|---|---|----|----|----|----|----|----|----|----|----|----|----|----|----|----|----|----|
| V |   |   | D | S | E |   |   |   |    | M  | I  | F  |    |    |    | Y  | U  | P  |    |    |    | L  | Z  |    |

Already DSE, IZV are such as to prove the hypothesis useless. But where are we to place
T . . . . R . . . . C . . . . K?
We would only get portions of random sequences. Let us try interval 7:

| 1 | 2 | 3 | 4 | 5 | 6 | 7 | 8 | 9 | 10 | 11 | 12 | 13 | 14 | 15 | 16 | 17 | 18 | 19 | 20 | 21 | 22 | 23 | 24 | 25 |
|---|---|---|---|---|---|---|---|---|----|----|----|----|----|----|----|----|----|----|----|----|----|----|----|----|
| V |   | Y | Z |   |   | L | E |   |    | S  |    |    | D  | F  |    |    | I  |    |    | M  | P  |    |    | U  |

We get sequences that seem possibly right—D F . . I . . M P . . U V . Y Z, and
elements LE and S of a French word. Let us see what we can do with TRCK. By placing C
before D, which will be its normal location if it is not in the keyword, we get CDF, KMP, and by
counting 7 places upward from C, RLE, TUV.

V . Y Z . R L E . . S . C D F . . I . K M P . T U .

The sequence AGQ will be located by putting Q between P and T; G will come after F; H of
NH will be placed between G and I; and thereafter the alphabet will be reestablished:

V X Y Z O R L E A N S B C D F G H I J K M P Q T U

We will close this digression on the reconstruction of the order of alphabets at this point;
the subject has been treated in detail by the great American establishment for cryptographic
studies, the Riverbank, in notes which have given us great help in the course of our studies on
this subject.

## CHAPTER X

## STUDY OF A CLASSIC SUBSTITUTION SYSTEM—BAZERIES SYSTEM

Substitution systems have engendered very numerous and interesting studies on new procedures, which their authors have often presented as indecipherable. We will develop in this chapter neither the description of these procedures nor the methods that have brought about the solution of many of them. However, to give an example of a very fine system, and to point out how a knowledge of the materials used in enciphering may influence the resistence of the cryptograms, by bringing to bear certain considerations, purely theoretical, which often serve as a basis for the contentions of inventors, we will elaborate on the Bazeries system.

Captain (later Major) Bazeries, when he offered this system to his government, was pointed out as an extremely perspicacious cryptanalyst, and his works bear out the opinion. He presented his device as yielding indecipherable cryptograms. Still, he met with a refusal. The reasons were probably various. It is probable that the question of the resistance to cryptanalysis of the cryptograms was not considered in particular by the examining committee in the conditions of perfect functioning in which Mr. Bazeries had built it, but rather it is probable that they considered the circumstances in which numerous poorly trained encipherers would have to manipulate a delicate instrument in actual difficult situations. After that, the author was very hard on "governmental red tape" in his works. There is found in the works of Viaris a method which indicates that his pretention to indecipherability was unfounded. We have also taken account, in the explanations that are going to follow, of certain remarks and procedures set forth by various cryptanalysts, particularly a study by General Cartier.

The Bazeries device [1] is composed of a shaft on which are mounted disks bearing numbers from 1 to 20—imagine a letter combination padlock without a handle. On each disk an alphabet of 25 letters (no W) is engraved. One of these alphabets is normal; the others are random and all different. Each disk bears a number and these alphabets are juxtaposed by arranging the disks on the shaft in an order fixed by the key. We form, by repeating a key word until we get 20 letters or by stopping a key sentence at the end of 20 letters, a literal key of 20 letters which we transform into a numerical key by enumerating the letters according to their relative order in the alphabet, and we place the disks on the shaft in such a manner that the sequence of their numbers reproduces the sequence of the numbers of the key. The device is then ready to function—we have the choice of as many different orders for the disks as there are permutations of 20 numbers, namely, $1 \times 2 \times 3 \ldots \times 18 \times 19 \times 20 =$ about 2 quintillions.

To encipher, we place the series of the first 20 letters of the clear text on a single generatrix of the cylinder formed by the total of the disks. Since each letter occurs only once on each disk, the position of each of them is perfectly definite. If we look over the cylinder and observe the 25 different generatrices as they aline the 25 letters of each alpabet, we read on one of these generatrices the beginning of the clear text. On the others, we read series of letters almost always random. We choose the 20 letters to represent the clear letters from any one generatrix; thus, we have a choice of 24 different representations. Once the beginning of the cryptogram is written, we assemble the next 20 letters of the clear text on a generatrix, and we encipher them by the 20 letters of any generatrix, whose distance from the clear generatrix will be preferably different from that of the generatrix that served to encipher the first 20 letters, etc. To

---

[1] This device is the same in principle as one invented in this country by Thomas Jefferson, and is similar to the cipher device, Type M-94, used by the U.S. Army.

decipher, we assemble the first 20 cipher letters on a generatrix, and a rapid inspection of the 24 others will reveal to us the one whereon the letter sequence will make sense. This is the clear text. We continue likewise with the following sets.

Considering the number of key combinations and the freedom of choice of generatrices, which give 24 different possible readings for a given section of cipher, the system presents a security that seems absolute to the inventor. Perhaps it *is* so if the device is kept secret from the cryptanalyst. Yet in cases where, as a result of circumstances which we must always consider normal before adopting a system for the war or diplomatic offices, the cryptanalyst may possess a description of the device and a copy of the alphabets, the finding of a translation becomes possible; for all that is then required is to find the key, and this can be done.

For the considerations that are going to follow, we will consider a device with only 10 disks. We can get an arrangement suitable for the study by writing the 10 alphabets (twice each in succession) on 10 strips of paper which we can manipulate in slits made in a big sheet.

The 10 alphabets that we will choose for this cryptograph (cipher device) among the 20 of Bazeries, are:

```
 1.  A B C D E F G H I J K L M N O P Q R S T U V X Y Z
 2.  B C D F G H J K L M N P Q R S T V X Z A E I O U Y
 3.  A E B C D F G H I O J K L M N P U Y Q R S T V X Z
 4.  Z Y X V U T S R Q P O N M L K J I H G F E D C B A
 5.  Y U Z X V T S R O I Q P N M L K E A J H G F D C B
 6.  E V I T Z L S C O U R A N D B F G H J K M P Q X Y
 7.  F O R M E Z L S A I C U X B D G H J K N P Q T V Y
 8.  G L O I R E M T D N S A U X B C F H J K P Q V Y Z
 9.  H O N E U R T P A I B C D F G J K L M Q S V X Y Z
10.  I N S T R U E Z L A J B C D F G H K M O P Q V X Y
```

We will not stop to recall a study by Viaris destined to retrieve the order of the alphabets— that is to say, the key—when the cryptanalyst knows the distance from the clear generatrix to the cipher generatrix. We do not see how, in practice, even when the encipherer pays no attention to this detail, such a case could arise.

We will, on the other hand, point out the following observation of Viaris. Let us construct a plain-text generatrix with E only; then the two neighboring generatrices will be (taking the disks in the order 1 to 10):

F I B D A V Z M U Z—namely, 1A, 1B, 1D, 1F, 1I, 1M, 1U, 1V, and 2Z's.
G O C C J I L T R L—namely, 2C's, 1G, 1I, 1J, 2L's, 1O, 1R, and 1T.

This example, on two generatrices, shows that the alphabetical composition varies from one generatrix to the other, and characterizes, so to speak, this generatrix, whatever the order of the disks may be. The disks can affect only the order of the letters and not their identity.

On a given generatrix, an E of the clear text will not be represented by just any letter, not even by just any letter chosen from 10 (10 alphabets) but by a letter chosen from 8 or 9 only (since the same letter will be found on several disks). With the Bazeries cryptograph using all 20 disks, a letter of a given generatrix is replaceable only by one of 12 or 13 of the remaining 24 letters of the alphabet.[1]

---

[1] Apparently Bazeries overlooked this idea, for he made no attempt, in the construction of his alphabets, to remove these repetitions. An increase in the number of strips, combined with a set of alphabets more scientifically constructed, flattens out the frequencies to a considerable extent.

In the explanations that are going to follow, we shall consider the cryptograph as ready to encipher; the disks arranged according to an unknown key, the 10 clear letters on a given generatrix. We will call this plain-text generatrix line 1, the next generatrix will be called line 2, etc.

Let the message be:

```
N C X I M Z U S L S    Y H L O E R T X V Z    I Q J O S V E J G U

C U V H F X X U F U    V I G E U F U F X A    T Y K G Q B N E
```

We have good reason to think that it contains the word DIVISION, and we will hunt for it.

Let us suppose that the word DIVISION was enciphered with line 2 (the generatrix next to the one whereon occurs the clear text); in that case, it will have been enciphered with the letters immediately following the letters of the plain-text word DIVISION. We do not know on what disk D was chosen; if it is on disk 1, D will be replaced by E; if it is on disk 2, by F; if it is on disk 3, again by F, etc., and if we place the letters following D one after the other on the 10 disks, we will get

```
D - E F F C C B G N F F
```

Let us do the same for every letter of the word DIVISION. The table of letters, which, for the 10 disks, follows each of the letters of the clear word, is:

```
       1  2  3  4  5  6  7  8  9  10
D  -   E  F  F  C  C  B  G  N  F  F
I  -   J  O  O  H  Q  T  C  R  B  N
V  -   X  X  X  U  T  I  Y  Y  X  X
I  -   J  O  O  H  Q  T  C  R  B  N
S  -   T  T  T  R  R  C  A  A  V  T
I  -   J  O  O  H  Q  T  C  R  B  N
O  -   P  U  J  N  I  U  R  I  N  P
N  -   O  P  P  M  M  D  P  S  E  S
```

So we see that if DIVISION has been enciphered with the second line, the only letters that can represent D are B, C, E, F, G, and N. We will draw up, according to the above table for the letters of DIVISION, the table of letters which can represent each of them by letting them occur once only, even when they occur several times in the table above.

```
D  I  V  I  S  I  O  N
B  B  I  B  A  B  I  D
C  C  T  C  C  C  J  E
E  H  U  H  R  H  N  M
F  J  X  J  T  J  O  O
G  N  Y  N  V  N  P  P
N  O     O     O  R  S
   Q     Q     Q  U
   R     R     R
   T     T     T
```

After having written the letters of the cryptogram at intervals equal to those of this table, let us slip along a sheet of paper bearing this table on it under our cryptogram. Let us stop at each of the letters that can represent D in clear, that is to say, at B, C, E, F, G, N. Let us see if the first letter to the right is contained in the list of those that can give us I in clear. If not, we will go further. If we are successful, let us verify the third letter, etc.

We do not find any place in the message where eight cipher letters in sequence coincide with eight letters taken from the separate columns of the preceding table; we cannot even make four letters coincide.

We conclude that the word DIVISION was not enciphered with the second line.

We could, in order to proceed faster, trust assistants with the task of carrying out this work simultaneously for each of the generatrices. Now, here is the work relative to generatrix 5:

```
      1  2  3  4  5  6  7  8  9 10
D  -  H  J  I  Z  U  H  K  U  K  K
I  -  M  B  L  E  M  S  B  T  F  R
V  -  A  E  E  R  O  L  R  L  H  N
I  -  M  B  L  E  M  S  B  T  F  R
S  -  X  Z  Z  O  Q  R  U  B  Z  E
I  -  M  B  L  E  M  S  B  T  F  R
O  -  S  C  M  K  N  N  Z  M  R  X
N  -  R  S  Q  J  E  G  V  X  T  U
```

and here is the table of letters capable of representing DIVISION placed in a position in which it seems applicable to the cryptogram:

```
. . . . . . S L S Y H L O E R T X V Z I Q . . .
              D I V I S I O N
              H B A B B B C E
              I E E E E K G
              J F H F O F M J
              K L L L Q L N Q
              U M N M R M R R
              Z R O R U R S S
                S R S X S X T
                T   T Z T Z U
                          V
                          X
```

Let us try, by applying the key to other portions of the message, to verify whether the solution is good or if it only happens to be an accident. In the latter case, we would continue our trials, and use other probable words if the attempts to place DIVISION on the 24 generatrices gave nothing.

Let us see from what disks the letters that give us the solution come. $H_c$ for $D_p$ comes from disk 1 (alphabet 1) and continuing, we find the key:

? 1 3 5 4 6 8 10 7 ?

We have encountered no uncertainty, each of the letters being met with only on a single disk in this example.   But if, for example, we had found that the $D_p$ was represented by $K_c$, we would have had to pick from the three disks 7, 9, and 10 which yield K on the fifth generatrix when D is on the first.   So, if several letters cause uncertainties, we may select from several keys. Trials on each of them would be made analogous to the one which follows.

Placing the disks, or strips of paper by which we represent them, in this order, the first set gives us, on the third generatrix above that on which we read the cipher NCXIMZUSLS:

? A T R O I S I E ?

Thence we deduce the text: LA TROISIÈME DIVISION SE PORTERA DEMAIN MATIN SUR RHEIMS STOP DÉPART À 7 HEURES, and the complete key

2 1 3 5 4 6 8 10 7 9

for in the other possible combination (disk 9 at the head), cipher letter N is not in the third place with respect to clear letter L, as it is on disk 2.

We had here a long and convenient probable word.   When we have none, we may simply seek a frequent trigraph or polygraph: EMENT, ERAIENT, IÈME, LES, etc.   We may then find several solutions, of which, for example, some are eliminated *a priori* as indicating the use of a single disk twice for the same set, and others are eliminated (if needs be; for in fact the word may occur several times and give several solutions) in the course of trials on other sets with the key being tested.   So much for that.   We have shown that in spite of the quintillions of theoretical combinations, it was not impossible to find a solution by the method of the probable word.

But, indeed, the analytical method may be applied.[1]   Let the cipher be:

S X B A P Z T P L F    S P R Z A R A D O A    D M R T

Let us suppose that the first disk to be put on the shaft is that of alphabet 1.   We will try to add on successively the 9 other disks, by placing alongside of S of the first alphabet the X of the 9 others, and by trying each time among the digraphs furnished by the 24 generatrices those capable of beginning a French sentence.   To these digraphs we will try to add a third letter, gotten by placing the B of the eight remaining disks on the same line as SX, and so on.   With a device, these trials would be rapid.   We will set the cylinder and make a table of it:

Alphabet 1   S T U V X Y Z A B C D E F G H I J K L M N O P Q R
Alphabet 2   X Z A E I O U Y B C D F G H J K L M N P Q R S T V

VE, EF, and OR are the only digraphs to consider.   Let us seek for trigraphs scanning all the other alphabets by considering only the three generatrices corresponding to the digraphs chosen, and by taking care to place the B on the same generatrix as SX.   We get:

| 1 | 2 | 3 | 4 | 5 | 6 | 7 | 8 | 9 | 10 |
|---|---|---|---|---|---|---|---|---|---|
| S | X | – | B | B | B | B | B | B | B |
| V | E | – | F | Y | Z | H | H | H | F | F |
| E | F | – | M | P | Q | E | Y | Q | V | V |
| O | R | – | X | F | G | R | I | S | T | Z |

---

[1] It is very doubtful that the process about to be described will yield any results for a larger number of disks. If, for example, the device involves 25 disks, as in the M–94, such an approach would be futile.

The only trigraphs to keep are ORG and ORI (we may reject ORT as scarcely probable at the beginning of a sentence, being free, however, to consider it again if nothing is gotten otherwise).

```
1  2  5    3  4  6  7  8  9  10
S  X  B -  A  A  A  A  A  A  A
O  R  G -  T  E  C  E  T  U  U
```

We will suppose that, for certain reasons, we are sure that ORGE won't be in the cryptogram. Then the solution 1-2-5 . . . yields nothing.

```
1  2  7    3  4  5  6  8  9  10
S  X  B -  A  A  A  A  A  A  A
O  R  I -  T  E  M  C  T  U  U
```

We cannot find a suitable tetragraph. We give up trying to place the second disk beside the first, and we try the third. We will pass over these trials in order to arrive at once at the assumption of a key beginning with 1-5 . . .

```
Alphabet 1   S T U V X Y Z A B C D E F G H I J K L M N O P Q R
Alphabet 5   X V T S R O I Q P N M L K E A J H G F D C B Y U Z
```

Digraphs kept: EL, GE, HA, OB, QU (we reject UT, which might, still, yield UTILE, in order not to overburden our explanations).

Let us seek trigraphs:

```
1  5     2  3  4  6  7  8  9  10
S  X -   B  B  B  B  B  B  B  B
E  L -   P  M  P  E  Y  Q  V  V
G  E -   R  P  N  I  O  O  Y  Y
H  A -   S  U  M  T  R  I  Z  I
O  B -   I  X  F  R  I  S  T  Z
Q  U -   U  A  D  N  U  U  A  A
```

We get many admissible trigraphs: ELE (éléments), GEN (général), HAT (hâtez-vous), OBS (obstacle). We should try them successively. In order to be brief, let us begin the trials with QUA; we have three possible solutions: 1-5-3 . . ., 1-5-9 . . ., 1-5-10 . . .

```
1  5  3    2  4  6  7  8  9  10
S  X  B -  A  A  A  A  A  A  A
Q  U  A -  X  C  U  L  N  T  Z
```

We are going to continue with 1-5-3 . . . to return in case of failure to 1-5-9 . . . and 1-5-10 . . ., which will go very quickly, since for trials of 1-5-9 and 1-5-10 we will already have the letters XCULNG, XCULNT of columns 2, 4, 6, 7, 8, 9, and 10, and since we have only to seek the letter of column 3, which will be X (corresponding to A on generatrix 1).

```
1  5  3  8    2  4  6  7  9  10        1  5  3  9    2  4  6  7  8  10
S  X  B  A -  P  P  P  P  P  P         S  X  B  A -  P  P  P  P  P  P
Q  U  A  N -  M  R  K  K  R  M         Q  U  A  T -  M  R  K  K  J  M
```

Let us continue with 1-5-3-9-4—

```
1  5  3  9  4     2  6  7  8  10
S  X  B  A  P  -  Z  Z  Z  Z  Z
Q  U  A  T  R  -  V  I  M  V  U
```

We arrive at:

```
1  5  3  9  4  6  8  10 7  2
S  X  B  A  P  Z  T  P  L  F
Q  U  A  T  R  I  E  M  E  C
```

By verifying the other sets, we find that the solution is correct: QUATRIÈME CORPS EST ATTAQUÉ.

This method may lead to very numerous trials; but, if we wish to save time without requiring the presence of qualified cryptanalysts, they can be done by clerks, beginning the studies simultaneously on each of the alphabets, as we did for alphabet 1, and except in case of errors in the text—such, for example, as occur in reception by wireless—they should succeed.

Therefore, in spite of the quintillions of combinations possible in theory on a 20-disk device, we will not agree that you can put unlimited confidence in the Bazeries cryptograph.

It is often the same for devices or cipher machines presented by inventors. Only after an examination of the machine itself, and after having been able to appraise the peculiarities of its encipherment by actually enciphering messages and by examining the functioning of the machine, can we see whether the relation wherein a letter depends upon the preceding one, because of the construction, cannot, in our calculation, cause a certain number of factors 26 (number of letters) to be replaced by factors 1 or 2, due to the fact that a letter is necessarily followed by one or two other definite letters and not by any other letter whatever.

We have given, with a proposed device of 10 alphabets, an example of what to do in solving Bazeries ciphers. The existence of 20 disks, the straddling of the probable word over two sets, the addition of nulls in the text, the use of a key of less than 20, leaving aside for each reading a certain number of disks according to a given law, would complicate the solution and lengthen the explanation. Since our aim is only to show that a system apparently very good may turn a weak flank to relatively simple processes of decrypting, we will not dwell on this subject, and we will close at this point the chapter on substitutions in which the letters are submitted individually to operations of encipherment.

## CHAPTER XI

## POLYGRAPHIC SUBSTITUTIONS

Instead of replacing the individual letters of a cryptogram by single plain-text letters or by groups of letters or figures, we may have to divide up the cipher into two, three, etc., letters. The enciphering components, instead of being only 26 as in the case of the letters, are very much more numerous, and identifying them becomes consequently much more complicated.

We will point out a few of the classic systems used in polygraphic substitution.

In the first place, a table with a double entry is conceived, in which the first letters of the digraphs occur on a horizontal line and the second letters in a vertical column (or vice versa), and in which every cell contains a group of two letters or of three digits, standing for the digraph indicated by the column and the row.

|   | A | B | C | D | E |   |
|---|---|---|---|---|---|---|
| A | 001 | 002 | 003 | 004 | 005 | . |
| B | 027 | 028 | 029 | 030 | 031 | . |
| C | 053 | 054 | 055 | 056 | 057 | . |
| D | 079 | 080 | 081 | 082 | 083 | . |
| E | 105 | 106 | 107 | 108 | 109 | . |
| . | . | . | . | . | . | |

The digraph CA is replaced by 003, DE by 108, etc.

As for the digraphs whose substitution is undertaken—that is to say, of the clear text—we shall form them by simply dividing the text up into sets of two; however, in order to avoid the repetition of the most frequent digraphs, we may intersperse nulls in the text.

If we intend for no law to appear in the shaping of the correspondence table (here AA=001, AB=002, AC=003, etc.), we will need an enciphering and deciphering table. However, these tables will be long, and systems have been invented to mask such visible relations as might exist between the letters of the digraphs and their equivalents, at the same time providing for easy legibility.

In works on cryptography are found tables of the type that follows, of which we include only a fragment.

|   | A | B | C | D | E | F | G | H | I | J | K | L | M | N | O |
|---|---|---|---|---|---|---|---|---|---|---|---|---|---|---|---|
| A | XZ | KJ | YJ | HP | PL | EL | VB | CI | DW | XN | ZL | YP | VN | HH | CC |
| B | LP | QT | HE | RS | UR | CR | ZH | GV | WC | HL | YN | KT | WT | MC | KH |
| C | DX | MN | AO | NH | SF | GI | WL | FN | AH | GR | BZ | HS | ZU | YM | WU |
| D | KM | YZ | RY | FP | TR | CT | XE | JK | NY | PO | GJ | JR | PE | MO | VB |
| E | QU | HP | QG | JQ | YQ | OB | SA | NL | PX | OP | VS | AF | XK | XR | UQ |

These tables are so composed that a given digraph being translated by a digraph, when we pass from the clear to the cipher, the latter digraph read as a plain-text digraph with its first letter in the first column and its second in the first row, reproduces the original digraph when we pass from the cipher to the clear.[1] Thus, by taking the digraph AF (A in the left-hand column and F in the row above), we see that it is translated by EL; by taking the digraph EL (E in the left-hand column and F in the row above), we see that it is translated by AF. Similarly, AO=CC, CC=AO. In the complete table, AA would be found at the intersection of row X and column Z, AB at the intersection of row K and column J, etc. So all the digraphs are reciprocal, and the table is read in the same way in decipherment as in encipherment.

We may use a system of movable strips such as this one, described in an American work:

```
        A B C D E F G H I J K              Fixed alphabets
A B C D E F G H I J K L M N O P            Movable alphabets
M A R S E I L B C D F G H J K M              on a slide
        P A R I S B C D E F G              Fixed alphabets
```

To encipher a digraph, we bring the first letter of the digraph, on the upper movable alphabet, to a position opposite the indicator A of the upper fixed alphabet; in the latter alphabet we find the second letter of the digraph and under it we read the two letters of the two lower alphabets.

Thus, the digraph EE will be translated CS, EI by HE, EK by KG, AA by MP, etc.

Simple square tables are also used, with alphabets usually sliding as follows:

```
  I.    A B C D E F G H I J . . . .
 II.    M A R S E I L B C D . . . .
III.
  A     P A R I S B C D E F . . . .
  B     A R I S B C D E F G . . . .
  C     R I S B C D E F G H . . . .
  D     I S B C D E F G H J . . . .
  E     S B C D E F G H J K . . . .
  F     B C D E F G H J K L . . . .
```

We encipher a digraph, chosen from row I and column III, by the letter in row II under the letter of row I, and by the letter of the table which is found at the intersection of the column of the first letter (in which the letter of row II has already been read) with the row of the second letter. Thus, IF is translated by CK, CC by RS, etc.

Orthogonal and diagonal digraphic substitutions.—A system which has been much used is the following one.[2] With a key, a square of 25 letters is formed. Let the key be LONDRES:

```
L O N D R E S
A B C F G H I
J K M P Q T U
V X Y Z
```

---

[1] This is equivalent to saying that the table is reciprocal.
[2] This is known as the "Playfair" system, in England and America.

and the square:

```
L A J V O
B K X N C
M Y D F P
Z R G Q E
H T S I U
```

Each digraph both of whose letters appear in the same column is enciphered by the letters just below these two. (If need be, the top row is considered as being underneath the lowest one.) AR is enciphered by KT. Each digraph both of whose letters appear on the same row is enciphered by the two letters to the right—LA is enciphered by AJ. If the two letters of a digraph are on different rows and in different columns, it is enciphered by the letter on the row of the first plain-text letter and in the column of the second, followed by the letter which appears on the column of the first and row of the second. (If a rectangle is constructed on the digraph it is enciphered by the two letters which are at the two unoccupied corners of the rectangle.) AG is enciphered by JR, ON by VC. On dividing up the plain text into digraphs, if a doublet is encountered a null is introduced into the text.

Example: ADRESSE is divided up into AD RE SK SE and is enciphered by JY GZ TX UG.

This system is sometimes designated by the name orthogonal and diagonal digraphic substitution.

**Trigraphic substitutions.**—Substitutions may effect groups of more than 2 letters. In order to work on trigraphs, tables like the one below have been suggested:

```
I.        A B C D E F G H I J K . . . . . . . .
II.       M A R S E I L B C D F . . . . . . . .
III. IV.
A    B    P A R I S B C D E F G . . . . . . . .
B    O    A R I S B C D E F G H . . . . . . . .
C    R    R I S B C D E F G H J . . . . . . . .
D    D    I S B C D E F G H J K . . . . . . . .
E    E    S B C D E F G H J K L . . . . . . . .
F    A    B C D E F G H J K L M . . . . . . . .
G    U    C D E F G H J K L M N . . . . . . . .
H    X    D E F G H J K L M N O . . . . . . . .
I    C    E F G H J K L M N O Q . . . . . . . .
J    F    F G H J K L M N O Q T . . . . . . . .
    etc.
```

For example, we encipher the first letter of the trigraph, chosen in alphabet I, by means of alphabet II; the second letter, chosen from alphabet III, by means of alphabet IV; the third letter, obtained by taking the intersection of the row of the second letter in alphabet III with the column of the third letter in alphabet I.

Thus, AFI is enciphered by MAK, AFE=MAF, DIC=SCG.

It is seen that the means of realizing a method of polygraphic encipherment are numerous. By making one of the alphabets occurring above on the left of the table movable and by shifting it by some law like a Saint-Cyr strip device, making the choice of the column or of the row in the table depend upon this shift, we will get polyalphabetic substitutions. Complications of these systems may lead to procedures extremely toilsome for cryptanalysis.

However, it seems that they are not often used, perhaps because of the necessity for using tables. The only system which appears to be currently used is that which uses the small table of 25 letters.

The decrypting of all these systems is based on an examination of frequencies. There are digraphic frequency tables, and we will rely upon them for our tests. However, when we know the principle of the system used, and when, for example, we do not have to find the key, we should carefully consider what the consequences of the method of encipherment are in the setting up of the substitution. Thus in trigraphic substitution, in the form we have indicated, the first two letters undergo a monoalphabetic and the third a polyalphabetic substitution. The result is that we may recognize the use of the systems described above when polygraphic repetitions lead us to imagine an encipherment by digraphs or trigraphs, by making a list of the frequencies of the letters of odd or even rank (digraphs), in which the letters of odd rank will give an almost normal frequency diagram; or, letters of rank $3n$, $3n+1$, $3n+2$ in which the letters of rank $3n+1$ and $3n+2$ will give almost normal frequencies.

**Example of solution.**—Since there are many more digraphs than letters, the consideration of frequencies or percentages would require much longer or more numerous messages in order to obtain any results than were necessary in the study of monoalphabetic substitutions. We will give only one example of studies in solution of the aforementioned orthogonal and diagonal digraphic substitution. In order not to lengthen the text unnecessarily, we have adopted a rather short cipher. Therefore, we will make some pretty bold assumptions, considering the paucity of text on which they will sometimes be based; we will grant ourselves this privilege, taking this example only as an exposition of the principles on which a better-founded theory would be based; but we must admit that in general such isolated and short messages would not enable us to carry a study through to completion under good conditions, except for good luck or a knowledge of contents easy to unravel (for example, probable words with syllables easily located).

We will recall only briefly the details of the procedure of encipherment. With a table of 25 letters, we encipher digraphs by letters in the common column or row of the two plain-text letters or by the corners of the rectangle constructed on these two letters.

```
A N G L E
T R B C D
F H I J K
M O P Q S
U V X Y Z
```

AT is enciphered TF; AG is enciphered NL; BO is enciphered RP.

We introduce nulls into the plain text to prevent the formation of a digraph by a repeated letter, as well as to separate words if deemed necessary (punctuation, ease of reading, etc.).

Let us now consider a cipher of this kind. Before trying to identify the digraphs by just using the message, let us see what help a knowledge of the procedure may give us.

According to the way digraphs are formed, a clear letter can be replaced by only five other letters of the table—the other four on the same row and the one just beneath it in its column.

```
X X X A X
      X
```

The frequency of this letter in the clear is hence distributed over five cipher letters. If it is very frequent it will augment the frequency of all or part of these five letters. We can say the same thing in other words. All the clear digraphs containing the letter A will be replaced by a digraph composed of letters found on the row or in the column of A, on what we might call "the bevel", after an expression used by Mr. Foucart in a study of this system. The frequency of A in the clear will therefore augment the frequency of the letters found on this bevel. We cannot say absolutely that every frequent cipher letter corresponds to a frequent clear letter, tying up these frequencies in a mathematical relationship, because several clear letters give digraphs in which the same cipher letter enters. But, in practice, we may say that the chances are good that a frequent cipher letter will be found on the bevel of a frequent clear letter and we will assume that this frequent clear letter is E, in order to begin our studies.

If we had very long messages, we might even try to combine the solutions by combining the frequencies. The eight letters on the bevel of E will be the ones whose digraphs among themselves and with E will reveal the normal percentage of E in the clear, each of these digraphs corresponding to an occurrence of E in the message. We would try out the sums of the most frequent letter combinations in the digraphic table, in order to approximate as closely as possible the proportions of 17 percent.[1] However, there is no use in following this route too far when we have just a few messages, because a method based on frequencies is liable to great error when there is not enough text.

Let us take a message 136 digraphs long and write it out in separate digraphs:

```
QA UJ ZO TC QI EO IE CY MQ EI CY EB ZB OE GT OA HE
MQ CZ ZO GT KH CG QP QA ZB HU MQ OZ QA YM GT MJ QM
VF YO YF QA TD OZ GI DT DE GT GL UV CD OZ HQ OZ AQ
QA OZ VO QI YG ZO EO RQ CY MZ MQ FQ EF CB CB XP TY
OZ IG YO EI QA YE ZA YJ OZ AQ OE MQ CZ KZ BF AI MQ
IG QP TO RQ EI YN OY GQ CE ZR OZ QA ZC CG XR OZ ZO
CG PQ TY IE OZ MV TG TY MQ KG GI OZ EH FB QA VO PG
OZ CM RG TG YM YC DT JU DE QM AO QM YG NA MQ QE GU
```

By reading the first letter in the row at the top of the table and the second in the column at the left, let us make a digraphic frequency table. The totals at the bottom of the columns indicate the frequency of the initial letter of the digraph and those at the right, that of the second letter.

---

[1] It is very probable that many sets of eight letters will be obtainable with the desired frequency properties. There are entirely too many possibilities for such an attack to be of real value, especially in English.

| | A | B | C | D | E | F | G | H | I | J | K | M | N | O | P | Q | R | T | U | V | X | Y | Z | |
|---|---|---|---|---|---|---|---|---|---|---|---|---|---|---|---|---|---|---|---|---|---|---|---|---|
| **A** | | | | | | | | | | | | 1 | 1 | | | 8 | | | | | | 1 | | 11 |
| **B** | | | 1 | | 1 | 1 | | | | | | | | | | | | | | | | 2 | | 5 |
| **C** | | | | | | | | | | | | | | | | 1 | | | | | 1 | 1 | | 3 |
| **D** | | | 1 | | | | | | | | | | | | | 1 | | | | | | | | 2 |
| **E** | | | 1 | 2 | | | 1 | 1 | 2 | | | 2 | | | | | | | | | 1 | | | 10 |
| **F** | | 1 | | | 1 | | | | | | | | | | | | | | 1 | 1 | | | | 4 |
| **G** | | | 3 | | | | | | 3 | | 1 | | 1 | | | 1 | 2 | 2 | | | | | | 13 |
| **H** | | | | | 1 | | | | | | 1 | | | | | | | | | | | | | 2 |
| **I** | 1 | | | | 3 | | 2 | | | | | 2 | | | | | | | | | | | | 8 |
| **J** | | | | | | | | | | | 1 | | | | | | 1 | | | | | 1 | | 3 |
| **L** | | | | | | | 1 | | | | | | | | | | | | | | | | | 1 |
| **M** | | | 1 | | | | | | | | | | | | | 3 | | | | | | 2 | | 6 |
| **N** | | | | | | | | | | | | | | | | | | | | 1 | | | | 1 |
| **O** | 1 | | | 2 | | | | | | | | | | | | 1 | | 2 | | | | 2 | 4 | 12 |
| **P** | | | | | | | | | | | | | | 2 | | | | | | 1 | | | | 3 |
| **Q** | 2 | | | | | | 1 | 1 | 1 | | | 8 | | 1 | | | 2 | | | | | | | 16 |
| **R** | | | | | | | | | | | | | | | | | | | | 1 | | | 1 | 2 |
| **T** | | | | | | | 4 | | | | | | | | | | | | | | | 2 | | 6 |
| **U** | | | | | | | 1 | 1 | | 1 | | | | | | | | | | | | | | 3 |
| **V** | | | | | | | | | | | 1 | | | | | | | | 1 | | | | | 2 |
| **Y** | | | 3 | | | | | | | | | | | | | | | 3 | | | | | | 6 |
| **Z** | | | 2 | | | | | | | | 1 | 1 | | 13 | | | | | | | | | | 17 |
| | 4 | 1 | 12 | 4 | 8 | 2 | 10 | 3 | 5 | 1 | 3 | 11 | 1 | 16 | 2 | 15 | 3 | 8 | 2 | 3 | 2 | 11 | 9 | |

The total frequencies of the letters are:

| A | B | C | D | E | F | G | H | I | J | K | L | M | N | O | P | Q | R | T | U | V | X | Y | Z |
|---|---|---|---|---|---|---|---|---|---|---|---|---|---|---|---|---|---|---|---|---|---|---|---|
| 15 | 6 | 15 | 6 | 18 | 6 | 23 | 5 | 13 | 4 | 3 | 1 | 17 | 2 | 28 | 5 | 31 | 5 | 14 | 5 | 5 | 2 | 17 | 26 = 272 |

The most frequent letters other than E (which cannot represent E) are Q, O, Z, G, Y, M, A, C, T, I. There is a strong likelihood that among these letters will be found those which are on the row and in the column of E, and which give, by their combinations, digraphs in which an E is found. Moreover, the most frequent digraphs are OZ, MQ, QA, ZO, GT, CY, CG, EI, IG, QM, TY, ... In order to abridge our study, we shall rely upon an observation which can be made on the normal frequency table, viz., that almost all the digraphs of E with any particular letter produce two digraphs of an appreciable frequency, in which E is the initial and the final letter respectively (ES–SE, ER–RE, etc.), and this peculiarity is much more infrequent in the case of other letters than E. Since, in the formation of digraphs by our methods, a reversal in the plain text causes a reversal in the cipher (if ES=KU, SE=UK), we shall begin by studying only the digraphs OZ–ZO, MQ–QM, QA–AQ, GT–TG, etc., leaving aside, for the time being, those which, like YT and CQ, gave no reversals in the message.

Next, we will try to identify the digraphs by means of their frequencies, their positions in the text, and their combinations with reversed digraphs (ELLE, CETTE, etc.), seeking first the digraphs containing E. When a digraph is identified we try to make use of it in reconstructing the table so as to profit by the letters set up in it in deciphering other digraphs. Now, if UK=AM, the possible arrangements in the table will be one of the three following:

```
A          U . . . A        A U . . . M K
U          .       .
.          .       .
.          M . . . K
M
K
```

The spaces which are marked and pointed off may be greater or smaller, and the rows and columns may be more or less separated, and the result of enciphering would not be changed. In the course of successive trials, it will be a question of reconciling the different assumptions on the three possible forms in each identification so as to reconstruct correctly a single table of 25 cells.

Guiding ourselves by the frequencies, we make the assumption: OZ=ES. The normal frequencies following those of ES in French are EN and LE. Here we have QA and MQ with the same frequency, 8. The normal frequency table gives us a greater difference between EL and LE (EL=½ LE) than between EN and NE (NE=⅗ of EN). Since AQ=¼ of QA and QM=⅗ MQ, we will adopt QA for LE. Then, too, the first group of the cipher is QA; we find the form AQQA= ELLE. Therefore, this hypothesis is, so far, acceptable.

Then we would get the following possibilities for arrangements in the table.

```
        E   A        E   O        E   M

        Q   L        Z   S        Q   N
or
          E            E            E
          A            O            M
          .            .            .
          L            S            N
          Q            Z            Q
or
    E A . L Q      E O . S Z      E M . N Q
```

One of the three arrangements of a particular digraph should combine with one for each of the others. We cannot get at the same time two of the columnar arrangements and two of the linear arrangements, since they all indicate the letter next to E, and since it is not the same letter. On the other hand, the three arrangements may be very well combined in a rectangle, by putting LN on the same line as Q:

```
        E      O A M

        Z      S

        Q      L N
```

Hence we conclude that ML=AN, and as assumptions, we may transfer to the cipher the values adopted ES, SE, EL, LE, EN, NE, AN (the other digraphs to be taken from this table by diagonals do not occur in the text).

Among the combinations of letters on which we made the assumptions which we have accepted up to the present, that is to say EOAM, which we suppose to be on the same line, our cryptogram contains EO and OE each twice; considering the few digraphs occurring in the table, these should be frequent since they are on a line with and contain E, except if there should be a repeated proper name with a peculiar form bringing in a digraph several times which would otherwise be infrequent. In a digraph thus formed, in order for a clear letter to appear in the cipher, it must be the middle letter of a group of three adjacent letters in the table, whose two extremes are the other letters of a clear and cipher digraph corresponding to one another. . A M K . on one line gives MK=AM and KM=MA. So if we suppose that EO is equivalent to a digraph containing the letter E, column O will be adjacent to column E. That is a new hypothesis which as yet is free from contradiction.

The E row will, therefore, be a permutation of the fixed pair EU, A, M, and a letter which is yet to be determined.

The arrangement E O M ? A, or E O ? M A would give EO=AE, an infrequent digraph for EA.

The arrangement E O A ? M or E O ? A M would give EO=ME which is not impossible considering the frequencies. Since the unknown letter may be a more frequent one than M (we have T in the list of possible letters in the bevel of E), we cannot make up our minds; however, we already know that A will not be to the left of E.

Among the letters that we have considered, by their frequencies and digraphs, as possibly appearing on the bevel of E, GYTI still remain. Of course, this list is not exclusive—it is just a guess.

Now, we have a frequent digraph EI-IE. If this digraph represents a clear digraph containing E, I will have to be beside E or beneath it. The latter place is open. We will get:

```
E O A ? M
I
?
Z S
Q   L   N
```

in which the positions of EO and EI alone are definitely located. As for the digraph EI, it could not represent any of the letters written in the table except ZE or QE. As a result, we must look among the unused letters for the letter to be placed above E or at the foot of the column. I is then immediately followed by Q or Z in the column. EI appears three times and IE twice. Only T could give us such frequencies (Y and G give only infrequent digraphs). Therefore, the column would be

```
E        or        E
I                  I
Q                  Z
Z                  Q
T                  T
```

We will agree to let EI=TE and IE=ET, and if we still keep Y and G as the only ones that can possibly enter into the bevel of E, since we have a digraph AO-OA and since the E digraphs with G are more frequent than the E digraphs with Y, we will suppose that G is the one on the horizontal branch of the bevel. Nevertheless, it is a somewhat hazardous guess; for this AO digraph might very well not represent **an E digraph** (its frequency is low but so are the frequencies of EG and GE. We would find very much more frequent clear digraphs with A or O on the same row). Therefore, we would get something like

```
E O M G A      or     E O G A M
I                      I
Q                      Z
Z                      Q
T                      T
```

The reciprocal positions of Z and **Q** are not yet definite. The letter that we were keeping unknown was supposedly G and prevented us from appraising the frequency EO=ME. Since **ME** is more frequent than GE, M is the letter to the left of E, and the E row must be EOGAM.

Let us return to the cipher, and apply our assumptions to EI and EO.

The beginning is :

$$LE_p \ UJ_c \ SE_p \ TC_c \ QI_c \ ME_p \ ET_p \ CY_c \ EN_p \ TE_p \ CY_c \ EB_c \ ZB_c \ EM_p \ . \ .$$

Moreover, we see the sequence ES EL EM EN appearing close to the middle of the cipher. This makes us think of the words LES ÉLEMENTS, and gives us the hope that at least a part of our guesses are right. The beginning suggests ordinal numbers, which often begin orders, taken as examples throughout this book. Therefore, **ME** would be preceded by IE, and ZI would be IE. This would reveal to us definitely the location of the different letters in the column, in which **E I Q** must follow each other. Now we get as a table

```
E O G A M
I
Q     L N
Z S
T
```

If the word ÉLEMENTS is right, $CZ_c = TS_p$. C will then be placed under S beside **T**. Continuing to examine the beginning, the groups

$$CY_c \ ENTE_p \ CY_c \ EB_c \ ZB_c \ EM_p$$

with the repetition $CY_c$, may be TRENTE—TROISIÈME. The digraphs $EB_c$, $ZB_c$ with a first letter (E, Z) coming from the I column and the same second letter make two digraphs ending **in I** plausible. Then, we would arrange quite a few components for the table. We would have to record the last result acquired,

```
E O G A M
I
Q     L N
Z S
T C
```

with the new results,

$$T_p \ C_c \qquad E_c \ O_p \qquad Z_c \ S_p$$

$$R_p \ Y_c \qquad I_p \ B_c \qquad I_p \ B_c$$

Putting B under O satisfies the last two. But the first is impossible as it stands. R no longer has a position in column T. We will therefore take the arrangement TCRY, and we will get

```
E O G A M
I B
Q     L N
Z S
T C R Y
```

Hence we find that $GT_c=ER_p$, $CG_c=RO_p$, $TO_c=CE_p$, $YE_c=TA_p$, $YG_c=RA_p$. Let us transfer these values (and their reversals) into the cipher.

Now we have the beginning:

$LE_p$ $UJ_c$ $SE_p$ $TC_c$ $IÈME_p$ $ET_p$ TRENTE TROISIÈME $RÉG_p$ $HE_c$ $ENTS_p$ $SE_p$ $RE_p$ $KH_c$ $RO_p$ $QP_c$ $LE_p$ . . .

They might be talking about the sixteenth regiment—$TC_c$ would then equal $IZ_p$, which is wrong, for T and C are on the same line and I is on another line. So it is the SEPTIÈME, $TC_c=PT_p$, and P is the last letter at the right of the last line of the table; so US must be the S of LES followed by a null. Hence U will be on the same row as S. HE will replace IM, hence H will be in the column between M and N. $KH_c$ is equivalent to $ND_p$, which we cannot yet place; but this leads us to think that K is on the N row; $QP_c$ is equivalent to $NT_p$, which definitely places P for us.

```
E O G A M
I B
Q     L N     (K is on this line)
Z S           (U is on this line)
T C R Y P
```

LES? SEPTIÈME ET TRENTE TROISIÈME RÉGIMENTS SE RENDRONT LE SI $HU_c$ ENESLE APER $MJ_c$ NE $VF_c$ CAVALE $TD_c$ ES $E_pI_c$ $DT_c$ $DE_c$ $ERA_p$ . . . ELLE $ES_p$ $VO_c$ $IERA_p$ $I_cE_p$ $SE_p$ $MET_p$ $Q_c$ $TRE_pZ_c$ $EN_p$ . . .

At last we have data enough to continue and finish the table. We have represented the untranslated passages of the cipher by a subscript "c". Sometimes there is only one doubtful letter, three of the corners of the rectangle being already known. This gives us one of the letters of the new digraph

```
E   G
.   .
I   ?
```

Finally we would reconstruct the table

```
E O G A M
I B D F H
Q J K L N
Z S U V X
T C R Y P
```

which was based on the  key **CRYPTOGRAMME** and the rest of the alphabet,

```
C R Y P T
O G A M E
B D F H I
J K L N Q
S U V X Z
```

We will remind you again that with short messages the work may be very much harder than in this example.   But looking for digraphs containing E seems to be a good method to follow, especially if we have a probable word containing E's at intervals easy to check.

## CHAPTER XII

# TRANSPOSITION SYSTEMS

In transposition systems, the encipherer mixes up the letters (or words) of the clear, according to a law known to the decipherer. By the reverse operation, the decipherer restores the order of the cipher letters or words in order to reproduce the clear.

As a result, the frequencies are normal, barring the addition of nulls or intentional errors in spelling.

**Transposition keys.**—Before going on, we will speak of transposition keys. These keys aim to indicate the numerical order in which the letters or columns are to be inscribed and transcribed. They are series of numbers, from 1 to another given number, in which none appears twice. They follow each other generally in a random order, and thus indicate the law whereby the letters or words must be inscribed and transcribed. These keys may be numerical: 5-6-3-9-1-10-2-8-4-7, and may be composed of the series of numerals in the order adopted for inscribing and transcribing the letters or words. First of all, we will pick out the element corresponding to 1 of the key, that is to say the fifth in order from left to right; next the one that corresponds to 2 of the key, namely, the seventh in order from left to right, etc. However, when the key is rather long and when we do not wish to keep it in writing (it is hard to remember a numerical key), we resort to a literal key, which may be turned into a numerical key when needed.

One of the universally known methods of converting a literal key—a word or a phrase of several words—into a numerical key is the following: We number the letters of the key in alphabetical order; if there is an A, we assign it number 1; if there are two A's we assign 1 to the one farther to the left and 2 to the other; if there are two A's, one B, no C, no D, and an E, we assign numbers 1 and 2 to the two A's, number 3 to B, number 4 to E, etc. If there are no A's, we assign the number 1 to the letter next in alphabetical order.

Examples:

```
A  M  B  A  S  S  A  D  E  D  A  L  L  E  M  A  G  N  E
1  15 6  2  18 19 3  7  9  8  4  13 14 10 16 5  12 17 11

M  I  N  I  S  T  R  E  D  E  L  H  Y  G  I  E  N  E
12 8  13 9  16 17 15 2  1  3  11 7  18 6  10 4  14 5
```

Thus, we get the key.

In inscribing the elements (components), we may follow a prearranged order other than the numerical order of the key but based upon these numerals (elements that are even—the reverse order, from the greatest to the smallest number, etc.). We may take the spelling of a number as a literal key (cent trente quatre: 2-3-7-12-13-10-4-8-14-5-9-16-1-15-11-6). In a word, we may use every means of foiling an enemy who might get a traitor to give him the key. However, the principle of the use of the key for transposition, indicated here, is applied to many and many a system of cryptography, and must be recognized by all cryptanalysts.

Let us get back to transposition systems.

Plenty of them have been invented, and we may invent as many more as we wish. All that is required is to adopt a suitable law to inscribe the series of letters forming the clear text, one by one, in an order different from that of the text.

An enumeration of these letters would do; sets of a given length may be used, and the letters may be taken in an order beginning with a set other than the first. For example, with the numerical key 4–2–6–3–7–1–5, we shall divide the text up into sets of seven letters. First we shall consider the total of the first seven sets and we shall inscribe the sixth set (the one corresponding to number 1 of the key) letter by letter in the order sixth, second, fourth, first, seventh, third, and fifth—that is to say, in the order of the key digits, in which 1 is the sixth of the numbers 4–2–6–3–7–1–5. Next we will inscribe the second set, which corresponds to the second key digit, etc. We shall skip the sets or letters missing at the end of the message when we get to the last set, if it is incomplete. Then again, we may first inscribe the letter bearing no. 1 in each set, then the one bearing no. 2, etc. We may inscribe the first set in the order of the key numbers beginning with 1, the second in this order beginning with 2, etc. So we see that pre-arrangements for the order of inscription are by no means scarce. Further on we will point out the general method of solving problems of this type. But let us say right now that when we get only one message of this kind and do not know how it was constructed, we have very little chance of ever succeeding in translating it, considering the extreme fantasy which may have been used in mixing the clear letters.

**Tabular transpositions.**—Quite often, too, transposition systems entail the use of a "table." The encipherer writes the clear text letter by letter in the cells of a table (sometimes called a grille, although this word ordinarily has a special meaning which we shall define further on), and some law or other determines the order in which the letters are to be inscribed in the cells. Varied tabular shapes may be imagined, any order at all for inscribing and transcribing; say a knight's move in chess, geometric figures, spirals from the center to the circumference, or vice versa. Here again the imagination may be given free play.

Still, there exist tables, much used and considered standard. We are going to speak of them now. The letters are inscribed in them in rows of equal length (save sometimes the last), so as to form columns. They are transcribed by columns in an order determined by a key.

When the last line is equal in length to the others, the table is said to be "completely filled." When it is not, the table is called "incompletely filled."

**The method of divisors.**—Under the title of "method of divisors", some data are found in works on cryptography on completely filled tables. Since the number of letters is the product of the number of rows by the number of columns, the length of the rows and that of the columns are divisors of the number of cipher letters. Hence, there results a tentative assumption as to the length of the columns. We will see the importance of this when we will have considered the problem as a whole. Under the title of double transposition, the said works allude to cases where the columns are inscribed in the table in an order determined by a key, and where the letters in each column are inscribed not from top to bottom in normal order but in an order likewise determined by a key, the same or different. (Sometimes the name "double trans-position" is used for another system which should be called "retransposition.") They speak of diagonal transcription, etc. It doesn't seem to us that there is any use to reproduce these data here. We shall take up in a general way only tables inscribed and transcribed by vertical columns, whether they be completely or incompletely filled. The considerations set forth on this subject may serve as a guide in the study of tables inscribed and transcribed in a different manner. Finally, the general method of studying transpositions will furnish a system of research applicable to all cases.

**Simple tabular transpositions.**—We define, then, as follows the system ordinarily called "simple transposition":

To encipher a clear text by simple transposition, we choose a key, usually literal, and transform it into a numerical key. We write the clear text in rows, each having a number of letters equal to the number of letters of the key. The letters of the successive rows, one under the other, form columns. We get the cipher by writing the letters in the order in which they occur from top to bottom in each column. The columns are taken in the order indicated by the key.

Example: Say we have to encipher "LA SIXIÈME DIVISION PARTIRA CE SOIR" with the key "MARSEILLE":

```
M A R S E I L L E
7 1 8 9 2 4 5 6 3

L A S I X I E M E
D I V I S I O N P
A R T I R A C E S
O I R
```

We get the following cryptogram, which we divide into columns to show the mechanism of the process:

AIRI XSR EPS IIA EOC MNE LDAO SVTR III

We will usually meet with it in sets of five letters:

AIRIX SREPS IIAEO CMNEL DAOSV TRIII

In deciphering, the key length and the number of letters in the message are known. By dividing the latter by the number of letters in the row (length of the key), we see how many whole lines there are (quotient) and how many more letters remain (last row incomplete). As these letters belong to the columns to the left of the table, it is easy to prepare, on cross-section paper, for example, a blank table in which the columns are ready to receive the same number of letters as those of the table made by the encipherer. The key is written above.

Here we have 30 letters, and the key has 9. So we will get 3 complete rows and 3 letters left over. We will, therefore, get three columns of 4 letters each and six of 3. The first are the three left-hand columns (7, 1, 8). We will then write the first four cipher letters one under the other in column 1, the following three in column 2, the following three in column 3, etc. We will thus build up a table exactly analogous to the enciphering table, and we will read the clear text normally.

Solution of simple transpositions.—The decrypting of documents of this nature rests essentially upon the consideration of digraphic frequencies. We strive to juxtapose two fragments of cipher from two neighboring columns and to reconstruct the clear text digraphs; then we juxtapose a third fragment to get trigraphs, etc.

Let the cipher be one of 78 letters:

TVCER NSMRY LEIQR EHOQC UDDEA URDSC AIUMR IEUPH

AMOUP AEIUR QENIS QUSIE RIICI ZAAEI SNOVE BRS

In this explanation of a general method, we will at first make no assumption as to the key length. We will seek, as we have said, to place the letters side by side. In order to get a good starting point, it is recommended that the least questionable digraphs be first chosen— if we took E as the first letter, we might successfully try to combine it with any consonant and several vowels. Then, too, we would have to make innumerable trials. So, as a starting point, we pick a letter yielding few digraphs: Z, which must be preceded by a vowel or N; X, which must be preceded by a vowel, preferably U or I; J, which must be followed by a vowel; or, best of all, Q, which must be followed by U.

Here we will take the letter Q. It appears four times in the cipher, whereas we find seven U's.

Each of these tests is based upon the following observation: As the clear text is written in rows, if we juxtapose a letter of a row in any one column next to the letter of the same row in the next column in the table of the encipherer, the letters above and below in the first column will likewise have to find their clear-text neighbor in the next column. Therefore, if we take a cipher letter sequence containing the letter Q, and another containing U, and if the two letters chosen are those that should give us the solution, the other letters of the two sequences, juxtaposed, must give us acceptable digraphs in clear text. One difficulty arises—that of limiting the sequences to the letters of a single column and of not taking simultaneously letters of the column where Q occurs and letters of another column. We will see how this difficulty diminishes as the work goes on. In the beginning, it is real, and demands great prudence in the trials.

Let us work with Q of the third group, then, and let us place column fragments containing the successive U's opposite the column fragment that contains Q. We will keep Q and U under observation:

| 1 | 2 | 3 | 4 | 5 | 6 | 7 |
|---|---|---|---|---|---|---|
| Y H | Y D | Y S | Y M | Y H | Y P | Y N |
| L O | L D | L C | L R | L A | L A | L I |
| E Q | E E | E A | E I | E M | E E | E S |
| I C | I A | I I | I E | I O | I I | I Q |
| Q U | Q U | Q U | Q U | Q U | Q U | Q U |
| R D | R R | R M | R P | R P | R R | R S |
| E D | E D | E R | E H | E A | E Q | E I |
| H E | H S | H I | H A | H E | H E | H E |
| O A | O C | O E | O M | O I | O N | O R |
| Q U | Q A | Q U | Q O | Q U | Q I | Q I |

Suppose that we have good reasons to believe that the letter Q at the bottom of the column is in the same column as the Q we are considering. We will eliminate combinations 2, 4, 6, and 7 in which this letter is not followed by U. We hold them in reserve, however, to be taken up again if we get no result with any of the three others. In this case we will put the end of the column above this letter.

Digraph II would force us to discard combination 3. However, it may be produced by the end of one word and the beginning of another. To decide among the three assumptions, we will resort to a method already pointed out as able to give useful information (we don't expect certainty), and we total up the frequencies by means of the digraphic table in chapter I.

| | | | | | |
|---|---|---|---|---|---|
| YH | 0 | YS | 0 | YH | 0 |
| LO | 4 | LC | 0 | LA | 12 |
| EQ | 1 | EA | 8 | EM | 20 |
| IC | 1 | II | 0 | IO | 10 |
| QU | | QU | | QU | |
| RD | 4 | RM | 3 | RP | 4 |
| ED | 21 | ER | 19 | EA | 8 |
| HE | 6 | HI | 0 | HE | 6 |
| OA | 0 | OE | 0 | OI | 10 |
| QU | | QU | | QU | |
| Total | 37 | Total | 30 | Total | 70 |

(We have not written in the frequeny of QU which is the same in all three columns.) So in order to continue the trials and to try to form trigraphs, we will adopt the combination furnished by Q of the third group with U of the ninth and we will consider that the greatest part of the third, fourth, ninth, and tenth groups are not suitable for new trials, having already been used in digraphs.

Let us consider our digraphs. The M of the third will probably be followed by a vowel, or by the consonants B, M, or P (see in the digraph table the letters following M); the QU digraphs will be followed by vowels, and OI probably by a consonant. In the cryptogram we will seek a sequence of the type ". . vowel or M or B or P . vowel ... consonant vowel"; or by letting "v" represent the vowels and "c" the consonants and by not considering the first two letters whose nature is doubtful: "v . v . . . c v." (If we get no result, we will replace the first vowel by M, B, or P.) We find, keeping sight of the groups already used—

```
E   A   U   R   D   S   C   A
E   N   I   S   Q   U   S   I
A   E   I   S   N   O   V   E
```

By juxtaposing these sequences, and the two letters preceding them next to our digraphs, we get:

| 1 | | 2 | | 3 | |
|---|---|---|---|---|---|
| YH | D | YH | R | YH | Z |
| LA | D | LA | Q | LA | A |
| EM | E | EM | E | EM | A |
| IO | A | IO | N | IO | E |
| QU | U | QU | I | QU | I |
| RP | R | RP | S | RP | S |
| EA | D | EA | Q | EA | N |
| HE | S | HE | U | HE | O |
| OI | C | OI | S | OI | V |
| QU | A | QU | I | QU | E |

At first sight, an examination of the trigraphs would indicate that series 1 and 3 are eliminated, because of the trigraphs IOA and RPR for 1, and IOE for 3. Moreover, the first trigraph of each column is inadmissible; that is, important only for the correct solution, and we cannot take advantage of this peculiarity in combinations 1 and 3, but we will take it into consideration in combination 2 in order to suppose that we have extended our trial sequence too high and we will leave this trigraph aside in what follows.

Although this first examination may seem sufficient, we are going to recur to the frequency test by considering the sum of the frequencies of the final digraphs of our trigraphs since we have no trigraphic frequency table.

| 1 | | 2 | | 3 | |
|---|---|---|---|---|---|
| AD | 1 | AQ | 1 | AA | 1 |
| ME | 19 | ME | 19 | MA | 3 |
| OA | 0 | ON | 28 | OE | 0 |
| UU | 0 | UI | 8 | UI | 8 |
| PR | 4 | PS | 4 | PS | 4 |
| AD | 1 | AQ | 1 | AN | 18 |
| ES | 42 | EU | 13 | EO | 0 |
| IC | 1 | IS | 8 | IV | 2 |
| UA | 7 | UI | 8 | UE | 8 |
| Total | 75 | Total | 90 | Total | 44 |

We will pick combination 2 in order to continue the trials (note that in case of very close totals it is better to give preference to the combination offering many medium frequencies, rather than to one coming up to the total only by virtue of a single very high frequency overbalancing the extreme lowness of the others).

Then our trigraphs are:

```
L A Q
E M E
I O N
Q U I
R P S
E A Q
H E U
O I S
Q U I
```

The occurrence of two Q's at an interval of six makes the discovery of a sequence containing two U's at an interval of six desirable.

We have two such: U D D E A U and U M R I E U.

Let us form tetragraphs:

| 1 | | 2 | |
|---|---|---|---|
| L A Q U | | L A Q U | |
| E M E D | | E M E M | |
| I O N D | | I O N R | |
| Q U I E | | Q U I I | |
| R P S A | | R P S E | |
| E A Q U | | E A Q U | |
| H E U R | | H E U P | |
| O I S D | | O I S H | |
| Q U I S | | Q U I . | |

We are one letter short at the foot of the last column in combination 2: the A which begins the ninth group and which ought to take that place has already been used as the second letter of the first tetragraph. If we accept this combination, it will, therefore, be necessary to sacrifice either the first or the last line. We prefer to choose combination 1, which, moreover, has no doubtful tetragraphs.

If we consider our cryptogram now, we see that we have taken four sets of 9 letters out of it—that it begins with a complete set of 10 letters, and that between the two sets, LEIQREHOQ and UDDEAURDS, there remains one single letter just as between the two sets AMOUPAEIU and QENISQUSI. These letters cannot remain unused. We have to attach them to the set preceding them by lengthening the table at the foot, or to the one following them by lengthening it at the top. As we have already curtailed one line of it at the top, we will try the bottom and will add a new tetragraph, by taking the tenth letter of our sequences now limited to nine, getting CREC, an acceptable tetragraph.

The cryptogram, therefore, contains in order: One set of 10 letters not used, two sets of 10 used, one set of 10 not used, 2 sets of 10 used, and 18 letters which can only represent two sets of 9, since the long columns never exceed the short columns by more than one letter. These two sets of 9 will represent two short columns of the table, and will, therefore, be at the right end of it, beside one another.

By juxtaposing them we will get two possible solutions:

```
R I          I R
I S          S I
I N          N I
C O          O C
I V          V I
Z E          E Z
A B          B A
A R          R A
E S          S E
```

The sum of the digraphic frequencies gives 109 for the left-hand combination, 63 for the right-hand one. We will choose the one on the left.

Two columns remain to be placed, to the right or left of our group of four or to the left of our group of two short columns,[1] or to the right of this group, but combining the letters in this last case not with those of the same line but with those of the line just above in the short column. As a matter of fact, the text continues from one line to the next, and plain-text digraphs beginning with letters in the last column of the table and in the first column on the line just below. This possibility must be kept in mind, because the letter with which we started might belong to the last column, and it would be necessary to take account of that when, as we have already done, we would be led to delimit the length of the columns in the cryptogram.

Let us continue: The two QU digraphs on the first and sixth rows of the group of tetragraphs call for vowels. The two columns to be placed are T V C E R N S M R Y and A I U M R I E U P H.

There is no doubt as to which one to choose, and we have finished the reconstruction of the table:

```
L A Q U A T R I
E M E D I V I S
I O N D U C I N
Q U I E M E C O
R P S A R R I V
E A Q U I N Z E
H E U R E S A B
O I S D U M A R
Q U I S P R E S
C R E C H Y
```

The numerical key which was recovered by considering the order in which the columns had been placed in the cryptogram was 2–5–6–3–4–1–7–8.

The problem is solved, for we will have the means of deciphering cryptograms enciphered with the same key. However, certain cryptanalysts insist on recovering the literal key from which the numerical key was derived. It is particularly a matter of intuition in which we try

---

[1] This is of course the same as the first case.

combinations of letters following one another in such a fashion as to yield a numerical key analogous to the one we have, and containing acceptable digraphs. Here we have the key "BORDEAUX."

**Use of the probable word.**—In the above, we have treated of the analytical method of solving simple transpositions.

The knowledge or the assumption of the existence of a probable word simplifies the solution considerably. With it we find a starting point for our trials. As a matter of fact, cryptograms may not contain a Q, or rather the digraph QU, too well known to cryptanalysts, may be disguised and replaced by K, for example. (In German the most apt digraph to start working with is CH, but there is a Morse signal for this digraph, so C and H are often grouped together, the combination is counted as a single letter, and it appears as one letter in the cipher columns.) When there is doubt as to the sequence to add to the columns already obtained, the probable word is a valuable aid. We didn't want to make a to-do about it, but the reader accustomed to our examples could have guessed the beginning LAQ . . . . IÈME DIVISION just as soon as the trigraphs were set up. This would have given him both the length of the rows (as a result of the number of columns) and the beginnings of all the columns. Just as soon as we can make assumptions about a word of which we have obtained but a few fragments, we ought to test and make use of them. In particular, if the letters of the probable word occur but once in the cipher, the mere juxtaposition of them solves the problem.

**Limitation of trials.**—The above exposition has shown us that the great difficulty is to determine the limits of the sequences to be juxtaposed. If, for example, we are certain that the U that we were going to try to place after Q is in the lower part of a column, while the Q is on one of the upper rows, we would not waste any time trying it. Consequently, everything that permits assumptions leading to simple rapid tests on the length and the limits of the columns is an aid to the cryptanalyst.

Among these fortunate items, we will first of all mention the certainty of dealing with a completely filled rectangle. If with this certainty we find a cipher of 96 letters, and if we suppose that keys shorter than 5 letters and longer than 30 are ordinarily avoided, the chances are that the table will have six columns of 16 letters, or eight of 12, or twelve of 8, or sixteen of 6, or twenty-four of 4. That will give us five tests to make; for 96 has relatively many divisors; but, having cut the message up into eight sets of 12 letters each, for example, it would only be necessary to try to form words on each row by juxtaposing the columns as they stand, without asking ourselves, "Do the letters we are trying to juxtapose really belong to the same row?" and without fearing a shift of one column against the other. If we write the columns on strips of paper, and if we make use of frequencies, as was done above, the task is usually simple.

We would be equally lucky if we knew the number of columns in the table, without being able to count on a completely filled rectangle. This may actually happen if an imprudent encipherer worked in our presence, too far off for us to be able to read his work, but at such a distance that we could distinguish and count the columns.

Let the cipher be the following, 52 letters long:

ASTNS  TUUSA  ANUOP  MTDEZ  LCECO  UDEAT  SEDDR  RREMC  QBOMP  ECEEO  NI

We know the table has nine columns. Dividing 52 by 9, we find that it has five complete rows and one row of 7 letters. As a result, there are seven long columns of 6 letters each and two short columns of 5. If we knew where the short columns appear in the cryptogram, we would cut the text up into sets of 6 and 5 letters, which would reproduce the columns of the table, and it would only be necessary to recover their order by writing them on strips of paper, and, using digraphic frequencies as before, to evaluate the worth of a particular juxtaposition trial.

We do not know the position of the short columns, but we can assign limits to each column.

As a matter of fact, suppose that in the actual table, the one used by the encipherer, the two short columns had been transcribed last of all. Cutting the cryptogram up into seven long columns followed by two short ones, we would get a copy of the columns in the actual table.

```
A  U  U  E  O  S  R  O  E
S  U  O  Z  U  E  E  M  E
T  S  P  L  D  D  M  P  O
N  A  M  C  E  D  C  E  N
S  A  T  E  A  R  Q  C  I
T  N  D  C  T  R  B
```

But our assumption may be wrong, and the short columns may be elsewhere. If the first column transcribed beginning with A were a short column instead of being a long column, the letter T, which ends it in this table, would pass to the head of the following column; that at the foot of this column, to the head of the third, etc.

If the two short columns had been transcribed first, the last 2 letters of the second column would pass to the third; the last 2 of the third, to the fourth, etc.

If the first column is long and the second short, the passage of a letter of one column to another will be effected, but we have considered the two extreme cases of short columns, at the end and at the beginning, and hence, the maximum possible shift of the letters.

If we set up the following table:

```
         a  t  e  a  r  q
      t  n  d  c  t  r  b  c
   A  U  U  E  O  S  R  O  E
   S  U  O  Z  U  E  E  M  E
   T  S  P  L  D  D  M  P  O
   N  A  M  C  E  D  C  E  N
   S  A  T  E  A  R  Q  C  I
   T  N  D  C  T  R  B
```

The table in capitals will represent the columns in one of the extreme cases, the table composed of the part of the table in capitals above the ruled line, and of the "crown" in little letters, will represent the columns in the other extreme case (considering each column separately, its letters, of course, not being placed on horizontal lines), and the letters contained on the first row and in the crown will be the only ones which may be found on the first row of the real table.

We would reason similarly for the second row, with a crown limited to one letter under the letter of the top of each column, since the letter of the second row is at an interval under that of the first row.

Thus, we succeed in greatly reducing the number of tests. The letter Q in the crown cannot be followed by any letters except one of the two U's of the first capitalized row if it is on the first row.

Hence, let us make the tests:

| | | | | |
|---|---|---|---|---|
| QU---------- | | QU--------- | |
| BU---------- | 0 | BO--------- | 2 |
| OS--------- | 7 | OP--------- | 1 |
| MA--------- | 3 | MM--------- | 1 |
| PA--------- | 6 | PT--------- | 1 |
| EN-------- | 39 | ED-------- | 21 |
| | 55 | | 26 |

We will choose the first set and underline the corresponding U.   However, for Q and U to be juxtaposed, we must arrange the long and short columns in such a fashion that Q and U will be on the same row.   We get this by placing the two short columns between the column of U and that of Q; for example:

```
A  U  U  D  E  A  R  Q  C
S  U  O  E  C  T  R  B  E
T  S  P  Z  O  S  R  O  E
N  A  M  L  U  E  E  M  O
S  A  T  C  D  D  M  P  N
T  N        E  D  C  E  I
```

We do not know which of the columns between U and Q are really the short ones.   However, we are sure that those of U and Q and those that are exterior to them in the table are certainly long.   By arranging the latter to the left and the other doubtful ones to the right, we have:

```
                  e  a
               d  c  t  r
Q  U  A  C  U  E  O  S  R
B  U  S  E  O  Z  U  E  R
O  S  T  E  P  L  D  D  E
M  A  N  O  M  C  E  D  M
P  A  S  N  T  E  A  R  C
E  N  T  I  D  C  T
```

Observing the five columns in which, we are sure, the letters are on their proper rows, we see the words OBUS and POST coming out:

```
U  Q  U  A
O  B  U  S
P  O  S  T
M  M  A  N
T  P  A  S
   E  N  T
```

and we can assume that column  U  O  .  .  .  .  has six letters and that the last fragment is DENT.

In order to seek the following column, we will take the probable word POSTE, and limit an E on the third row.  Taking the rest of the table with the crown of the third row:

```
            a
        c   t   r
    E   O   S   R
    Z   U   E   R
    L   D   D   E
    C   E   D   M
    E   A   R   C
    C   T
```

We see that we have only two E's able to come on the third row, the one in S E D and the one in R R E.

By trying the S E D column, we see the word "COMMANDE" outlining itself on the fourth row.   Only the O of the C E E O column can fit in and furnish us:

```
C   U   Q   U   A   T
E   O   B   U   S   S
E   P   O   S   T   E
O   M   M   A   N   D
N   T   P   A   S   D
I   D   E   N   T   R
```

By taking the first C of the  E Z L C E C column which alone will do, we see enough plain text appearing to finish the solution:

```
R   E   C   U   Q   U   A   T   O
R   Z   E   O   B   U   S   S   U
R   L   E   P   O   S   T   E   D
E   C   O   M   M   A   N   D   E
M   E   N   T   P   A   S   D   A
C   C   I   D   E   N   T
```

We have thus demonstrated how it is possible, knowing the number of columns of the table, to speed up our experiments by limiting the zone in which we are to seek the second letter when we have chosen the first letter.

This method has an interesting application when we know a word in the cryptogram.

Several times during the war, the wireless stations intercepted conversations of this sort:

Station X to Station Y: ISSTE PNLES UOSCO AFMER UEORN OPRTC UTPEY G

Station Y to Station X: Telegram garbled.   What is the word before FOUG?

Station X to Station Y: NANCY TOUL.

We must, of course, find the letters of these names in the cipher. Some of these letters are found once only. Let us place them at the intervals they must occupy, putting them in a column with the neighboring letters: [1]

```
O . T E . . . N
A . C Y . . . L
F . U G . . . E
```

We see that C and Y are 5 letters apart in the cipher; therefore, the columns will have either 4, 5, or 6 letters. Moreover, according to the series NANCY TOUL FOUG, in which the Y and the G are in the same column, the key has 8 letters, which decides us in favor of four completely filled rows and one row of 4 (36 letters divided by 8), say four columns of 5 and four columns of 4.

Let us, therefore, lengthen the preceding columns toward the top:

```
S . P T . . . E
C . R P . . . P
O . T E . . . N
A . C Y . . . L
F . U G . . . E
```

Referring to the cipher, we see that this last column must be stopped at L; for only three letters would be left over for the following column before SCO. In order to complete NANCY and FOUG, we rely upon the sequence EORNO. The necessity of finding T, O, and U of TOUL at the foot of the columns, and the division of the sets already inserted into the cipher, immediately yields the solution: "SEPTIÈME CORPS SE PORTERA SUR NANCY TOUL, FOUG."

However, we may not be able to find so many letters easy to place definitely as a result of their occurring only once in the message.

Take a cipher of 47 letters:

RTEUR DLNLB TGRIL EINTA IDAEE YNARR IRMUD EAHAA TRIQE EB

in which we suspect the occurrence of the name of the village TRAMBLY. Let us use this assumption as a means of seeking to determine the length of the key. According to what we know about the habits of the authority who gave this key to the encipherer, it will probably not have more than 10 nor less than 5 letters.

We will first try to imagine how a table of 47 letters can be constructed with keys of 6, 7, 8, 9, and 10 letters; then, in this table, we will see if we can fit the word TRAMBLY into the cipher, by using the letters B and Y (Y occurs only once in the message; B, twice). We will not use M which occurs only once, in order not to recur to the preceding example. In reality, we should naturally use it.

The cryptogram of 47 letters will be broken up with a key of 6 letters into five columns of 8 letters and one of 7; with a key of 7 letters, into five columns of 7 letters and two of 6; with a key of 8 letters, into seven columns of 6 letters and one of 5; with a key of 9 letters, into two columns of 6 letters and seven of 5; and with a key of 10 letters, into seven columns of 5 letters and three of 4.

The two intervals from B to Y are of 16 and 21 letters, respectively.

---

[1] There are actually two C's in the text of the message, but the author apparently overlooked one of them.

These intervals may be realized (in order for B and Y to be juxtaposed):

| Key length | Interval 16 | Interval 21 |
|---|---|---|
| 6 | 2 columns of 8 | Impossible. |
| 7 | Impossible | 3 columns of 7. |
| 8 | Impossible | Impossible. |
| 9 | 1 column of 6; 2 of 5 | 1 column of 6; 3 of 5. |
| 10 | Impossible | Impossible. |

Let us try the key of 9, and break up our cipher into two columns of 6 letters and seven of 5 letters.

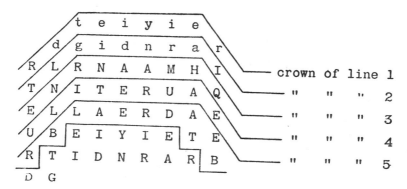

Let us make the crown, supposing that the cryptogram begins with the five short columns.

We see that Y might be on the first row, but then we have no B to put with it. It might be on the next to the last one, and we have a B on the same row, plus an L on the row above which we can shift down, by arranging for one column of 6 and two of 5 between B and Y:

```
R  D  T  I  D  N  R  A  R
T  L  G  N  A  A  M  H  I
E  N  R  T  E  R  U  A  Q
U  L  I  A  E  R  D  A  E
R  B  L  I  Y  I  E  T  E
   E                    B
```

However, as the contours indicated (and that made the construction of the last table practically useless), if we found TRABLY on the contour of the crown of row 4, we couldn't have gotten M on it. For the same reason, we will not succeed with the second B, when we will have brought Y to the same row by arranging the intermediate columns in three columns of 5 and one of 6:

```
R  L  G  I  D  N  M  H  I
T  N  R  N  A  A  U  A  Q
E  L  I  T  E  R  D  A  E
U  B  L  A  E  R  E  T  E
R  T  E  I  Y  I  A  R  B
D              R
```

The examination of the crowns might, therefore, have saved us the construction of these two tables.

The key of 9 gets us nowhere.

Let us try the key of 7.

```
            r   a   n   u
        l   i   i   a   d   t
    R   N   L   D   R   E   R
    T   L   E   A   R   A   I
    E   B   I   E   I   H   Q
    U   T   N   E   R   A   E
    R   G   T   Y   M   A   E
    D   R   A   N   U   T   B
    L   I   I   A   D
```

We know that we cannot bring the first B next to Y. As for the second, the last letter of the message, the lower contour shows us immediately that it can be placed there. The only L that we could find for the trigraph is the one in the first column. The B must then be lowered one row, and the Y, two. This is possible by leaving the L where it is, since we have two columns between L and B to give the two letters of the crown. As for the rest of the name, TRAM, we likewise have its letters in the limits of the possible downward shifts, and on different columns, but the necessity of keeping two columns short does not allow us to shift all the letters of the contour downward simultaneously to the same line. Our word will have to fall on two rows, and we will get the table:

```
    R   N   I   A   N   U   T
    T   L   L   I   A   D   R
    E   B   E   D   R   E   I
    U   T   I   A   R   A   Q
    R   G   N   E   I   H   E
    D   R   T   E   R   A   E
    L           Y   M   A   B
```

The reconstruction of the order of the letters in TRAMBLY yields the cryptogram (key: ROSALIE).

```
    U   N   T   R   A   I   N
    D   A   R   T   I   L   L
    E   R   I   E   D   E   B
    A   R   Q   U   A   I   T
    H   I   E   R   E   N   G
    A   R   E   D   E   T   R
    A   M   B   L   Y
```

At this point we will stop these examples of experiments on simple transpositions in which we endeavored to draw the reader's attention to numerous observations which may make it easier to get the results. We may say that it takes much more experience and special aptitude to succeed in solving transposition problems than for the relatively simple substitution problems that we have described. Beginners seem generally at a loss to know "at which end" to take hold of a transposition, when they have no probable word, no Q's followed by U's, and no indication of the length of the key. We cannot overemphasize the fact that, instead of wasting time contemplating the cipher day in and day out, you must make assumptions, and try something or other. Often a wrong starting point leads to considerations or to juxtapositions of letters which get us on the right track.

The use of strips on which the assumed columns which we are trying to juxtapose are written often reveals groups of interesting letters which finally bring about the solution.

When we know the habits of encipherers in constructing the key, we must observe that it is a good idea to begin by using the greatest possible columnar lengths. For example, if the encipherer is in the habit of using keys from 15 to 25 letters long, and we have a message of 150 letters, we will know that the columns have from 6 to 10 letters. Very long sequences of consonants, which according to normal frequencies must be very often followed by vowels, will probably bring about a sequence in which the vowels will be in the majority, and we will look for it in the cryptogram. Two or three M's in a sequence of 10, and M's, B's, or P's at intervals equal to those of the M's will be interesting to bring together if the columns have more than 10 letters. They will no longer interest us if the columns are very short, because there is very little likelihood that the columns are juxtaposed in the same order for the first M, which comes from one column, and the last, which comes from another.

As soon as we have almost certain trigraphs, we will make assumptions on the length of the columns, and the beginnings of the sets that correspond to them. This will enable us to look for the U which we are trying to place after a Q supposed to be in the third row of the table at about the third letter of the assumed set, and to reject the U's occupying places too far away in the sets, etc. And as soon as we see the components of probable words appearing, we must take them into account. A knowledge of the questions with which the correspondents may be concerned, of the map for military operations, of the names of political personalities in the case of diplomacy, etc., is very much more necessary, we think, when we are working on transposition systems than on substitution systems, granting an equal complexity in both systems. That is why, in our opinion, transposition systems are usually more secure than substitution systems, when we wish to have people who could hardly be called experts encipher numerous messages.

**Grilles.**—We will pass on to another classic transposition system, the one that uses grilles.[1]

The grille is a piece of cardboard containing perforations such that, if we place it over a sheet of paper, certain parts of this sheet are visible through the perforations or holes and others are hidden. Suppose we write a sentence in these holes by letters or words, and then remove the grille. Then suppose we fill in the lines on the sheet of paper between the inscriptions made through the holes by means of well-chosen letters or words: It might be impossible to distinguish the inscriptions made through the grille from those made afterwards, and thus the words or letters of the clear message are concealed in a series of enveloping letters or words which will prevent the meaning from being found out. The sheet of paper treated thus will be sent to the correspondent, who, provided with a grille just like the one the encipherer used, will place it over the message and will read the sentence he is looking for through the holes, all the characters added afterwards being hidden.

A system of this sort may be used in telegraphy provided the cipher text is written on cross-section paper or checked so as to replace each letter in the same position in which it was found in the original of the encipherer.

In this form, the method requires the sending of all the useless enveloping text written after removing the grille in order to conceal the real message. This is, therefore, not very practicable, especially for telegrams.

---

[1] According to our way of thinking, the term "grille" is sometimes wrongly used for simple transposition tables, particularly in digits rather than in letters.

The order in which the characters are written into the cells may be fixed by a prearrangement. The text may be inscribed in rows or columns, or else numbers above the cells may determine the order in which they are used.

In order to lessen the number of nulls, it is advantageous to utilize the greatest number of useful cells—openings in the grille. However, if the letters, written in these openings, are too close or in a simple order, by rows, for example, the words will be guessed in spite of the nulls that they contain. That is why the openings are sometimes numbered in a variable manner so that the successive letters of a word will not appear on one row or in one column. Again, we may simply use a table with numbered openings, superimpose a piece of transparent paper, and write the plain-text letters in numerical order using all the openings. The cryptograph used in the French Army in 1886, made of sliding strips on which numbers were inscribed and with the strips placed in an order corresponding to a key, indicated by the succession of its numbers the order in which the letters written in a cross-section table were to be transcribed. Along these lines, grilles are sometimes used merely to determine the order in which letters are to be transcribed from a message, the letters being inscribed normally and transcribed by columns. That results in a transposition table in which blanks exist on the rows and in the columns, and where, consequently, the juxtaposition of neighboring columns becomes exceedingly difficult. Nulls are no longer trifled with, and the text thus inscribed is transmitted by telegraph.

Example:

```
L  .  A  T  R  .  O  .  I
S  ·I  .  E  .  M  E  .  D
.  I  V  I  S  .  I  O  .
N  .
```

```
LSNII  AVTEI  RSMOE  IOID
```

The same result, obtained by the above-indicated system using a table with numbered cells, that is to say the complete use of all the openings and the suppression of nulls, may be also obtained by the simultaneous use of several grilles, whose openings never correspond and such that, if placed successively on the same piece of cross-section paper, they will finally expose all the openings after each of the grilles has been set in its proper position. We begin to write in the openings of the first grille alone; we remove it, then we put the second one down and write in its openings which reveal parts covered by the first grille and cover up all the cells revealed by the latter. The same thing is done with a third grille which exposes only blank cells, etc. At length, after using the last grille, we get a mixture of letters belonging to successive sections of the message, which we can write down and send without bothering with useless nulls.

We will not dwell on the decipherment of these systems; it will come under a general head that we shall study later on. The mixture of letters obeys nothing but absolutely arbitrary prearrangements. However, following up the use of multiple grilles, opening up all the cells in turn on the encipherment sheet, we will examine the case of revolving grilles.

A revolving grille is usually a square one, perforated so that all the cells of the table have been exposed once each when it is placed over an enciphering table in the successive positions obtained by rotations of 90°. The exposed openings in the grille are hence equal in number to one-fourth the number of cells.[1]

---

[1] This statement is correct if the square has an even number of cells on a side; if this number is odd the number of openings in the grille when multiplied by four is one less than the number of cells in the square. This is due to the fact that the center square remains unfilled in the *odd* case.

The use of such a device entails a certain number of consequences. Let us take a grille with four cells on a side, in its four positions,

| I | II | III | IV |
|---|---|---|---|
| 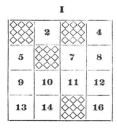 | 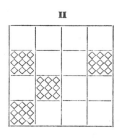 |  | 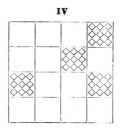 |

and let us number the cells normally from 1 to 16. We see the following open cells: position I—1, 3, 6, 15; position II—5, 8, 10, 13; position III—2, 11, 14, 16; position IV—4, 7, 9, 12.

Every open cell in position I has a symmetrical one in position III, so that to the succession of letters 1, 3, 6, 15 corresponds another succession 2, 11, 14, 16. Recognition of a clear tetragraph in the four cells 1, 3, 6, 15, hence, entails the recognition of another in the cells whose numbers individually make totals of 17 with the numbers of the first, but taking them in reverse order (the tetragraph will be read in the order 2, 11, 14, 16, while we have to read in the order 16, 14, 11, 2 to get totals of 17). The positions II and IV lead to the same remarks.[1]

Now, the grille permits a message of 16 letters, hence if we can succeed in distinguishing in the cipher the letters coming from one of the four sets of clear text, we should find the letters coming from the symmetrical set. Every acceptable digraph must have a reasonable digraph to correspond to it.

Let us take the message:

NVCOS  RITIY  SXEII  ETEMO  STUNR  OSNEU  DAIEL  P

enciphered with a revolving grille. We suspect that the word DIVISION is in it. We are choosing, in this case, a probable word; otherwise, we would resort to successive tests just as in a transposition table in which we had no evident breaks. But that would not be practicable unless we had more material. Let us note too that, when grilles are used, we often get a message longer than the number of openings in the grille. Then we have to divide up the text into sets equal to this number of cells, filling in the last part with nulls. The property of messages always having a length equal to the same number—a perfect square—indicates the use of a revolving grille.

We are going to write the cryptogram on two lines symmetrical with respect to one another, in order more easily to apply the symmetry we have just pointed out as a result of which each cell, in one of the positions III or IV, is symmetrically placed with respect to a cell in one of the positions I or II; the second line is formed by writing the message in reversed order.

NVCOS  RITIY  SXEII  ETEMO  STUNR  OSNEU  DAIEL  P
PLEIA  DUENS  ORNUT  SOMET  EIIEX  SYITI  RSOCV  N

Each digraph formed on one of these lines by two successive plain-text letters corresponds on the other line to the reversal of a second plain-text digraph.

---

[1] There actually is a symmetry existing in all four positions so that the determination of one digraph in the box leads to the knowledge of three others by a process of rotation.

Let us now place the cryptogram in a table of 36 cells which will reproduce the enciphering table:

| N | V | C | O | S | R | | 1 | 2 | 3 | 4 | 5 | 6 |
|---|---|---|---|---|---|---|---|---|---|---|---|---|
| I | T | I | Y | S | X | | 7 | 8 | 9 | 10 | 11 | 12 |
| E | I | I | E | T | E | | 13 | 14 | 15 | 16 | 17 | 18 |
| M | O | S | T | U | N | | 19 | 20 | 21 | 22 | 23 | 24 |
| R | O | S | N | E | U | | 25 | 26 | 27 | 28 | 29 | 30 |
| D | A | I | E | L | P | | 31 | 32 | 33 | 34 | 35 | 36 |

We know that there are nine open cells, probably one or two to each line. Therefore, the successive letters of a word are probably separated by no more than one line—i.e., 6 spaces.

Supposing the word DIVISION to be in the plain text, let us look for it.

There is only one D—31. The first I after D is I (33), then comes I (7) which is too far away.

The digraph symmetrically placed with respect to DI is OR—a good one. Since DI is on the last line, the rest of the word has been enciphered in a new key position. We will note at once that, in this new position, the open cells 31 and 33 are moved to 36 and 24; but that, as a result of the construction of the grille, the cells 16 and 6, which ought to be open in the third position, and the cells 1 and 3, which ought to be open in the fourth, are certainly closed; if then we were to find a V in cell 1, 3, or 6, it would certainly not be the one we are seeking.

We have V (2). For the I that follows, we hesitate between I (7) and I (9); for S, we can use only S (11); then a new doubt between I (14) and I (15), and finally, the chances are that we will have O (20) and N (24).

Let us see what the positions symmetrical to each of these assumptions give:

V (2)  I (7)  S (11)  I (14)  O (20)  N (24) = ETUOUL
V (2)  I (9)  S (11)  I (15)  O (20)  N (24) = ETTOUL

We see that the solution is

V (2)  I (7)  S (11)  I (15)  O (20)  N (24) = ETTOUL

With the exception of a single cell, we have reconstructed the grille. Arranging it in the table and reducing it to the first position, we see at once that the open cell is 29 and we have:

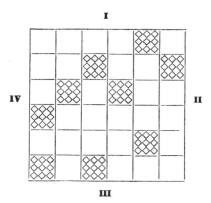

with the message: SIXIÈME DIVISION SE PORTERA SUR NANCY ET TOUL.

Sometimes we have succeeded quite quickly with a relatively long probable word, i.e., long with respect to the key. When the data are less advantageous, we need to take care to avail ourselves fully of all the elements for study; as soon as we have formed an assumption concerning the grille, we must observe whether or not this assumption occasions a useful observation in any one of the four positions. Particularly, we must take care to restrict the field of assumptions by noting which cells will be opened up *in another position* by the openings we have just discovered in the grille, and by considering that, consequently, *these cells are open* in the present position and cannot furnish any component of the clear text in a second position.

**Anagrams.**—Aside from these particular cases, we do not know how to solve transposition systems except by *a priori* juxtaposition of letters in them to form words, at best, and without any special procedure—that is to say, by the formation of an anagram constituting plain text.

When we are in possession of but one cipher for this work, we may sometimes form quite a few anagrams without anything happening to indicate the right one.

When we have another message as a check, we may escape this stumbling-block. Most transposition systems are such that if we work on two messages of the same length, each letter of one undergoes exactly the same operations as the letter that occupies, in the other, the same rank from the beginning; and is found in the same place in the cipher. However, just as soon as we deal with messages of different lengths, the letters of one undergo operations that often carry them very far away from the place that letters of the same rank in the other clear text occupy in the other cryptogram. Therefore, in most cases, we may work profitably on cryptograms with the same number of letters, in order to check every assumption made on one by the other.

Let two ciphers be, for example:

```
NNYCT   OUAIL   PPDLU   ATEOR   R
BUGRI   LAOQS   ATAUA   NVTRS   D
```

In the first one, we see that part of the letters form the words NANCY and TOUL in the first groups. There remains IPPDLUATEORR.

Given the fact of the occurrence of the names of regions and the letters which we are to arrange, we will again anagram—this time for DE and POUR. There now remains IPLATR = IL PART.

But is he leaving for Toul from Nancy or to Nancy from Toul? The second telegram will straighten this out:

IL PART DE gives us, by placing in the same order the corresponding letters: QUAND VA T.

The letters corresponding to TOUL give ILAS.

Those corresponding to NANCY give BOURG and to POUR, TRAS.

We must then read: IL PART DE TOUL POUR NANCY, and QUAND VA–T–IL À STRAS–BOURG?

In order to anagram, when we get several cryptograms of the same length, we may utilize the points that are known about the sums of the frequencies in order to try digraphs, and handle the problem without needing a probable word, starting in one of the messages with a probable digraph and by checking in the other messages.

In the case of tabular transpositions the shifts undergone by the letters from one cryptogram to another when the messages are of unequal lengths are subject to laws simple enough for us to be able to study two cryptograms of different lengths. Supplementary letters are added at the feet of the columns in the case of the classic tables, like the one we have examined. Two or three letters more in one of the messages than in the other might, therefore, leave a good many columns unchanged, and if these are the first ones transcribed, the letters at the same distances from the beginnings of the two plain-text messages will be at the same distances from the beginnings of the cipher. If one of the messages is double or triple the other, the columns will be two or three times as long. If there are ten columns for example, the letters of the first line in both cryptograms will be in positions differing by at most one letter from one another when the messages are divided up into ten equal sets. When we have probable words for the beginning or end of a message, we have a means of limiting our studies in each cipher to different regions corresponding to each other. But, practically speaking, all this has a very restricted application.

**Search for the Key.**—When we have found it possible to restore a clear message by ana-gramming, it is of the greatest importance to recover the key, since that is what will enable us to translate ciphers of different lengths from that of the message solved. The work will vary according to the process of encipherment and we must make a detailed analysis of the system used in passing from the plain text to the cipher.

To briefly give an idea of the manner in which a study of this type may be carried on, suppose we know the enciphering process and that all we have to do is get the key. Suppose the method is as follows: Above the plain text, the repetitions of a keyword are written and the clear letters corresponding to the same key letter are inscribed successively, the letters of this key being taken in a given order (for example, alphabetically). Thus we get a cipher which we will call the first cipher. We treat this in the same way as we treated the clear in order to get the final cipher.

Example:

```
First operation_____   AMIENS   AMIENS   AMIENS   A
                        LACINQ   UIEMED   IVISIO   N

First cipher_____   LUINI   MSCEI   AIVNE   IQDO

Second operation____    AMIENS   AMIENS   AMIENS   A
                        LUINIM   SCEIAI   VNEIQD   O

Final cipher_____    LSVON   IIIEE   UCNIA   QMID
```

Having at hand a message of 46 letters enciphered in this system, we will suppose that we have obtained a solution by anagramming, and we will try to answer the following question: Knowing the cipher and the plain text, how are we going to find the key?

Suppose the problem is solved and that the key is BORDEAUX. Let us replace each letter by the number of its position in the plain text, and subject the series of numbers thus obtained to the two successive operations. Thus we will find the position that each clear letter occupies in the cipher.

```
B  O  R  D  E  A  U  X  B  O  R  D  E  A  U  X  B  O  R  D  E  A  U  X
01 02 03 04 05 06 07 08 09 10 11 12 13 14 15 16 17 18 19 20 21 22 23 24

B  O  R  D  E  A  U  X  B  O  R  D  E  A  U  X  B  O  R  D  E  A
25 26 27 28 29 30 31 32 33 34 35 36 37 38 39 40 41 42 43 44 45 46
```

First cipher: 06 14 22 30 38 46 01 09 etc. . . . .

```
B  O  R  D  E  A  U  X  B  O  R  D  E  A  U  X  B  O  R  D  E  A  U  X
06 14 22 30 38 46 01 09 17 25 33 41 04 12 20 28 36 44 05 13 21 29 37 45

B  O  R  D  E  A  U  X  B  O  R  D  E  A  U  X  B  O  R  D  E  A
02 10 18 26 34 42 03 11 19 27 35 43 07 15 23 31 39 08 16 24 32 40
```

Final cipher: 46 12 29 42 15–40 06 17 36 02–19 39 30 41 13–26 43 24 38 04–
21 34 07 32 14–25 44 10 27 08–22 33 05 18 35–16 01 20 37 03–
23 09 28 45 11–31

Let us analyze the successive operations. The first cryptogram is built up in sets of numbers which differ by 8 (the key length). This progression of 8 from one number to the one following is interrupted only at changes in the key letter. To compose the final cryptogram, we form sets or sequences each containing a letter of each set in the first cipher. These letters follow each other in the same order. There is a parallelism between these sequences: If the first letter of one, corresponding to A in the keyword BORDEAUX, differs by 8 or by 16 from the first letter of the other, corresponding to E or D, the other letters corresponding to the A of successive keywords differ by 8 or by 16 from the letters of the same rank in the sequence corresponding to the E's and D's of the keywords (unless there be a break in the progression of the first cycle). So that by adding 8 or a multiple of 8 to the different numbers of one sequence, we should find the succession of numbers in another or at least a part of this succession. Starting with this observation, let us note that conversely, if we make successive tests on a set of the cipher (composed by means of a key of unknown length), by adding the same quantity to each number of this set and if we chance to get in this way another cipher set, we will probably have found the length of the key. Suppose that, in this case, we were ignorant of this length. Let us try to add 7, 8, 9, 10, etc., to each of the numbers of a cipher set (for example the last 20 numbers). We see cipher sequences appearing on the line which corresponds to 8.

|   | 44 | 10 | 27 | 08 | 22 | 33 | 05 | 18 | 35 | 16 | 01 | 20 | 37 | 03 | 23 | 09 | 28 | 45 | 11 | 31 |
|---|----|----|----|----|----|----|----|----|----|----|----|----|----|----|----|----|----|----|----|----|
| 7 | 51 | 17 | 34 | 15 | 29 | 40 | 12 | 25 | 42 | 23 | 08 | 27 | 44 | 10 | 30 | 16 | 35 | 52 | 18 | 38 |
| 8 | 52 | 18 | 35 | 16 | 30 | 41 | 13 | 26 | 43 | 24 | 09 | 28 | 45 | 11 | 31 | 17 | 36 | 53 | 19 | 39 |
| 9 | 53 | 19 | 36 | 17 | 31 | 42 | 14 | 27 | 44 | 25 | 10 | 29 | 46 | 12 | 32 | 18 | 37 | 54 | 20 | 40 |

18 35 16–30 41 13 26 43 24–09 28 45 11 31–17 36–19 39.

We have 46 letters in the message and 8 in the key; the sets will, therefore, have 6 letters each for the first 6 letters of the key and 5 each for the last 2 key letters. The reestablished successions of 6 and 5 letters conforming with those which we have been able to draw in toto from the final cryptogram will then probably be whole sets corresponding to a key letter; 18 35 16 will be the end of a set, and 17 36 will be the beginning of a set, since it follows a complete set.

However, with barely a few exceptions, a final cipher sequence should have its numbers equal to those of the preceding letter of the keyword augmented by 8. The sequence corresponding to the letter to the left of the one that gives 30 41 13 26 43 24 should hence be 22 33 05 18 35 16. We actually have this sequence in the cipher. Thus, step by step, the order of the sets is reconstructed, and the numerical key whose length we already have will be recovered.

Getting back to our problem, in which the known data are the plain text, in which letters occur in the order 01, 02, ... , 46, and the cipher in which these letters are mixed, we see how we can try to add the same number to a cipher sequence to get another sequence by replacing the cipher letters by the numbers that they bear in the clear. These are 46 12 29 ... 11 31. In practice difficulties may arise from several sources. It may be hard to identify a clear letter, an A for example, with a given cipher A if there are several of them; therefore, the order of numbering the cipher will be doubtful and the sequences confusing. This obstacle will be surmounted if we get several anagrams of the same length, the uncertainties in one being removed in another. We will find ourselves in an equally disadvantageous position if the key is long and the breaks in the sequences of the first cryptogram are very numerous in very short sequences. But the principle of the method remains the same.

We will not continue this study any further, and we will not generalize. We just wanted to show how a transposition system may be analyzed, and, supposing the problem solved, the method of finding the unknown key by means of a cryptogram, a translation of which is at hand. This last condition is usually the hardest to find in actual practice. The slips of the encipherer sometimes bring the cryptanalyst important help along these lines. However, it is particularly on the knowledge of the language of the message and on a wide technical experience that the cryptanalyst must count to succeed with anagrams.

We have said that transpositions, particularly of the grille type, might not only apply to letters but also to polygraphs or words. We will not dwell on these matters: Certain historical novels make a to-do about messages in which three words in four are nulls, the text and the nulls together making sense and the real message being composed of only the words in positions $n$, $n+4$, $n+8$, ... . Transpositions of the words of a clear text often give quite sufficiently incomprehensible messages to form interesting problems. We must almost always turn to the method of anagramming, counting ourselves lucky if a second message enables us to check the assumptions we make on the first.

## CHAPTER XIII

## SUPERIMPOSITION OF SYSTEMS

When correspondents do not find that the security obtained by one encipherment of a message is great enough, they often subject the first cryptogram, considered as a plain message, to a second encipherment, which is sometimes called a superencipherment. When both systems are well chosen, a great increase in security results; but, sometimes, the result is illusory, and the security is only equal to that offered by the first system, if not even inferior.

We make no pretention to examining all of the possible systems. Besides, in this case, we no longer have introductory studies to cryptography, but cryptanalytical studies requiring quite a wide knowledge and experience with cryptograms. Therefore, we will take just a few examples, in order to point out the lines along which these systems are conceived, how they should be considered before adoption, and how they may occasion the researches of cryptanalysts.

**Simple substitution.**—When a message is enciphered in simple substitution, a superencipherment by another simple substitution results in nothing more than just another simple substitution. If $A_p$ is represented by $E_c$ in the first cryptogram, and if $E_p = N_c$ in the second substitution table, clear A will be represented by cipher N in the final cryptogram.

Therefore, it is not without astonishment that we will find in a volume edited in 1922 a system of this type described as preferable to the known procedures "which do not yield an absolute security." At the end of the Rudolf Mosse Code,[1] the use of the following procedure is recommended: To write out the message to be enciphered by means of some steganographic script (like the so-called "Freemason" alphabet, in which the letters are formed by two or three lines belonging to the sides of a square or triangle) in which there is one character per letter of the alphabet, to turn the page upside down, which places the steganograms upside down, and make them represent in this position other letters of the alphabet than when they were right side up, to translate the characters in this position, and write down the text thus obtained.

This is equivalent to three simple substitutions. Turning the characters upside down is nothing but a substitution.

**Simple substitution and polyalphabetic substitution.**—Superimposing simple substitutions upon polyalphabetic substitutions, or vice versa, may obliterate all the advantages which normal alphabets for the polyalphabetic substitution would offer the cryptanalyst, in case such alphabets were used. He finds only random alphabets when, having discovered the key length as for an ordinary polyalphabetic substitution, he seeks to find the clear for the cipher letters.

**Superimposed polyalphabetic substitutions.**—By successively using polyalphabetic substitutions with given key lengths, we obtain, after the second substitution, a polyalphabetic substitution with a period equal to the least common multiple of the lengths of the two keys.

Let us first take up the case in which the keys have exactly the same length. Let us encipher a message with the key 1–3–2–4 in the Gronsfeld system, and then superencipher it with the key 0–1–4–2. We get:

```
Clear_____ L A P R E M I E R E D I V I S I O N
First encipherment_____ M D R V F P K I S H F M U L U M P Q
Second encipherment_____ M E V X F Q O K S I J O U M Y O P R
```

---

[1] This has been deleted from the later editions of this code.

The same result is gotten as if the clear message had been enciphered with the key 1–4–6–6, the same in length as the two original keys. It will be noticed that the successive encipherment of messages amounts to enciphering the two keys one by the other (1–3–2–4 enciphered with the key 0–1–4–2 becomes 1–4–6–6) and applying the new key to the clear message. When we are working with literal keys, we may thus use two successive encipherments with clear keys in order to succeed in getting an encipherment with a random key, resulting from the encipherment of one of the keys by means of the other with the square table used.

It is easily seen that a message obtained by enciphering with a key of 4 and a superencipherment with a key of 6, or vice versa, would give a period of 12. We will show this again in the case of keys in the Gronsfeld system.

Let the keys be 1–3–2–4 and 1–0–1–2–0–3. By applying them successively, the shifts of the one with respect to the clear (letter of the text $+n$) being added to the shifts of the other (letter of the text $+n+n'$), we get:

$$
\begin{array}{l}
1\ 3\ 2\ 4\ 1\ 3\ 2\ 4\ 1\ 3\ 2\ 4\ 1\ 3\ 2\ 4\ 1\ 3\ 2\ 4\ 1\ 3\ 2\ 4 \\
\underline{1\ 0\ 1\ 2\ 0\ 3\ 1\ 0\ 1\ 2\ 0\ 3\ 1\ 0\ 1\ 2\ 0\ 3\ 1\ 0\ 1\ 2\ 0\ 3} \\
2\ 3\ 3\ 6\ 1\ 6\ 3\ 4\ 2\ 5\ 2\ 7\ 2\ 3\ 3\ 6\ 1\ 6\ 3\ 4\ 2\ 5\ 2\ 7
\end{array}
$$

Therefore, we find a period of 12. Now, we know that the system of Gronsfeld, in its principle is absolutely analogous to the system of Vigenère; the alphabets to be taken to encipher each letter are indicated not by their initial letter but by a numerical interval. Our reasoning is, therefore, general. By combining key lengths which are prime to one another, we may obtain very long periods, and hence cryptograms hard to decipher if they occur as single samples. We are not going back to questions of how to solve polyalphabetic substitutions with very long keys.

**Retranspositions.**— As we have said, transpositions might assume various forms, and the prearrangement adopted might cause a mixture seemingly void of any law other than the one consisting in a chance enumeration of the letters by the correspondents. The operation of again transposing the letters already mixed up by the first encipherment will in nowise change the principles we have laid down for the study of transpositions. A simple transposition system may be applied several times, for example, the tabular system, and 2, 3, etc., transpositions may be made. Doubtless, several successive simple transpositions might occasion a methodical study like the ones we presented further back. However, in the majority of cases, we must resort to anagramming as the only method of solution.

**Transposition and substitution.**—The combinations of substitutions and of transpositions still remain. They may assume various forms. We will cite several of them.

By writing the message out in a table with a given number of letters per row, and by considering the digraphs formed in each column by two successive rows, one type of system can be obtained by applying a digraphic substitution to these digraphs. Example:

L A Q U A T R I E M
E D I V I S I O N

We take the digraphs LE, AD, QI, UV, AI, TS, etc., and encipher them. It is seen that the digraphic frequencies no longer help us, and that the discovery of the meaning of some of them no longer enables us to guess those which precede or follow them.

When substitutions involving groups of letters or digits are used, after a convenient transposition system is chosen, we may return to a representation of each group by a single letter and thus avoid transmitting cryptograms appreciably longer than the clear message. For example, let the substitution be made with this table:

```
            Z Y X V T

        M   A B C D E
        N   F G H I J
        O   K L M N O
        P   P Q R S T
        Q   U V X Y Z
```

Message _____   L A Q U A T R I E M E D I V I S I O N
First cipher ____  OY MZ PY QZ MZ PT PX NV MT OX MT MV NV QY NV PV NV OT OV

Now let us apply any kind of a transposition whatever, either by means of a geometric figure or simply by leaving the first and last letters alone and by grouping the last letter of each digraph with the first letter of the following. Let us replace each new digraph by the letter it represents in the table:

```
O YM ZP YQ ZM ZP TP XN VM TO XM TM VN VQ YN VP VN VO TO V
O  B  P  V  A  P  T  H  D  O  C  E  I  Y  G  S  I  N  O  V
```

and we will get the cryptogram OBPVA PTHDO CEIYG SINOV.

The most frequently encountered combinations of substitution and transposition involve transposition diagrams. But even so, the number of possible variations is very great; for each plain-text letter may be represented by one or two characters, and in the latter case, the transposition may take place before or after the substitution and may be applied to single characters or to pairs. Besides, the substitution may be either monoalphabetic or polyalphabetic. We will cite some of these possibilities, indicating in a summary fashion what ideas may be utilized to obtain the solution.

In general, given only one message to study, the chances of recovering the key are quite small. With a greater amount of text at hand, we may find messages of the same length, or having identical beginnings, and may avail ourselves of the ideas applying in such cases. It may even happen that we are in possession of the plain text of certain of the cryptograms.

Quite often the greatest difficulty is encountered in finding the number of columns in the transposition rectangle. Cryptograms having the same beginnings permit us to obtain the lengths of columns from which information we may get an idea of the kind of table used and which are the long and short columns. The examination of additional messages in the same key permits the elimination of some of the incorrect hypotheses. Sometimes we can even arrange the columns into long and short ones, and then with several cryptograms of different lengths which also differ as to the number of long columns, it may happen that we can reconstruct the order of some of the columns. Other observations, as we will see, may help in this research.

When the substitution is monoalphabetic, letter for letter, and the transposition is effected by means of a design, the order of the two operations is immaterial; we may substitute before transposing or else substitute after the first cryptogram has been obtained by transposition.

Such a cryptogram yields a frequency table analogous to that for a monoalphabet, and in most cases E can be picked out without difficulty. But the characteristic grouping is lacking for finding digraphs which would permit us to fit columns together.

If we know the number of columns in the rectangle, an attempt may be made to guess a probable word using considerations of the type presented in the chapter on transpositions. The frequencies of the cipher letters will serve as a guide in identifying those letters which make up the probable word.

However, this identification and the determination of the portion of the table which corresponds to the probable word are very difficult except in the case when the probable word is very characteristic either because of very frequent letters or, better still, because of very infrequent letters. Although the encipherment involved is quite simple, it, nevertheless, yields cryptograms of a high degree of security especially if the key is long and the cryptograms are short.

In order to study cryptograms built up by first substituting numbers for the letters and then transposing the individual digits, we will first suppose that the substitution table is the one given below:

|   | 1 | 2 | 3 | 4 | 5 |
|---|---|---|---|---|---|
| 1 | A | B | C | D | E |
| 2 | F | G | H | I | J |
| 3 | K | L | M | N | O |
| 4 | P | Q | R | S | T |
| 5 | U | V | X | Y | Z |

Each letter is enciphered by setting down the number of the column, followed by that of the row, in which it is found. We will now try to elucidate what takes place in the transposition.

After this last operation has been completed, we will have a cryptogram containing only the first five digits which give it a characteristic appearance.

It would be a good idea to begin by counting the frequency of each digit.

Let us make a remark on this point. If the frequency of each letter is entered into the enciphering table and the sums obtained for each row and column, we find:

|  |  |  |  |  | Total |
|---|---|---|---|---|---|
| A 7 | B 1 | C 4 | D 4 | E 17 | 33 |
| F 1 | G 1 | H 0 | I 7 | J 0 | 9 |
| K 0 | L 5 | M 3 | N 9 | O 7 | 24 |
| P 3 | Q 1 | R 7 | S 7 | T 7 | 25 |
| U 7 | V 2 | X 0 | Y 0 | Z 0 | 9 |

Total_____ 18   10   14   27   31

The 1's in the cryptogram arising from a column (as the first figures of a group), together with those resulting from a row (as the second figures of a group) have a normal frequency proportional to $33+18=51$.

Similarly the remaining digits will have frequencies proportional to the figures given below:

| No. | Frequency |
|---|---|
| 2_____ | $9+10=19$ |
| 3_____ | $24+14=38$ |
| 4_____ | $25+27=52$ |
| 5_____ | $9+31=40$ |

If, then, the cryptogram at hand has been enciphered with a table analogous to that which we have chosen, with the letters in the same place as in our example, the frequencies of the digits will be proportional to the above numbers.

Another remark is the following: If the transposition rectangle has an even number of columns, the first line will contain an exact number of cipher digraphs; if the table has an odd number of columns, one digraph will be cut in two, the first figure being in the last column of the first line, the second figure being in the first column of the second line. In the first case (even width) each column of the table will contain only initial figures of cipher digraphs or else only final figures. In the second case (odd width) there will be a mixture in each column, the odd lines beginning with an initial digit, the even lines with a final digit.

If, then, in the first case we suppose the columns to be known and separated in the resulting cryptogram, the odd columns will yield frequencies based on the initial figures of digraphs, the even columns will yield frequencies based on the final figures of digraphs. Now for certain figures these frequencies are considerably different. 5 as an initial is much more frequent than as a final (31 against 9); 1 as a final is quite a bit more frequent than as an initial (33 against 18). These characteristics in the columns of the cryptogram will show up even though they are not sufficiently clear to permit the determination of the end of one column and the beginning of the next. In the case of a rectangle of an odd number of columns, this characteristic disappears, the distribution being practically uniform, but it will be discovered if we consider the digits in the even places of a column and the digits in the odd places provided the columns are sufficiently long for some law to be discovered.

It is, therefore, possible, given several messages, to determine the number of columns in the rectangle, at any rate after some trial.

When this has been accomplished, we may try to pair off the columns on the basis of frequency, granting that the best pair is that one which gives the greatest number of E's.

Suppose we have the following cryptogram:

```
25534   45414   51143   13441   13353   11423   13121   55135   35341
24244   12141   45311   45525   45322   55
```

By means of the 5's and the 1's, we can with a sufficient degree of approximation distinguish six columns in the following order: 1 odd, 2 even, 1 odd, 1 even, 1 odd. As the total number of letters is divisible by 6, the rectangle is completely filled and we will not have any hesitation about long and short columns (a hesitation which it must be admitted will arise and will require trials to be made on a number of messages in order to permit us to make hypotheses about the beginnings and ends of columns).

Let us, therefore, cut the given cryptogram up into six equal columns:

```
        I—255344541451          IV—513535341242
       II—143134411335           V—441214145311
      III—311423131215          VI—455254532255
```

and try to fit the columns together. In making this trial, we may suppose the odd and even columns known and will consequently try to fit together only an odd and an even column. If, however, we were not sure of the parity of the columns, we would make our trials on all the columns.

Let us successively set columns II, III, and V next to I, IV, and VI:

| A | | B | | C | | D | | E | | F | | G | | H | | I | |
|---|---|---|---|---|---|---|---|---|---|---|---|---|---|---|---|---|---|
| I | II | I | III | I | V | IV | II | IV | III | IV | V | VI | II | VI | III | VI | V |
| 2 | 1 | 2 | 3 | 2 | 4 | 5 | 1 | 5 | 3 | 5 | 4 | 4 | 1 | 4 | 3 | 4 | 4 |
| 5 | 4 | 5 | 1 | 5 | 4 | 1 | 4 | 1 | 1 | 1 | 4 | 5 | 4 | 5 | 1 | 5 | 4 |
| 5 | 3 | 5 | 1 | 5 | 1 | 3 | 3 | 3 | 1 | 3 | 1 | 5 | 3 | 5 | 1 | 5 | 1 |
| 3 | 1 | 3 | 4 | 3 | 2 | 5 | 1 | 5 | 4 | 5 | 2 | 2 | 1 | 2 | 4 | 2 | 2 |
| 4 | 3 | 4 | 2 | 4 | 1 | 3 | 3 | 3 | 2 | 3 | 1 | 5 | 3 | 5 | 2 | 5 | 1 |
| 4 | 4 | 4 | 3 | 4 | 4 | 5 | 4 | 5 | 3 | 5 | 4 | 4 | 4 | 4 | 3 | 4 | 4 |
| 5 | 4 | 5 | 1 | 5 | 1 | 3 | 4 | 3 | 1 | 3 | 1 | 5 | 4 | 5 | 1 | 5 | 1 |
| 4 | 1 | 4 | 3 | 4 | 4 | 4 | 1 | 4 | 3 | 4 | 4 | 3 | 1 | 3 | 3 | 3 | 4 |
| 1 | 1 | 1 | 1 | 1 | 5 | 1 | 1 | 1 | 1 | 1 | 5 | 2 | 1 | 2 | 1 | 2 | 5 |
| 4 | 3 | 4 | 2 | 4 | 3 | 2 | 3 | 2 | 2 | 2 | 3 | 2 | 3 | 2 | 2 | 2 | 3 |
| 5 | 3 | 5 | 1 | 5 | 1 | 4 | 3 | 4 | 1 | 4 | 1 | 5 | 3 | 5 | 1 | 5 | 1 |
| 1 | 5 | 1 | 5 | 1 | 1 | 2 | 5 | 2 | 5 | 2 | 1 | 5 | 5 | 5 | 5 | 5 | 1 |

If we then consider the frequencies of the various digraphs, we have:

| | A | B | C | D | E | F | G | H | I |
|---|---|---|---|---|---|---|---|---|---|
| 11 | 1 | 1 | 1 | 1 | | 2 | | | |
| 12 | | | | | | | | | |
| 13 | | | | | | | | | |
| 14 | | | | 1 | | 1 | | | |
| 15 | 1 | 1 | 1 | | | 1 | | | |
| 21 | 1 | | | | | 1 | 2 | 1 | |
| 22 | | | | | | | 1 | 1 | |
| 23 | | 1 | | 1 | | 1 | 1 | | 1 |
| 24 | | | 1 | | | | | 1 | |
| 25 | | | 1 | 1 | | | | | 1 |
| 31 | 1 | | | | | 2 | 3 | 1 | |
| 32 | | 1 | | 1 | | | | | |
| 33 | | | 2 | | | | | 1 | |

| | A | B | C | D | E | F | G | H | I |
|---|---|---|---|---|---|---|---|---|---|
| 34 | | 1 | | 1 | | | | | 1 |
| 35 | | | | | | | | | |
| 41 | 1 | | 1 | 1 | 1 | 1 | | | |
| 42 | | 2 | | | | | | | |
| 43 | 2 | 2 | 1 | 1 | 1 | | 2 | | |
| 44 | 1 | | 2 | | | 1 | 1 | | 2 |
| 45 | | | | | | | | | |
| 51 | | | 4 | 3 | 2 | | | 4 | 5 |
| 52 | | | | | | 1 | | 1 | |
| 53 | 2 | | | | | 2 | 3 | | |
| 54 | 2 | | 1 | 1 | 1 | 2 | 2 | | 1 |
| 55 | | | | | | | 1 | 1 | |

We observe in this table, in which the correct solutions are B, D, and I, that the highest frequencies are those of E (51), and that the incorrect pairings do not often present a higher frequency (the digraphs spreading out over the whole scale of numbers). It does, however, happen that the combination which corresponds to E will not exhibit this property in an incorrect pairing except for a few accidental cases the chances for which decrease as the length of column increases.

Keeping that remark in mind, let us apply it to the case in which the alphabet has been entered normally into a square but for which we do not know the number scheme adopted for the rows and columns. In other words, we do not know the key of the substitution table. We have the means of discovering E. It will be the group corresponding to the greatest frequencies obtained by coupling each column successively with all the others, remembering, of course, that we must expect errors as the result of chance.

When the columns have been coupled together in this way and E has been discovered, we have the means of obtaining new letters on the basis of frequency since each number digraph represents one letter. We already know, if the alphabet has been inserted normally, which letters are on the same row and which are in the same column with E, also which of these are frequent and which are infrequent. The determination of each new letter will give additional hypotheses about its row and its column. For example, J corresponds to a group whose first figure is the same as that for E. Among the letters having the same second figure as J, only I is frequent. Therefore, the row F G H I J will correspond to an infrequent letter in the E column and will have one frequent letter in it. One will also observe that in the row K L M N O, only the letter K is very infrequent. If, then, one row involves four frequent letters, the fifth being absent, it will probably be the third, and the column corresponding to the absent letter will be the first one.

Once several plain-text letters have been obtained, an attempt is made to obtain the transposition rectangle by setting the paired columns next to each other in their proper relationship. We will thus have solved the following problem: Reconstruct the transposition key and the coordinates at the side and top of the substitution square, given the alphabet which has been inscribed in the square.

If we found that the transposition key involved an odd number of letters, then it would be necessary to use the even letters in each column first with one column on the right and then with that same column on the left, after which it would be necessary to treat the odd letters in the same way. We would thus have to make four trials for each one of the preceding cases.

The reasoning, of which we have given but a short sketch above (with an attempt to stray as little as possible from general considerations without getting into problems in cryptanalysis which are beyond the elements of that science), is based upon the inequality of the frequencies of the rows and columns of the enciphering square. Thus, we were able to use the characteristic frequencies of the 5 and the 1 to draw conclusions about the make-up of the transposition diagram.

An attempt has therefore been made to construct a table in which the total frequencies of the rows and columns would be practically the same, without making the alphabet a secret or variable element and permitting us to keep it in writing with the possible risk, of course, of having it fall into the hands of the enemy. The following table satisfies that condition:

|   |   |   |   |   |   |   |   |   |   | Total |
|---|---|---|---|---|---|---|---|---|---|---|
| E | 17 | K | 0 | H | 0 | V | 2 | Y | 0 | 19 |
| G | 1 | L | 5 | I | 7 | R | 7 | J | 0 | 20 |
| Q | 0 | C | 4 | N | 9 | B | 1 | T | 7 | 21 |
| X | 1 | D | 4 | F | 1 | S | 7 | U | 7 | 20 |
| Z | 0 | A | 7 | P | 3 | M | 3 | O | 7 | 20 |

| Total | 19 | 20 | 20 | 20 | 21 |
|---|---|---|---|---|---|

The difficulty of cryptanalysis has been considerably increased and in particular the difference in frequencies of the 5 and 1, which was pointed out in the preceding system, no longer appears. We can, however, still attack messages based on such a procedure by making various trials based on different hypotheses as to the lengths of the columns in the rectangle unless the comparison of several messages gives more precise means of obtaining that information. The work is based on this observation that E is the only frequent letter in its row and column. When an attempt is made to couple two columns, the correct result, viz, that one which yields the greatest number of E's, will show very few other combinations using the same initial or the same final digit as E.

It is, therefore, seen that a system of nonvariant simple substitution and of transposition may, in spite of its complexity, be attacked by a cryptanalyst with good chances of success. The best safeguard will be to furnish for study a minimum number of messages, enciphered with the same keys by changing the arrangement of the letters in the square and also the transposition key.

We may also resort to variants, having several indicators for each of the columns and rows of the square. In such a system, so far as we now know, it appears almost absolutely impossible to find the keys if we have nothing but cryptograms at hand. According to General Cartier, who has devoted himself particularly to studies of superencipherment, the key to the transposition table and the substitution may be found when the plain text of a cryptogram and the number of columns in the transposition table are known. But this author himself makes the observation that it is never possible to reach any result except with a sufficiency of messages, provided that skillful encipherers do the work without falling into the common error of consistently choosing certain equivalents in preference to others.

**Polyalphabetic substitutions and transposition.**—People have used systems consisting of a polyalphabetic substitution and a transposition. We have particularly often encountered Gronsfeld substitutions in this connection, in which the alphabets used were few and close to the clear alphabet. Will we begin with the transposition? If we do, the resultant text is submitted to a substitution with successive alphabets determined by a key. If we have plenty of cryptograms, we may seek the alphabets involved by treating the letters which have been acted on by the same key element. We write the messages one under the other, and assuming a Vigenère or Gronsfeld system, we can find the alphabet from the most frequent letter unless that letter is not a definite plain-text E, in which case we can use a series of the type ERASINTULO. (See p. 9.) If we discover the key and the alphabets, we are back again to the problem of transposition.

As we have usually seen, if the substitution is performed first and the transposition afterwards, it will be noted that the transposition table will assume different shapes according as the number of letters per row is equal to the length of the substitution key (or to a multiple of it), or is different from it. In the first case the periodicity of the key brings back the same alphabet to the same column of each new row. This does not happen in the second case, however. The problem may be treated in a general way and we will point out the observations leading to solution by means of a very simple particular case.

We will suppose that the message was enciphered by means of a Gronsfeld system with the key 0–1–2, so that if the clear text were AAAAAAAAA..., the cipher would be ABCABCABC...

If the transposition key has a length equal to a multiple of 3, the first column of the table will be composed of plain-text letters only (AAAA ...), the second of letters one removed from the clear (BBBB ...), the third of letters two places removed from the clear (CCCC ...) the fourth of clear letters (AAAA ...), etc., and the cipher will be of such a type as BBBBAAAACCCCBBBBCCCC, etc.

If the key has one letter more than a multiple of three, the table will be of the type:

```
A B C A B . . . .        A B C A
B C A B C . . . .        B C A B
C A B C A . . . .        C A B C
A B C . . . . . .
```

and we will have sequences of the ABC type in every column. The cipher will be of the type:

```
A B C A A B C A C A B C B C A C A B C
```

The break in the ABC series results from a change of columns.

If the key has two letters more than a multiple of three, the table will be of the type:

```
A B C A B . . . .     A B C A B
C A B C A . . . .     C A B C A
B C A B C . . . .     B C A B C
A B C . . . . . .
```

In every column the series ACB will be found, and the cipher will be of the type:

A C B A A C B A B A C C B A

Classifying a cipher in one of these three groups, we will be enabled to make an assumption about the number of letters in the transposition key which will make it much easier to reconstruct the key since the columns begin with a clear letter or one shifted one or two places against the clear, and must follow each other in order. At the same time, the substitution problem will be solved.

But when we are dealing with a real cryptogram, instead of the letters ABC, we have difficulties in distinguishing the clear letters from those that have been changed. We have to resort to frequency considerations.

A given cipher letter, N, may represent N or M or L. We will suppose that each cipher letter always represents the most frequent of the three letters which it may replace, and in this schematic representation of the cipher we will designate the letters which are themselves the most frequent of the triplet by A (here, $N_c = N_p$); by B, those which would be the result of enciphering the most frequent letter with the key $+1$ (for example $F_c$, since it follows the most frequent letter in the set DEF); by C, those which would result from the key $+2$ (for example $G_c$, since it is two removed from the most frequent letter of the set EFG). A table containing a list of the letters and the type under which they fall may be drawn up according as the most frequent letter is the letter itself, the preceding one or the one before that, in each case.

```
A B C D E F G H I J K L M N O P Q R S T U V W X Y Z
A B C A A B C A A B C A B A B C C A A B C C C B C
```

Now, by studying a certain number of cryptograms constructed along these lines with a view to seeking their peculiarities, it is recognized, as Captain Painvin has pointed out, that in most cases the cipher belongs to type I, II, or III, according as it contains a majority of sequences of types AA, AB, or AC.

Let the cryptogram be constructed of 48 letters:

VKTKU  BFTEB  VGQTG  VUIPM  CLMNA  NOJJF  ESSFG  GPNRS  TNUBW  BPZ

By replacing each letter by the index of the type it belongs to, we get:

CCBCC  BBBAB  CCCBB  CCACB  CABAA  ABBBB  AAABC  CCAAA  BACBC  CBC

Sequences of type AA, BB, and CC are 20 in number.
Sequences of type AB, BC, and CA are 14 in number.
Sequences of type AC, CB, and BA are 13 in number.
Therefore, we conclude that the number of letters in the transposition key is a multiple of 3.

In most cases, a single cryptogram cannot give any more complete information than this. However, if we have several, we may successfully estimate the length of the columns by comparing the beginnings and endings. Thus, we can see more or less clearly the point where the **CCC** series yields to the **BBB** or **AAA** series, which will belong in our cryptogram to the second column transcribed (or, if the first columns are of the same type, to a following column). In this case, the third letter **B** is probably an accident, and the first column ends with the first group; however, aside from the fourth and fifth groups, the separations of the columns are no longer clear by any means.

As we have said, the key is a multiple of 3. A key of 9 would cause columns of 5 and 6 letters, and a key of 15 would cause columns of 3 and 4 letters, which might also fit. We will suppose that we have other messages and that more beginnings have definitely indicated a 9-letter key. It would give us the following succession of columns:

CBCAABCAB (a column of type C inscribed first, and one of type B, second). In the same way we would see which are the long columns by a consideration of possible different length of columns with the different lengths of cryptograms and the key of 9. We would finally place the cipher in sets as below:

| Type C: VKTKU, | B: BFTEBV, | C: GQTGV, |
|---|---|---|
| A: UIPMC, | A: LMNANO, | B: JJFES, |
| C: SFGGPN, | A: RSTNU, | B: BWPBZ |

Immediately we get the first three columns (the long columns) in **ABC** order:

| L B S | which gives on translation, | L A Q |
|---|---|---|
| M F F | | M E D |
| N T G | | N S E |
| A E G | | A D E |
| N B P | | N A N |
| O V N | | O U L |

The two other columns of type A, tried as the fourth column, give the digraphs:

| Q R | Q U |
|---|---|
| D S | D I |
| E T | E P |
| E N | E M |
| N U | N C |

The digraph QU makes us adopt the second solution. Going ahead step by step, we retrieve the text: "LA QUATRIÈME DIVISION SE PORTERA DEMAIN DE NANCY SUR TOUL."

The cryptogram:

```
BSTBD   URQEC   RFBIT   EOTFP   KSAUL   FPNVU   GTMUS   RMGBU   VFVJA
PFHSW   TGWOU   KFNNJ   JNGZA   W
```

gives as its scheme:

```
BABBA   CACAC   ABBAB   ABBBC   CAACA   BCACC   CBBCA   ABCBC   CBCBA
CBAAC   BCCBC   CBAAB   CACCA   C
```

Sequences of type AA=16; type AB=23; type AC=25.

It is, as a matter of fact, enciphered with a key of 11 letters. The plain text is: "LA QUA-TRIÈME DIVISION SE PORTERA DEMAIN DE NANCY SUR TOUL. DEPART A TROIS HEURES."

In this example of superencipherment, we see how the superimposition of the substitution system on the transposition facilitates the reconstruction of the transposition table. Therefore, it is feasible to ask ourselves if the complication of the encipherment is justified by the advantage obtained from the point of view of the complexity of the system. If we are content to change the transposition keys without modifying that of the substitution, and if traffic is heavy enough for the cryptanalyst using formulae tabulations to reconstruct the lengths of the columns and their positions on the basis of several messages, with a good approximation, the solution of the problem of the transposition key becomes almost mechanical.

We have shown from these few examples, how, when we have identified a complicated system, or when we know by any means that it is such, we should dissect it in order to see how to treat it, and reduce it to simple cases which we know how to solve by the usual steps, which form the successive stages of the problem's solution. As for the great difficulty—that of identifying the systems which produced the cryptograms received by the cryptanalyst without complementary explanations, we solve them, when they can be solved, by a knowledge (due to experience) of the results given by the transformation of a plain message into a cipher by means of the systems we have had occasion to work with before, and by trials on messages which we ourselves encipher by different systems, in order to reproduce the same peculiarities as those in the cryptogram. Should we be contending with experienced encipherers, masters of complicated systems, who frequently change their keys, and even their general systems, we must not be astonished if we do not succeed in breaking the seal of secrecy with which they have desired to stamp their correspondence.

## CHAPTER XIV

# CODE SYSTEMS—DESCRIPTION OF SYSTEMS AND SUPERENCIPHERMENTS

**Generalities.**—Code systems are substitution systems in which the elements of the correspondence tables—comprising letters, syllables, words, and sentences—are so numerous that it is not possible to learn them by heart nor to reconstruct them when needed and it is necessary to make written lists of them. The totality of these lists forms what is called a code, or a repertory, or an enciphered dictionary, or enciphering tables. We might perhaps establish differences among these words, according to the external appearance of the document and its size. Here we will use one or another of these terms indifferently.

For commercial purposes, code books have been publicly printed. When we wish to keep the correspondence tables secret, we must have recourse to codes specially composed and kept secret—big corporations and government bureaus, therefore, have their own codes.

In all documents of this nature, a certain number of words occur in their various linguistic forms; sometimes, on the same line, a radical is followed by several endings which correspond, for example, to a verb and a noun, to an adjective and an adverb (commenc-er, -ement; facile, -ment).

The meaning, or a special prearrangement, indicates whether, in deciphering, we must translate the first or the second of the words which occur next to one another in this way.

Certain phrases or clauses, or combinations of frequent words also occur in the code.

But there are some words and proper nouns that do not occur in it. They are broken up into their alphabetic or syllabic components which we encode successively. Many codes contain prearranged groups, the use of which is explained in the preface, to facilitate this operation. Words enciphered by components are frequently designated by the expression "les syllabés."[1]

The more words or expressions there are, and the less we need to resort to the syllabary, the more complete we say the code is.

When the two lists in the correspondence tables—words and their equivalents—are both alphabetically or numerically regular, we say that the code is orderly.[2] To encode, we look up a word in its alphabetical place in the table, and we write in the cryptogram the equivalent for this word occurring opposite it; to decode, we look up this equivalent in its alphabetical or numerical place *in the same table*, and we find the clear text word opposite it.

But, in substitutions, we saw that the use of a random substitution alphabet complicated the task of cryptanalysts considerably. We get the same result by introducing randomness in the order of the equivalents in the case of code. In this case, instead of being able to use the same table for looking up words to encode or equivalents to decode, we adopt *different* tables: One in which the words to be encoded are in alphabetical order and the equivalents without order, the other in which the equivalents are in alphabetical or numerical order and the clear words without order. Thus, we avoid long researches, which would be necessary if we had but a single list to retrieve in decoding, for example, an equivalent buried in a long random list.

---

[1] We have no corresponding word, using instead the phrase "words that must be spelled out." The best equivalent to be found in the Funk and Wagnalls unabridged dictionary is "syllabicated words."

[2] We call such a code a "one-part code."

The two tables are called the encoding list (or encoding table) and the decoding list (or decoding table). The code is often called a disordered or random code.[1]

An example from a page of a one-part code:[1]

| | | | |
|---|---|---|---|
| 2000 | Corse | 2050 | couronner |
| 2001 | Cortège | 2051 | courrier |
| 2002 | Cortès | 2052 | par le courrier |
| 2003 | Corvée | 2053 | cours |
| 2004 | Corvette | 2054 | au cours |
| 2005 | Coryza | 2055 | cours moyen |
| 2006 | Costume | 2056 | dernier cours |
| 2007 | Cote | 2057 | course |
| 2008 | Côte | 2058 | court |
| 2009 | Côté | 2059 | courtage |
| 2010 | à côté de | 2060 | courtier |
| 2011 | de tous côtés | 2061 | cousin |
| 2012 | du côté de | 2062 | couteau |
| 2013 | coter | 2063 | coûter |
| . . . . | . . . . . | . . . . | . . . . . |

An example of pages from a two-part code:

| Enciphering table | | Deciphering table | |
|---|---|---|---|
| piège_____ | 4367 | 1020 | madame |
| pierre_____ | 1025 | 1021 | convoi |
| pierrerie____ | 9872 | 1022 | accord |
| piété_____ | 0013 | 1023 | marne |
| pile_____ | 1421 | 1024 | heure |
| pillard_____ | 5718 | 1025 | pierre |
| piller_____ | 6884 | 1026 | porteur |
| pilote_____ | 4321 | 1027 | repos |
| . . . . . . . | . . . . | . . . . | . . . . . |

Finally, in some cases, mixed codes are found. All the words are in alphabetical order, and the great majority of the groups are in order, so that a single table might suffice. However, for reasons that will be explained further on and which result from the method of solving one-part codes, it is preferable for certain words not to be represented by a group corresponding to their alphabetical place; thus, in French, it is bad for "A" to be represented by 0001.

Then, in its alphabetical place opposite "A", we write some group or other, and we reproduce this group in its numerical place by writing opposite the number the word "A." The plain-text group is no longer in its alphabetical position. This requires two lines of the code for the words thus treated and breaks the order of the tables, but we can facilitate the reading by typographical artifices. Such a system does not burden the editors of the code with the toilsome task of cross-referencing which two-part codes require, and enables us to economize on paper and printing, since only a few words occur twice, in actually encoding and decoding, while in the two-part code all the words occur once in the encoding table and again in the decoding table.

Example:

| | | | |
|---|---|---|---|
| A_____ | 1404 | dilapider_____ | 1401 |
| ab_____ | 0002 | dilater_____ | 1402 |
| abaisser_____ | 0003 | dilatoire_____ | 1403 |
| abandon_____ | 0004 | A_____ | 1404 |
| abattre_____ | 0005 | dilemme_____ | 1405 |

---

[1] We call such a code a "two-part code."

**Code words and groups.**—We have spoken of the equivalents of clear words. These equivalents are, in general, groups of digits or groups of letters, or words.

Up until late years, it seems that groups of digits have had the preference. A very common arrangement was the one-part code with 100 pages of 100 lines each, in two columns, thus: 10,000 words, with equivalent groups of 4 digits, which were telegraphed either in sets of 4 digits or in sets of 5 by joining all the sets of 4 and dividing the result into groups of 5. Attempts to use letter codes had not met with great success, perhaps because, in Morse telegraphic transmissions, two letters, if misread, may be received as two other letters or even as one single letter. This increased mistakes. While digits, every one composed of 5 signals succeeding each other in a special order, might indeed cause an error (frequently, however, a single error), two of them could not be confused and read as one.

The codes which did not use groups of digits often used complete words, borrowed from spoken tongues, and included in the repertory of the Berne Convention which contains all the words issuing from languages admitted in international correspondence and charged for at the rate of one word. Transmission errors in these words were usually quite apparent.

For some years the raising of the prices of telegraphy has given a great importance to everything that can shorten telegrams. Now, although a group of five digits or a word of the Geneva [1] list is taxed as one word, a combination of 10 letters, forming any word at all, even absent from the Geneva list, is counted as one word provided it is pronounceable. [2]

Attempts have, therefore, been made to set up equivalents in the form of groups of five letters only by choosing vowels and consonants in such a way as to yield a pronounceable combination (since these may be joined two by two to form 10-letter words, thus cutting the cost in two).

The equivalents of plain-text words are often called code words or code groups. Pronounceable code groups of five letters are now in actual use.

Toward this very end of economy, the most recent codes sold to commercial firms contain a very great number of sentences of quite a few words, relating to business dealings. Some of them even specialize in particular kinds of business (the wine business; mines, etc.). In these codes, the end aimed at is not chiefly cryptography, to hide the meaning of the message from third parties, but it is rather the economy of having to transmit only one code word instead of a clear sentence. Still, such messages may often fall into the hands of a cryptanalyst who will strike difficulties, coming first from the uncertainty of what code was used (even if no change has been made in the meaning of the code groups); then, too, from the cryptographic processes which a correspondent desirous of hiding his communications from the indiscreet, from his competitors, or from his employees, who may know his code, may have used to modify these groups. The recognition of the code used requires long practice, supplemented by a special library, thoroughly furnished, in which are included the codes of all nations, procurable in commerce, and aided by repertories of the characteristics of codes bearing upon points which we will discuss later on. As to the systems used on the code groups, that takes us back to the cryptographic studies which form the principal object of the present work and we will say a word about them.

In order to be able to introduce an order into the study of codes, we will commence by distinguishing (a purely superficial distinction) those which contain as code groups nothing but groups of digits. Thence, we will pass on to those which are made up of letter code groups.

Furthermore, we will strike the same difficulties as authors before us in expounding general theories concerning the solving of code problems, and we will have recourse only to explanations

---

[1] Geneva in the original, but should be "Berne."

[2] The International Telegraph Conference of Madrid in 1932 completely eliminated all restrictions upon the construction of 5-letter code groups.

and examples bearing upon particular cases, not being able to deduce therefrom any general methods. We will refer the reader, desirous of fuller documentary study, to the second volume of the work of Valerio, in which that author gives several examples of code solution.

**The Sittler numerical code.**—The numerical code with digit code groups most used in France during the period from 1900 to 1920 was certainly *Sittler's Numerical Telegraphic Code*. It is a volume of 100 pages, each of them comprising two columns of 50 lines, and the 100 lines thus obtained on each page numbered from 00 to 99. The words in it are arranged in alphabetical order, important expressions under caption occurring after the word (agree, agree with, to agree; act, act so as to, you act, etc.). The letters and infrequent syllables which occur in the code are in their alphabetical place. A certain number of blank lines at the end of each list of words beginning with a given letter of the alphabet enables the correspondents to make a few additions suitable for their business.

The pages are not numbered.

The usual manner of using this code is to adopt a prearranged pagination. The simplest method is to call any page at all 00 and to continue the numbering from that page on. Thus, we get the same result as by adding a constant number to the pagination obtained by numbering the pages of the code from beginning to end from 00 to 99; it is an orderly numerical substitution of the simple normal alphabetical type.

Being given a cryptogram, how are we going to find the pagination used by the correspondents?

Just as in the study of alphabetical systems, the first thing to do is to list the frequencies of the letters to try to get a basis for guessing the system, likewise, in code telegrams, but not for the same reason, it is advantageous to list the different groups to verify their frequencies and sometimes their combinations. For long-winded studies, these lists are made in the form of indices on which every line is enumerated and corresponds to a group, and after having grouped together the messages to be studied in a series, and having paginated this series, we write down on the index the reference to the pages upon which each group occurs, so as to be able to find each repetition of this group quickly, when we are making guesses as to what it may mean. For our first researches, we may content ourselves with writing the groups of the telegram by columns beginning with a given digit, so as to make a first arrangement and to be able to count the frequencies easily.

These lists will then reveal frequent groups. Among these groups, prepositions and punctuation marks are usually found. Sometimes, with respect to their role, we classify the words of a language into *full* words, which give a meaning to discourse, and *empty* words—conjunctions, articles, prepositions, auxiliaries, pronouns, etc.—which enter into sentences whatever subject is treated of. Valerio even gives a list of the frequencies of empty words. We will remember only that it is these empty words that are the most frequent.

Now, in the method of using Sittler that we have indicated, the two digits representing the lines of the work are unchanged. Doubtless, we may write the two digits of the page before, or after, the two digits of the line. But when we have taken note of the line of a certain number of empty words, we soon find the two digits of this line in the most frequent groups (et, 33; par, 68; pour, 63; etc.), and by identifying the word with a group, we get the number of a page. In the case of a continuous pagination which we have expounded, that is enough to enable us to read the whole text. The assumption must naturally be verified on the basis of other groups.

It is to be noticed that we have but rarely found the articles or the preposition "de" among the most frequent words. Under pretext of "telegraphic style" the correspondents ordinarily suppress them.

Although the paragraph that is going to follow is not in its proper place here, and had better been interposed in the chapter on superencipherments, we will point out right away one of the methods, often used, to increase the secrecy of Sittler, that is to say, a transposition bearing upon the four digits of a group. If we represent the two digits of the number of the page by **PA**, and the two digits of the line by **LI**, we find, besides the combinations **PALI** or **LIPA**, all the combinations of these four digits, such as **PLIA**, **PILA**, etc. Often we will have to try guesses on several combinations of this nature before finding the right one, by successively coupling together the digits of the groups two by two in order to seek to identify a theoretical line number with a word as we have said above, when, as often happens, we have not got enough messages to get evident frequencies.

In the case where the numbering of the pages is normal and continuous, a knowledge of a single group brings about the solution of the problem. But, often, this numbering is not normal and continuous. We sometimes find a certain order in the numeration—for example, the pagination from 99 to 00 in reverse order; the use of all the even numbers, then of all the odd numbers; the use of the 10 numbers ending with 0, then of the 10 numbers ending with 1, etc.

But often the randomness is carried further (order being kept within each 10, but the tens being mixed, for example) to the point that a correspondence table is required for the correspondents themselves to replace the natural pagination of the code by the adopted pagination, and thus we tend toward absolute randomness.

Then we begin our attempts at solution by using the probable word, and we endeavor to determine the page of a certain number of words and to find a relation among the numbers of these pages and the natural pagination of the volume. The researches are greatly facilitated by preparing in advance a register in which are brought together on a single page the 100 words which correspond to a given line in the code, which is called "a Sittler by lines."

Some guesses as to the meaning of groups may, of course, be based on their position in the cryptogram. Many correspondents end their messages with "period" (line 31) and many also with "best regards" (96). "Letter (98) follows (52)", is also a frequent ending, while, on the other hand, "I have received (49)", "answer (76)", are often found at the beginning. Among the advantageous sources of conjectures, we must further cite the whole series of words expressing the idea of telegraphing, and the words which express values (francs), weights (tons), and numbers.

With regard to the latter, we will make a remark on the composition of Sittler in particular and of codes in general. We have said that, in Sittler, the expressions derived from a word come after that word; thus, after HUNDRED we get TWO HUNDRED, THREE HUNDRED, etc. The occurrence of these numbers among the words from which there are code equivalents should lessen the frequency of HUNDRED in messages. In practice, it is scarcely lessened at all. Having to encode TWO HUNDRED, the encoder who is not a specialist is going first to encode the word TWO, and when next he finds TWO HUNDRED next to HUNDRED he doesn't erase the group already written, and immediately after it he encodes HUNDRED. Thus, in codes the real place for all the expressions ought to be the alphabetic position of their first word. But still, when too great a number of them are included, encoders do not take the trouble to read the list. From a practical point of view, and when it is not a question of codes made to lessen the price of the telegram by the inclusion of ready-made sentences corresponding to a single code word, it is, in our opinion, useless to insert too many phrases or formulae into the text.

We have pointed out the permanence of the line number and a knowledge of this number for the frequent words as a method of decoding Sittler. So the procedure against decryptment will be the modifying of the line number, either only for frequent words, which are permuted with other words of the page, or by a general substitution with respect to the line number as the one which refers to the page. When this substitution is simple, such as the one which results from the addition of a given number to all the line numbers, the comparison of all the frequent code groups, among which, by the subtraction of a given number, we may make the line number reappear (PAR and POUR are 5 lines apart; LA, LE, and LES, on the same page are 53 and 30 lines apart), sometimes suffices to give us grounds for guessing the meaning of certain groups. A frequency graph of the normally ordered Sittler and of the cryptogram may be made. This sometimes yields results. However, if the lines are subjected to a substitution by a random table used at the same time for the page or the reversals of the latter, or still something else, then the cryptanalyst finds himself confronted with serious difficulties, and can hardly count on anything but the accumulation of workable data to make useful observations.

We have said that Sittler is composed of groups of four digits. In practice, telegrams in Sittler are often sent in sets of five by dividing the total of the groups into sets of five. When the final group does not contain five digits, some correspondents leave it as it is or complete it with zeros, which attracts attention. But some take the precaution to complete it with null digits other than zeros, which may cause uncertainty to reign as to the use of a 4- or 5-digit code. This uncertainty, when the message is not too short, is removed by the consideration of repetitions. By dividing the text into sets of four digits, we see repetitions of groups appearing, while they are not apparent, or not so much so, in groups of five digits. This research into the number of digits in the groups is to be made in all cases before attempting to list the groups of telegrams.

In order to deceive as to the identity of the code, some correspondents use Sittler with five digits. This is very easily accomplished by several methods:

First, the use of nulls—the interposing of a null digit in a prearranged position in the group of four digits. This method ordinarily betrays itself very quickly in the examination of the frequent groups, unless used with a rare mastery. It does diminish the frequency, since the fifth digit differs from repetition to repetition, but the sameness of four digits finally attracts the attention of a cryptanalyst suspecting the occurrence of such methods.

Next, by the use of a page enumeration in groups of three digits. If only one number per page is used, the use of at most a hundred numbers occurring alone in the lists finally shows up. However, if the digits of the line and of the page are well mixed in the group, the cryptanalyst may have to look long before classifying the groups enables him to discern the method. If several numbers per page are used, to be taken indifferently, the difficulty increases still more.

Or yet again, with methods permitting the reconstruction of a 2-digit number from one of three digits by the use of an arithmetical operation. Example: Replace the first digit of the line number by a group of two digits such that the units digit of their sum is the first digit of the line (7 will be replaced by 07, or 16, or 25, etc., or 89). Add to the line number any digit which is written after it (16 is replaced by $259 = 25 - 9 = 16$; of $171 = 17 - 1 = 16$).

Thus, we see that there is no end of methods throwing cryptanalysts off the track. They, as we have said, can only depend upon a sufficiency of messages which, by dint of repetitions, may yield bases for certain assumptions.

Even this line of attack may be denied by modifying the prearrangement or the key from one telegram to another.

We can point out methods to be changed daily or even with each telegram, either in a given order or by making them known to the correspondent by a prearranged word or group. Among these methods, we have seen the following one used: The correspondents agree upon a word in the code, taken as a keyword, and encipher it at the beginning with the method used for the telegram; for example, by adding a given number to each group of the telegram, or by adopting a given order for the four digits of the group.

We will not say anything more on this subject. However, we see that a very simple commercial code, suitably "camouflaged" by an experienced cryptanalyst and used by skilled people, may be an excellent means of secret communication. To tell the truth, we have not often seen Sittler and similar codes thus used. Those who use them are almost always satisfied with changing the pagination, or with adding a given number, called an "additive key", to the groups. Let us observe that, in the latter case, some correspondents take care not to write the 1 of the tens of thousands if the addition makes it appear, while others do not take this precaution, which attracts attention. In the use of additive keys, it often happens that, instead of adding the number formed by PALI to the key, taking into account all the tens digits, we add only each digit of one of the numbers to the corresponding digit of the other without carrying anything: 4597 plus 2068 gives 6555 and not 6665. This is a prearrangement to be determined upon by the communicants.

**Other codes with four digit groups.** —We do not pretend to list all codes here, not even those we are familiar with. And these are far from forming the majority of those that have been introduced into commerce. We will only cite a certain  number of them as types.

Beside Sittler, we may place the *Bazeries Codes*, two almost analogous documents called table no. 1 and table no. 2. Bazeries provides three different numberings for the pages: Ordinary, reserved, and special. Some correspondents indicate the pagination used by one of these words in clear, and thus furnish an assumption as to the code. One of the weak points in the Bazeries tables is the punctuation marks, grouped in one division of 10 on the same page  page 1 in table 2 and the last page in table 1. The syllables are grouped at the beginning of each letter. When we are looking for proper names or probable words, as we will see later, and when a name has two syllables beginning with the same letter, this may give a starting point. However, the great number of formulae composed of a preposition or of a conjunction and an article, and the distribution of the numbers which occur in the alphabetical position of the first number given ("two hundred" is under "two"), in our opinion makes the Bazeries codes cryptographically securer documents than Sittler. This is especially true when we are content with simple methods of numbering the pages without trying to find already complicated cryptographic methods of which we have just spoken and which give even to Sittler a security of first rank.

The *Nilac Code* also has 100 pages but the only digit which occurs in the printed text is a number from 0 to 9, opposite each of the 10 words or expressions separated by the printing arrangement which make up the 10 series occurring on each page. Therefore, the correspondents must agree not only on the two page digits but also on the digit of the group of 10. The cryptanalyst then has only one printed digit to go by, and that only when no other cryptographic method has been used to mask it. The expressions follow the word to which they are closely akin in meaning, and not in the alphabetical position of their first word. The compound numbers occur under their first element ("two hundred" under "two").

We find a new arrangement in the Nilac. Beside the series of ordinary words and expressions occurs a second series composed of syllables and geographical names. Therefore, two different translat  correspond to a given group of four digits on a given line. The meaning is usually sufficient to tell which to take in decoding, but in case of doubt the encoder announces that the second translation is to be taken, by means of special groups translating: "begin proper names", "end proper names"; or "begin syllables", "end syllables."

Let us observe in passing that amateur encoders have a tendency to use these special groups even when the meaning does not require it, and the reappearance of coupled groups (beginning—end), when the cryptogram contains many proper nouns or syllables, attracts the attention of the cryptanalyst, and may furnish a basis for an assumption on the significance of these groups. They, therefore, give what is called "an entry" into the code.

**Use of the fifth digit.**—This column of proper nouns and syllables is found in certain private codes, but sometimes other means than a special group are resorted to in order to point out their use in the text. Some 4-digit codes admit of the use of a fifth digit, placed before or after the group of four, in order to point out the use of a special column or the use of the second or third word of the line (hunt, to hunt, hunter), or again, grammatical inflections (plural, feminine, past participle, present indicative, etc.). Cryptograms then present some groups of four digits and some of five digits, sometimes even of six, seven, and eight in the case of encoders who are prodigal with grammatical details (feminine plural; second word of the line, past participle, feminine plural). The listing of the groups, permitting the recognition of 4-digit groups and these same groups with their additional digits, reveals the method. This method is known under the name of "*Use of the fifth digit.*" Let us observe that some codes regularly entail the use of groups of four and of five digits, and that, consequently, at first sight, the use of the fifth digit may encourage researches into other codes than those of the 4-digit type.

The *Telescand Code*, a French code of 100 pages for words in current use, with a supplement for proper nouns, uses a fifth digit in this way. It is always 0, and indicates the use of a column of expressions adjoining the column of words. Starting with a code of a certain completeness, this multiplies its contents by two. This code was only published in 1914; now in 1923 it does not seem to us to be used very extensively.

**Foreign codes with digit groups.**—Among the foreign codes sold for commercial use, a certain number (*Chiffrier-Wörterbuch*, by Friedmann in Berlin, for example) are of the Sittler type. However, we meet with variations of this type which we are going to point out.

The *Chiffrierbuch* by Stern and Steiner (Vienna, 1892) and the *Dizionario per corrispondenze in Cifra* by Baravelli (Turin, 1896) contain a principal part or "code" of 100 pages, analogous to those of Sittler, with 100 lines to the page, on which occur words and expressions. However, at the beginning of the volume are found 3 tables. The first, called table of vowels and punctuation marks, comprises but one page with 10 lines numbered from 0 to 9. The second, of one page with 100 lines, comprises the isolated letters, the pronouns, the conjugational endings, and the auxiliary verbs. The third, of 10 pages with 100 numbered lines to the page, comprises the syllables. According to the examples given by the authors, the expressions of the first table occur in the cryptogram in 1-digit groups; those of the second, in 2-digit groups; those of the third, in 3-digit groups; and those of the code in 4-digit groups. We are free to regulate by prearrangement the numbering from 0 to 9 of the pages of table III, and the numbering from 00 to 99 of the code. In practice, sometimes the correspondents figure that they increase the security of the communications by modifying the printed tens digit of table II and the single digits of table I.

So cryptograms composed by means of these codes usually contain a majority of 4-digit groups, but also groups of 1, 2, and 3 digits. They may not be transmitted in sets of 5 digits, as would be possible if all the groups were equal. Words encoded by syllables occur under the form of sequences of groups of 1, 2, and 3 digits, entirely characteristic of the codes of this type.

In order to avoid this characteristic aspect, and in order to facilitate the operations of superencipherment of which we will speak later on, some correspondents change all the groups into 5-digit groups by adopting a pagination with three digits which includes all four parts, taking care to represent the lines of table I by 2-digit numbers. The joining of the syllables in the same page sometimes enables us, nevertheless, to discern the nature of the code used, when the attention fixes itself upon series of groups issuing from pages very close to one another.

**Codes of more than ten thousand words.**—It seems that, in all these codes, the authors have endeavored not to exceed 10,000 words or expressions, and have confined themselves to more or less ingenious secondary methods of increasing the completeness of the code (several words to the line, two columns, etc.). The authors of a whole series of codes, among which are the *Nuovo Cifrario*, Mengarini (Rome, 1898), the *Cifrario per la corrispondenza segreta* by Cicero (Rome, 1889), the *Diccionario Cryptographico* published at Lisbon in 1892, the *Diccionario para la correspondencia secreta* by Vaz Subtil (Lisbon, 1871), etc., have been satisfied to write the words they deemed useful on 100 lines, without troubling themselves *a priori* about the number of pages, which reaches nearly 300 in some of these works. According to the instructions at the beginning of these volumes, it behooves the correspondents to establish the prearranged pagination for the inscription of which a place is reserved in certain works, or to apply to the existing pagination or to the numbers occurring in groups of four or five digits opposite each line, a key to assure the secrecy of the correspondence (a mixture of the digits of a group, considering the thousands digit as forming a number of one or two inseparable digits, adding a number to each group, etc.).

Thus, these codes yield cryptograms of 4-digit groups and of 5-digit groups which begin, barring transposition, with the first digits 1, 2, and 3. Sometimes correspondents standardize the form of the groups by having 0 precede the groups of 4 digits. Sometimes, also, individuals called upon to use these codes adopt a pagination in 3 digits, extending from 000 to 999, not necessarily using every number and using several numbers for each page. However, many telegrams present the appearance that we have cited above, and comprise some groups of four arbitrary digits and some groups of five, beginning only with the first few numbers.

Since there are cases when correspondents are led to place a zero in front of the groups of four, the authors of some codes have had this 0 printed, and thus get codes with 5-digit groups. The *Clave telegrafica* by Darhan (Madrid, 1912) contains a series of groups running from 00001 to 32400, each line being represented by a complete group. Its author, moreover, according to the preface, had not intended it to be used for transmissions in groups of digits, but it was to serve to replace a clear text word by another word of the table serving as a conventional word, the relation between these two words resting upon prearranged mathematical operations connecting the numerical group representing these two words. However, we have seen the Darhan used as a code with figure code groups with changes in the order of the digits (transposition within the code group).

*Slater's Code* (London, 1906) with 25,000 groups, is conceived with the same object in view as the Darhan, and the same observations apply to it.

A certain number of codes which contain code words also contained code groups in digits, beginning with 00001 and running on to the end of the code (75,800 for *Lieber's;* 103,000 for *A.B.C.;* 379,300 for *Western Union*, etc.—thus, we may come across some groups of six digits), and sometimes in telegrams we find these groups used, but more often than not the groups are used in these codes only to permit of operations facilitating the usage of a cryptographic method, leading to the transmission of code words in letters.

Finally, as a type of code of 5-digit groups, we will call attention to the *Dictionnaire chiffré Diplomatique et Commercial* by Airenti (Paris). This code is beginning to grow old, since it contains many proper names, chosen from the financial, political, and commercial world, of notables now dead, out of business or office, or supplanted. However, it is very complete and has been used very extensively.

The Airenti comprises groups of five digits from 25,001 to 84,200; hence, it contains no groups beginning with 1 or 9 or with 20, 21, 22, 23, and 24. This is one of the means of recognizing it. It often happens that the order of the digits in each group is permuted, so it is a good idea, when we suspect the Airenti, to try to find out whether some one of the sets of digits in the first, second, third, fourth, or fifth positions of the groups does not reduce to the numbers from 2 to 8. Some encoders use another numbering: The 5-digit groups contain on each page an immutable part, the first three digits, the last two digits being the only ones that change lineally from 01 to 00, in ascending order. Then, at the top of the page occurs a pagination beginning with 101. The hundreds digit, the thousands digit, and the ten-thousands digit of each group are often replaced by the three digits of the page number. Then the numbering of Airenti runs from 10,101 to 69,300. The method recommended for cryptography by the inventor is the addition of numbers to the code groups in digits, either the same for each group, or different, according to a certain law. Further on we will return to these methods.

Here we will stop our remarks about codes with figure code groups.

**Codes with letter groups.**—As codes with groups in letters, we will cite first some old documents in which letter groups were used to get a greater number of combinations than groups of digits of the same length yielded (26 letters instead of 10 digits), without seeking to avoid payment for characters per word.

The *Mamert Gallian Code* (Paris, 1874) thus contains nearly 17,600 ($26^3$) "ternaries" or groups of three letters. The cryptographic system recommended is a transposition within the group or a simple substitution with a normal alphabet applied to the letters. However, Valerio, in the second volume of his work, observes that all the operations of substitution with periodic keys with any alphabets at all may take place on the letters formed by a Mamert Gallian telegram; he studies some solutions of problems of this nature, in which he has recourse to some extremely interesting considerations of frequency. We cite this as a study to be remembered. It may be useful to analyze it as an exercise insofar as it may serve as a stimulus for certain researches in complicated superencipherments; however, we have never met with the use of the Mamert Gallian Code.

The *Chiffrier-Wörterbuch* by Katscher (Leipzig, 1889) comprises code groups of four letters of which the first and the third are A, B, C, or D, excluding all the other letters of the alphabet (except sometimes E in the first position); the other two letters are arbitrary.

We will not dwell on these old documents, but will pass on now to the more up-to-date codes with pronounceable code groups of five letters.

As we have said, the aim of the authors of these works is to economize on the telegraphic rates. People have not hesitated to compose very large and also costly volumes (the *Western Union* has 1,800 pages), in order to include all common phrases and expressions for which any use could possibly be imagined, and which comprise more than one word: The dates for the 365 days of the year; prices, counting by halves, in pounds, dollars, francs, rubles, etc.; weights; the names of the banks of all countries; the prices of stocks quoted in the stock market; etc. The savings that result from the charges on two of these formulae for a single word (two groups of 5 letters forming a pronounceable 10-letter code word) rapidly repays the cost of the volume when there is much correspondence. Many of these codes include at the end of the volume a table of code words classified alphabetically according to their last letters—if errors in transmission alter the code word, we have two tables to look up the correct word in: The code itself in the hope that the beginning of the word is unaltered, and the final table for cases where, though the beginning is changed, the end is intact.[1] Then too, in choosing code groups, the authors frequently impose the condition that a group used must differ from every other group in the code by at least two letters, which makes errors less to be feared.

We cannot give many details concerning these codes which are already extremely numerous and are still multiplying every day. They are distinguished from one another by certain peculiarities of the code words, and by the groups representing the most frequent words, to such an extent that we can succeed *a priori* in recognizing telegrams in which one of these

---

[1] The process of correcting errors in code groups is greatly simplified by the use of a permutation table. Such a table is found incorporated in practically all of the most recent code books, and insures the two-letter difference mentioned by the author in the next sentence.

codes has been used. Take for example the groups of *Bentley* (English), one of the codes most currently used (1923). These groups begin indifferently with vowels or consonants. In it, we meet with sequences of two vowels, and of two consonants and doublets (ABBIG, ABJIN, CYAPT); but if the first letter is a vowel, the second is a consonant, and, save rare exceptions, gives quite pronounceable digraphs (CL, CH, FE, KL). If the first letter is a consonant, the second is a vowel; the letters Q and X are not used; and initial Y and Z are found only in supplementary groups to be filled in by correspondents, hence rarely used. The "period" is encoded by TUGNY.

In the *A.B.C.*, 6th edition (English), are found sequence of two vowels or of two consonants in the first two places (AETMA, BJAUL, BRUWN). The letter Q is used, but followed only by U (QUAWD, QUUOJ) and the groups succeed each other in order up to ZYZYO.

In the *Code interprète Veslot* (French) there are code groups of four letters representing syllables, and code groups of two and three letters for the grammatical forms. Therefore, the words of the telegram have variable lengths. All the 5-letter groups are of the type consonant-vowel-consonant-vowel-consonant; the only final letters are C, D, G, L, N, R, S, T, X, Z (10 in all). The letters H, K, Q, W, X are not used as initials. The code, properly speaking, ends at NENEL, and the remainder comprises only supplements. This code, like some others, has editions in various languages, but while a single table suffices in French for the basic code, it requires encoding tables in other languages (in which the words are in alphabetical order and in which the code groups are in the order imposed by both their meaning in French and the foreign word which translates this meaning), and decoding tables (in which the code groups are in order).

The *Rudolf Mosse Code* (German, Berlin, 1922) has 5-letter code groups in which Q is not used. The groups are of very diverse forms (ABKRU, ABOOW, AEBOA, DAOOL, DAOUD, DEASS, HEUUR, TROPT) and follow each other to Z. The same volume contains a reduced code with 3-letter groups which are transmitted in groups of 10; that is, three groups of 3 and a check letter. The use of the check letter is encountered in various forms also in other works; for example, in the *Code international Lugagne* (edited in Paris), in 7 languages, which contains more than 6,000 groups, all of 3 letters. Its aim is to reveal errors in transmission. For example, in the Rudolf Mosse Code, each group of 3 is filled out with a digit picked at random from 1 to 9, thus: AHM 1, AUP 4, EVI 6, written below. When three groups have been enciphered, for example, AHM AUP EVI, the sum of their digits is gotten $1+4+6=11$. On each page of the code is found a table giving the correspondences of the letters of the alphabet in numbers from 3 to 27 ($1+1+1$ to $9+9+9$). Opposite 11 is found Z: We write AHMAUPEVIZ. Let us suppose that the telegrapher sends AHNAUPEVIZ. The recipient gets the total (AHN=4) $4+4+6=14$, Z gives 11, so there is an error, and it leaves no confidence in the meaning of the phrase.[1] Certain parts of the Mosse Code with numerical equivalents may occasion the use of a condenser (see further on), causing a saving of 50 percent in the transmission cost, and the 10-letter words of the condenser are formed of vowel-consonant or consonant-vowel digraphs.

*The Marconi Code* (English with two other languages per volume) has 5-letter groups of varied forms, which, in the great majority of cases, do not begin with two vowels nor two consonants nor with Q. H, J, Q, V, W, X are never final letters. Some groups, standing for numbers, according to another table, begin with two consonants or QU followed by syllables of 2 letters.

---

[1] The idea of a check letter or check number, which has been introduced in this fashion and which is to be found in condensing systems, can do no more than indicate the existence of an error. (It is of no aid in correcting such an error.) It must also be noted that under particular circumstances the check figure or letter may be correct, even though an error exists.

The *Western Union* (American) includes on each line two 5-letter code groups to be used at discretion, one pronounceable, the other composed of any 5 letters, pronounceable or not. The letters Q and X are not used as initials, nor is the letter Z in pronounceable groups which correspond to numbers, dates, values, etc., from R on. This code is very complete. It contains nearly 380,000 groups.

We will not go on with these examples. We have seen enough to perceive that the different codes have their own individual characteristics and that certain code groups may occasion the assurance that they do not come from a given code even when we do not have a collection of codes at hand.

Some other codes, published for the most part before the increases in telegraphic rates which followed the war of 1914–18, use code words taken from spoken tongues, of such a length as to be counted as one word each. However, errors are less to be feared in them than in artificial code words, because the words of spoken tongues are usually more easily reconstructed than the latter.

The French *AZ Code* used code words taken only from Dutch, with the object, so the author says, of making the *AZ* more easily recognizable, and also to prevent confusion between the words left in clear by the encoder and the code words (the Dutch language is very little used).

The *Lieber* uses code words from all tongues, beginning with A, B, C, D, E. It is published in several languages, and, in order to avoid all difficulty inherent in the scheme of the clear words in alphabetical order, it is divided into short chapters relating to a given subject. The alphabetical table of these subjects, in whatever language the particular copy of the code may be, is at the beginning, and refers to the proper pages. However, words and formulae are not in alphabetical order on these pages. On the other hand, the code words are strictly in this kind of order.

The *A.B.C.*, 5th edition (English), likewise uses code words from all tongues, and it uses the whole alphabet from A to Z as initial letters in the principal part or in the various supplements.

We will not point out any more of this type. We will remark, however, that a great number of commercial firms have codes with words agreed upon among themselves, such as trade names for engine parts, etc. There exist little codes for sending news to people who are away, for engaging hotel rooms, etc. A library of this literature, ever necessary to an important cryptanalytic office, is almost always very incomplete. The majority of these codes, too, have characteristic aspects; thus, The *Marconi's Wireless Telegraphic Code*, which contains nearly 12,000 formulae, has code words beginning only with A (Abaissaix to Alumbrado).

Sometimes these codes contain artificial code words of more than five letters. The *Engineer Code* by Galland (German), which has about 1,000 pages, uses code words of seven letters, beginning with the letters from A to M.

It is the same arrangement as is found in the Telescand, which we have already spoken of as a code in code groups of four digits. The author of this work invented code words of nine letters capable of being increased to ten with a prearranged letter to indicate the use of the second column of the page or particular conjugation; the words are formed from artificial 6-letter radicals followed by 3-letter endings. There are only six of these 3-letter endings (ABA, BEC, CIE, DEN, ERU, ION). Their origin is, therefore, particularly easy to recognize.

Here we will terminate these observations on a few of the numerous types of codes found in commercial use. Secret codes, by and large, fall into analogous classes.

**Cryptographic methods—Superencipherment.**—With reference to Sittler, we pointed out a number of cryptographic methods used with codes. We are going to take this subject up again and develop it.

The application of a cryptographic system to the cryptogram obtained by replacing clear words by their code equivalents constitutes a superimposition of systems which we have called a superencipherment.

We will recall first the systems already mentioned with reference to Sittler: A transposition of the components of a group and substitutions bearing on either some or all of the components of a group. As we have seen, these substitutions may be of the single equivalent type, based on a correspondence table, or of the variant type, a number being represented by the result of an arithmetical operation of which we write down the terms, and these terms may vary; or, a page may bear several numbers.

Substitution often occurs in a form slightly different from that which we pointed out above. We showed, especially, substitution of the page or line number by another number of two digits. It often occurs in the form of numerical tables, yielding a new digit to substitute for each digit from 0 to 9, an operation which does not take place except after the initial encodement. It is to be pointed out that this sort of operation does not change the formula of a group. If the first, the third, and the fifth digits of a group, for example, are the same, we will find three identical digits in the group after the substitution. If a single substitution table is used, recurring groups will occasion repetitions. Hence, people have been led to change the substitution table often in order to suppress repetitions. Even in the course of one cryptogram, we may seek to change the formulae of the groups by using different tables for the different positions in the group (first, second, third, etc.). This amounts to a polyalphabetic substitution, and with this system, in order to avoid repetitions of groups which would result if there were as many tables as digits in each group, since each one of the digits of a repeated group would be replaced by another *identical* letter in the repetitions, we can use a polyalphetic substitution with a key of a length different from that of one or more groups.

Among ideas along the same lines as substitutions, we will point out additive and subtractive keys. Sometimes a certain number is added to each group. In order to avoid repetitions, we may change the number to be added from group to group. To avoid as far as possible adding the same number to repetitions, we may also choose the number of digits of the additive key as different as possible from the number of digits of one or more groups. Again, we can get indefinite keys by choosing an auxiliary document which gives long lists of digits (a table of logarithms, or a two-part code itself). Finally, we can make up auto-keys. In order to operate from left to right, in all these systems, it is better to simply add the digit of the group to the digit of the key, without even considering remainders.

Treating the succession of groups taken from the code as a message, we can subject it to all imaginable kinds of transpositions. Among these we may point out, as being convenient for use, tabular transpositions with successive transcriptions of the columns in the order indicated by a key, either taking all the columns from top to bottom, or according to a prearranged law.

In addition, we often meet with transpositions based on the mixture of digits from two lines superimposed upon the sequence of groups written in lines of a prearranged length.

When they adopt superencipherments, the correspondents take into account the possible cumulative effect of transmission errors. The omitting of one or more groups by the telegrapher may in certain cases result in making the telegram absolutely incomprehensible. For this reason, with certain methods, we try to limit the mixture of the digits to what is strictly necessary for avoiding repetitions and concealing code groups, reserving, all the while, the means of translating at the very least a part of the text in case of accident. Too general a mixture of the digits of the document would not permit of this.

Among the methods of cryptography used on codes and recommended by their authors, we will mention those which occur in the Darhan key and several others. A group corresponds to the word to be encoded. This group is subjected to an operation: Addition, subtraction, transposition of certain digits, etc. We get a new group to which there corresponds in the code a word of the language. That is the word which we write into the cryptogram. Among the operations provided for by Darhan is found division into sets of four digits of the series of groups of five digits gotten by the translation of the clear, and the replacement of each of these groups by a word from the code which is always found on the first pages, and which consequently begins with one of the first letters of the alphabet. This gives an assumption as to the method. It has appeared to us that this system of cryptography is the one most used with codes using arbitrary words. The code word is replaced by another code word generally chosen at a given interval from the first.

**Use of books.**—Before passing on to general observations on the solution of codes, we will say one word more about the use of printed works which are not intended for encoded correspondence, and combinations or condensers.

Just as we can look for the equivalent of a definite letter on the page of a book by the number of the line wherein it is found and the place it occupies in this line, so also can we look up a word in a book and represent it by its coordinates in the book. In the case of special subjects and in encoding only certain words, we can refer to any book at all, say directories, such as *All Paris (Tout Paris)*, in order to encipher names and addresses. However, we may always rely upon a dictionary which contains all the words of a language, and, profiting by the enormous number of dictionaries, either monolingual or bilingual, which contain an alphabetical list of the words, place the cryptanalyst in the face of a great difficulty if he wishes to hunt for the dictionary used. The use of these methods is revealed usually by the form of the groups in the cryptogram, in which the interval between the page and line numbers usually stands out, and in which the number of the line or of the word on the page rarely reaches 99. Thus, the cryptanalyst finds that he has to solve the problem of reconstructing a one-part code.

Also in the case of the ordinary dictionary, a procedure similar to the one mentioned above with respect to Darhan, is used—the replacing of the clear word by another word bearing a definite relation to the first (five above, same number on preceding page, etc.). This yields apparently incoherent text.

**Code combinations.**—We have seen that the cost of telegraphy made the transmission of pronounceable code words in letters less onerous than that of groups of digits. Hence, some have been led to replace the digit groups of old codes by letter groups. For a long time, tables for substituting two letters for groups of two digits (easily gotten by combining the 5 vowels and 20 consonants), and pronounceable trigraphs for groups of three or four digits, have been in commercial use (Pierron Bottin [Foreign volume], Voller's 12-Figure system, published in Hamburg, etc.). These combinations, like the codes, have their characteristics concerning the use of letters, enabling us to recognize whether a message could have been encoded with one of them or not. Their use amounts to a substitutional superencipherment, and combinations of this sort may be invented by the correspondents and modified so as to make repetitions of groups disappear.

The Rudolf Mosse Code, for example, though composed of 5-letter groups, offers a condenser at the end of the volume for the use of certain numerical indicators of two or three digits. In technical matters, we may substitute these indicators for indicators of the same nature composed of groups of 5 letters, so that 10 digits will replace four groups of 5 letters.

We then "condense" them into a new 10-letter group. This condenser has two different digraphs to represent each of the numbers from 00 to 99. The use of any of these digraphs for each set of two is regulated according to the total of the numerical values of the digits by means of a special table. This is intended to control transmission errors; however, it is a pretty complicated process, and the advantage of this complexity is not very evident.

Although, as a general principle, these combinations have been provided only to effect savings, they may still constitute methods of secret writing, and be quite annoying to crypt-analysts, because of the great number of systems they make up which can be superimposed on a great number of codes.

## CHAPTER XV

## GENERAL IDEAS FOR SOLVING CODE SYSTEMS

We can give only inexact directions on the procedures for solving code systems. The problem, simple enough when we are sure of the code used, becomes extremely complicated when we are ignorant, not only of the code and its nature, but also of the language of the correspondents. In our opinion, it is not by keeping within the realm of pure cryptographic science that we can ordinarily solve it. From a military, naval, diplomatic, or police point of view, cryptography is only one element of information service, and all the elements of this service should contribute to the solution of a cryptogram.

Using several classic examples, we will point out how information of a general nature gave cryptanalysts their bearings.

Nevertheless, to be able to use the information, or even have it sought for, it is necessary that the cryptanalytic agency have material and bases for guessing prepared. It is of this preparation that we are going to speak first, drawing upon our memories and upon our experience. Of course, the procedures that we are going to point out because of having applied them or having seen them applied are given only under the heading of examples. They may not be the best, and could not be offered as rules.

**Examination of cryptograms.**—The first test to put to a cryptogram is to find out whether it is superenciphered or not, and if the code used is known. To do this, we will look for repetitions of groups or fragments of groups, if needs be, making a complete list of every group by columns, according to the first letter of each word (every group beginning with 0, every group beginning with 1, etc.), or if, from repetitions, we suspect the existence of groups of 3 or 4 letters, then according to the first letter of each such group. If we have no repetitions, superencipherment must be feared, and we keep this assumption for future study. If we have repetitions and are not sure that we are dealing with a secret code, we seek to find in the list of frequent groups in the codes we know whether elements of these repetitions will allow us to identify words and pages, as we said with reference to Sittler.

**Words in clear mixed with cipher.**—Let us notice that hunting the identity of a group and of a word is greatly facilitated when we have reasonable *a priori* assumptions as to the meaning of the word represented by the group, and when we are not forced to examine possibilities based only on the list of words found, for example, on a line of Sittler (listed by lines; see above). Now, the presence of words in clear makes these guesses much easier. The habit of encoding only a few words of a message that we wish to keep secret is deplorable from the point of view of the security of the cryptogram. It is forbidden in all cipher bureaus. Still, a very skillful encoder may intentionally venture to keep words we have defined as *empty* words in clear: Prepositions, conjunctions, articles, etc., whose encodement gives frequencies and information to the cryptanalyst. He may thus deprive the latter of this information. We will not, however, advise that the difficulty be played with in this way.

The occurrence of clear words proves to the cryptanalyst that superencipherment including the whole document (tabular transposition, for example) has not been used. It tells him, barring cunning on the part of the encoder, the language used in the encoded portions. (This trickery is met with perhaps even without forethought, in the case of certain commercial dealings in which the correspondents take the words to be encoded from a single code book, and in which one of them, located in a foreign country, uses that language for the clear. This is a sort of anomaly, but it is met with.) As we have said, the clear especially fosters the guessing of the meaning of groups according to the context. Often, when clear words are very infrequent, and when the use of a given code is suspected, the occurrence in this code of a word left in clear in the cryptogram must make us renounce the theory; for the encoder, supposedly conscientious, left in clear only those words that he could not find in the code. Thus, "obus" (bomb) is found in Bazeries and not in Sittler. A rather long message in which the only clear word is "obus" is probably not encoded in Bazeries, but it might be in Sittler.

Listing of groups. -When this preliminary examination makes it possible for us to determine on a basis of repetitions, that a code has been used and the length of the groups, and when no ray of light has revealed the identification of the code used and the simple cryptographic system applied to this code, it is time to proceed to a "listing" (or to "the inscription") of the groups. If many messages are available, or if it is foreseen that they can be available, and if it is desired to proceed to a reconstruction of a code, we will do well to begin this listing on a register immediately by enumerating the messages and by noting, opposite the line of the register that bears the number of the group, the number of each message in which the group appears (simple registers may be made on cross-section paper. The sheets should be enumerated and the lines marked by 10's). If we believe, because of the correspondents, that we are dealing with a commercial code and that we will discover it by looking over only a few messages, we make a simple list on a sheet of paper divided into columns, placing the groups more or less high up in the columns in order to place them little by little in their numerical position as the list progresses.

These listings show us: first, the frequencies; and second, the combinations, if we are careful to note its former appearances each time we write down a group previously encountered.[1]

The combinations usually correspond either to sets of code words repeated several times in the text or to words spelled by syllables. Among the first, company names, quantities of merchandise, sums of money . . . , are frequent subjects; broken sequences, in which some similarly placed groups are different while others are the same, suggest the possibility of numbers (one thousand three hundred and fifty francs, one thousand three hundred and fifty-two francs. Only the groups representing 50 and 52 will differ). Among the syllables, a knowledge of the subjects that interest the correspondents may give ideas about the words represented. Telegrams from agents coming from a city where a conference is being held are apt to contain the names of politicians, for example.

If we study the frequent groups, we may find that by calculating the distance separating two of them in the list (by a subtraction), we will happen upon the distance separating two frequent groups in a known code, and that, therefore, we are dealing with nothing but an additive key affecting just one group at a time in a code which we possess. By studying the frequent groups and their combinations we can guess at certain words. If I had 5202 5383 0073 2289 4203 as a frequent sequence in an April telegram coming from Genoa, and if 5204, 5257, and 5285 are frequent in this telegram, I wouldn't be afraid of trying L . LO . Y . D George and LA, LE, and LE's, for the meaning of these different groups, and I would look up the Sittler PALI with the key +102.

When we cannot alight upon a known code, we are forced to reconstruct the code.

Reconstruction of a one-part code.—When the code is one-part, this operation does not usually offer insurmountable difficulties; the smaller it is, the less difficulties it provides. Never-

---

[1] The necessity for returning to all the previous occurrences of a group in order to study its combinations may be avoided by listing a number of the groups occurring on both sides of the group in question at the time it is indexed.

theless, in the case of commercial codes of the recent sort in which whole pages are devoted to expressions of sums of money varying by 10 francs, for example, and where the sentence "I have (such and such an article)" is found one line away from "I do not have (the said article)," the difficulties can be overcome only by a very exact technical knowledge of the subjects concerned.

It is nearly always advantageous, when we can, to have a known code with about as many groups as the code we are studying, and in the same tongue. Thus, we take into account the approximate position the frequent words occupy, and, if the pagination does not begin with 00 on the first page, which often happens (so as not to begin the code in French with the frequent A), that allows us to guess forthwith at the shift by means of a sort of frequency graph on which we mark on a straight line, for the known and unknown codes, successive segments proportional to the number of groups separating two frequent groups.

In studies of this kind, we have almost always looked for punctuation marks first. Telegrams often end with a punctuation mark. Often punctuation precedes certain of the repetitions of a group occurring at the opening of a telegram, because it begins a phrase. When, according to these remarks, and according to the position in the messages of certain groups which seem to be repeated at such intervals as would suggest them playing the role of the period or the comma, and which are not juxtaposed, we have come to definite conclusions on the identification of punctuation marks, we appeal to linguistic peculiarities in guessing at words beginning and ending sentences, at articles, pronouns, auxiliaries, past participles of verbs, etc. Lists grouping the sequences preceding and following a group that we are studying and permitting comparisons among them are often useful. When a cryptanalyst himself does all this work without entrusting it to aides under pretext of needing clerical assistance, it thoroughly acquaints him with the cryptograms he is studying, and enables him to notice things which engender new assumptions.

It has often proven useful for us to list the first 10 or 20 groups of cryptograms and the last 10 or 20. In these we have seen a certain number of sequences or group repetitions appear, which direct subsequent investigations. Signatures are found at the ends often preceded by a punctuation mark and by "close quotations." At the beginnings we find references, formulae such as: "For Mr. . . . ." "I address this telegram to . . .", or, "I have received the following telegram . . ." Best of all we may discover a precious element: Numbers. Many correspondents encode numbers and sometimes the dates of their telegrams. So in the series of messages, between certain groups changing at each tenth for the numbers and each month for the dates, we see some groups, succeeding one another and changing each time, but periodically reappearing and giving successive numbers. Now, numbering is a very good basis of attack on a code.

When we thus get hypotheses on a certain number of groups, we seek to extend them, on one hand in the code by giving meanings to groups numerically adjacent, and on the other hand, in the cryptogram by seeking to construct sentence elements. There are no more directions to give here on the method of procedure. We can only recommend boldness. Our own experience, and that of our instructors, have often shown us that gross mistakes in our first guesses have not hindered success. The main thing to do is to lend to "groups" some significance or other in "words" in order to give them in subsequent investigations an existence, so to speak, a personality distinguishing them from the troop of other groups, thus focussing attention upon them, and permitting ideas which give rise to initial guesses in the cryptogram; the corrections come later. It is at this juncture in the study that we consider the composition of the code; that we discover if it has tables apart from the "code" proper: syllables, geographical names, auxiliary verbs, numbering, etc. (see the description by Baravelli), all of which are artifices adopted by the compilers to try to prevent the cryptanalyst from utilizing frequent words or too evident extended repetitions, both of which are more easily translated than the general text, with the view of getting starting points in the alphabetical list of the words.

**Dangers in code compiling.**—These artifices, depending on whether they are used by a skillful encoder or not, risk defeating their own purpose. Example: The author of the codes which we have just mentioned used to place a list of the equivalents of the most frequent words on the last page of his book (at the same time leaving other equivalents for these words in their alphabetical position). There were several codes in service at the same time, and the combinations of keys would change very frequently. However, the frequency of the number of this page was so much higher than the others (seeing that the encoders almost never used any save the list easiest to find, and no other) that all the transpositions and all the additives affecting one group were easy to identify on the assumption that the two most frequent digits in the code groups represented the number of that page. Apart from that, the very presence of too many groups issuing from a given page betrayed the use of the said code. Separate tables of easily recognizable syllables (Baravelli) occasion researches into a very short syllabary adjoined to a large code, and for that very reason easy to reconstruct (ends of words spelled out, probable proper names, etc.). Once this result is obtained, we have the meanings of a certain number of groups, permitting us to extend the translation, just as if the encoder had left plain text. The use of a fifth digit often makes the verbs recognizable, when, for example, it is used for the past participle, present participle, or the imperative, which gives three different inflections for verbs with three fifth digits over and above the group of four digits, representing the infinitive, while substantives have only one or two (plural, second word of the line). The certainty that a word is a verb limits our researches, and permits the finding of auxiliaries, pronouns, etc., thanks to the rules of sentence structure.

While we are on this subject of precautions, we will also point out the system whereby a method of alphabetical encipherment is used for words not found in the code; for example, a letter for letter substitution. We have met with this system, combined with the use of codes in groups of letters, wherein the change of system was indicated either by special groups opening and closing the alphabetical encipherment, or by the use of an infrequent letter which did not occur in the code isolated at the beginning and end of the alphabetical encipherment. The testing of the sequences of one of the spelling indicators, in the first case, or of many groups beginning with the infrequent letter, in the second, made the constant occurrence of the second group or of the second letter show up, occurring nowhere else. This gave us a clue to the system. But we have also met these encipherments by letter substitution in code messages made up of figure groups. They caught the eye immediately, and immediately gave the cryptanalyst his bearings.

So it is seen that at times precautions taken by the authors of codes react against the security of their work. Insofar as they concern cryptographic studies and the work of cryptanalysts, we cite these examples to show what sort of things to notice in making lists in a code, which may serve to reveal an entry into the document.

**Research and use of plain-text translations.**—The cryptanalyst must naturally not neglect anything that may facilitate the identification of groups with clear words. Among the means sometimes afforded him to give him excellent information on this subject, we must count the more or less exact translation of the cryptogram.

More especially if we have documents of noteworthy information—agencies, diplomacy, war, etc.—it often happens that newspaper articles, for example, allude to objects treated in encoded telegrams, and even reproduce information transmitted in secret messages. A comparison between the repetitions of a proper name and the repetitions of a sequence of groups; the division into paragraphs resulting from punctuation when the latter has been determined or left in clear, which sometimes happens; and numbers when they occur, are, along with many other factors, elements of identification. A cryptographic workroom must, therefore, have in its library one or two collections of information media to make it possible to seek information on the possible contents of telegrams of given origin and date. Experience proves, too, that quite often seemingly incomprehensible difficulties are experienced in finding certain information in newspapers or business house pamphlets, but this is a part of this type of work.

A still greater boon to cryptanalysts is the possession of the same message sent to different addressees in different systems or different codes, one of which is known. This question of telegrams, called bilingual even though their plain text is one and the same, is one of the most interesting to cryptanalysts, because they are enciphered in several secret languages.

**Working with two-part codes.**—Leaving advice on the reconstruction of one-part codes, we have at length arrived at considerations extending to the reconstruction of all codes. If the cryptanalyst is materially aided in his researches by a knowledge of the probable first letters of the plain text equivalent of a group (which information he draws from the position of the group with reference to the alphabetical arrangement furnished by the groups already translated), and if this resource fails him in reconstructing a two-part code, the principle of the method still remains the same. Here again, we try to guess the meaning of certain groups according as they are either frequent or otherwise characteristic, and we seek to identify punctuation and particular words. Only, as we do not have to respect the restraint of alphabetical order, we can take a far flight into the realm of hypotheses. Thus we can adopt a definite meaning for a word only after it has been checked several times in different sentences. And, in our opinion, in order to be sure of messages thus translated, it is necessary to have been able to verify several translations made by the cryptanalyst on the basis of translations obtained elsewhere (newspapers, for example) or on the basis of a series of historical facts leading to a perfect similitude between the documents and the actual facts with which they are concerned. Verifications of this nature were often obtained in the course of the war, and, thanks to regiment numbers and dates, it was discovered that certain two-part codes had been used to encode military communications, which permitted of identifying the great majority of the words with perfect certainty.

It must also be noted that, in a code, there is an enormous number of words which are almost never used, and, therefore, we must not be too quickly frightened when we see that a code may have 100,000 groups, for example. The listing of the groups in cryptograms will generally narrow our studies down to an incomparably smaller number.

Before speaking of the means whereby we succeeded in revealing certain superencipherments, we will make an important observation on the construction of two-part codes.

As we have said, the starting point for such studies is the listing of the groups and the consideration of frequencies. Variants for frequent words present a primary consideration to confuse the cryptanalyst in codes as in alphabetic substitutions. Even in one-part codes, variations are striven for by including expressions in which the frequent word occurs, but often these expressions happen next to one another on consecutive lines (and, and to, and the, and that, etc.), and, if they suppress the evidence of the frequent word, they allow a region to remain in the list wherein many neighboring groups appear. This gives the cryptanalyst something to study. In two-part codes this hazard no longer exists, and the compilers are not afraid to increase the number of equivalents for the same group or for homophones. It is by a study of the repetitions of sequences, when he has enough data, that the cryptanalyst sometimes succeeds in identifying among these several variants for the same word. In the study of random codes, we must not be scared off on meeting several groups having the same meaning, and, when we possess the probable translation of a cipher, we should not be astonished at not finding repetitions of groups in the places where we expected them according to the plain text.

**Examples of solutions.**—Very often telegrams are superenciphered. These superencipherments must be discovered before passing on to the reconstruction or to the identification of the code.

We are not able to give complete practicable rules, but we will cite some examples, showing how we have profited by the mistakes of encoders or mistakes in transmission in solving problems. Therein will be seen the necessity of following very attentively the reception and the classification of the messages and of making a summary study of them and a rapid comparison with the contents of files, so as not to let the chances which are offered the cryptanalyst by the clumsiness of the enemy escape him. These examples are not purely imaginary, and many comparable elements for study are found in the repetitions caused by bad wireless transmissions. We have only to recall that at the present hour the number of encoded messages which are sent by wireless and can be listened to by whoever wishes, permits us to borrow, without at all departing from reality, all the examples we desire of this kind of correspondence.

First example: The two telegrams which follow have been intercepted:

> X to Y—No. 485. —9 groups—05690 99355 82354 49717 82103 01729 60224 24389 8592

> X to Z—No. 486. —14 groups—05690 92718 99355 82356 55114 49717 82600 22103 01729 61129 02242 43893 32598 592

These two telegrams have common parts separated in the second by parts absent from the first. Such an appearance might result from a simple transposition table, with columnar transcription and with which a certain message was enciphered for Y; for Z, however, a sentence was added to this same message. Thus, we would find in the second cryptogram the columns of the first, differing in length by at most one letter with "tails" prolonging each of these columns. But the end of the telegram is the same in the two messages (so there is no tail to this column). The first common sequence has 6 digits; the second has 8; the third has 8; etc. Therefore, we must conclude that the transcription has taken place alternately from top to bottom and from bottom to top. As there is a 9 at the head of the second common part or at the tail of the first, we have put the break in the wrong place. The first common sequence has only 5 digits: 05960, and the second, has 8: 99355823. The columns, then, have 4 and 5 digits.

Let us juxtapose them in the following order:

```
0  5  8  7  1  1  7  2  4  2
5  5  2  9  7  0  2  4  3  9
6  3  3  4  8  3  9  2  8  5
9  9  5  4  2  0  6  2  9  8
0  9        1     0
```

(When we have had 9 digits to distribute between two columns, we have always written the two sets in the order 5–4; however, the order 4–5 is possible.)

Let us try to reconstruct the columns of the second cryptogram by adding "tails" to those of the first: we have 68 digits to distribute in 10 columns, 8 columns of 7 and 2 of 6.

Between the first and the second columns, we have to distribute five figures, namely, 92718. That is impossible without forming a column of 8, so our second column is too long. We should have adopted the order 4–5.

```
0  5  5
5  3  8
6  9  2
9  9  3
0     5
```

Between the third and the fourth columns, we have to distribute 65511; 2 digits in the third column and 3 in the fourth give us two columns of 7.

Between the fifth and the sixth: **60022**; 3 digits in the fifth and 2 digits in the sixth.

Between the seventh and the eighth: **1129**, two apiece.

Between the ninth and the tenth: **33259**, 3 in one of them and 2 in the other.

Thus, we have distributed our columns in 3 sets: those which are long in both cryptograms; those which are short in the first and long in the second; and those which are short in both. Still nothing guarantees that our distribution is absolutely right; between the last two columns, for example, we could have distributed the sequence of 5 digits as 2–3 instead of adopting 3–2.

```
0 5 1 2    5 7 1 4    7 2
5 8 0 4    3 9 7 3    2 9
6 2 3 2    9 4 8 8    9 5
9 3 0 2    9 4 2 9    6 8
0 5 1 0  | 8 1 6 3    1 9
9 6 2 9    1 1 0 3    1 5
2 5 2 2    7 5 0 2
```

If we meet with more material for study of the same kind, we will be enabled to define the limits of the position of each column. We will suppose that we know the code used for encoding and that it is Sittler. We seek only the key. We will make the following assumption: A punctuation mark has been placed between the first and second parts of the cryptogram: 8163 would, therefore, equal a punctuation mark. In Sittler, according to the natural order of pages, 6831 means *period*. Sittler being used here in groups of 4, the slice from the middle of the unequal lines (10 columns to the table) will be a group from Sittler in which the digits will be transposed as in 8163. We find 1547 (first line) cinquième (fifth); 8984 (third line) sur (on); 0725 avec (with).

To put the columns of the first set back in order, we look for what may precede fifth. We will find 5102=la (the). The last two digits of the first line form the page numbers of a word whose line number is 80. We will find Division, and the table will be reconstructed.

We might say that the supposition that we possess the code is not too audacious, even in the case of supposedly secret codes. Sometimes superencipherment is adopted in actual practice, only as a result of doubt as to the security of a code too long in service, copies of which have vanished and cannot be replaced. Then, too, many encoders imagine that a superencipherment even on a code known to the cryptanalysts assures a sufficient security. We think so, too, barring accident or mistakes like those we have just shown or like those of the following example, and these can be guarded against with a unified personnel and a somewhat extended play of keys or systems.

Second example: The following telegrams have been intercepted:

1st May—X to Y—485—9 groups—05690  53285  79442  87110  30169 27539  90224  84389  8592

2d May—X to Y—485—9 groups—05690  99355  82354  49717  82103 01729  60224  24389  8592

Too superficial an examination of the first and last groups may lead us to imagine simply a repetition, as they are constantly seen passing by wireless. A closer examination reveals great differences in the messages. The second group of the first telegram, 53285, gives place to 58325 in the second; then 7944 gives 4497, etc. The beginning of the second group of the telegram is found reversed, 5399, and the ends of the two messages are the same.

The encoder of the first telegram made a mistake in transforming the literal key into a numerical key in a transposition table in which the columns are transcribed alternately from top to bottom and from bottom to top. The correspondent was unable to translate it, and requested a repetition; and the same table was transcribed without making any errors this time in the order of the columns: The column transcribed the first time as No. 2, from bottom to top, was then transcribed as No. 3 from top to bottom. The error did not begin till the second column and ended at 0224.

Thus, without any possible confusion, we have the composition and the length of the first column transcribed and of the 6 following ones, of which there are 3 of five digits and 3 of four. In the last 3 columns, there are 1 of five and 2 of four; we cannot make the distribution.

This discovery, in itself, is not sufficient to permit the translation. It gives at least information of prime importance on the system employed, on the length of the key, and the construction of the rows of the table.

We will stop this chapter here. In this work, we wish to confine ourselves to general notions. In questions of code, and especially of codes used with superencipherment, it is difficult to establish the limit between general notions and applicable particulars, considering the extent of the domain in which the encoder as sole arbiter may choose the code and the superencipherment, the number of fundamental code groups (100,000 groups of 5 digits, for example, among which N groups may represent a single word, and which, in a two-part code, may be chosen at hazard), and the possibility allowed him with indefinite keys to admit no general law for either the code or the superencipherment. General notions in cryptography have for their aim learning to establish laws. When there are none, we must have recourse to the other aids of the cryptanalyst—knowledge of commercial codes, obtaining other codes by means outside cryptography, errors of encoding, plain-text translations of cryptograms, etc.

# Chapter XVI

## CIPHER MACHINES

**Sliding strips, disks, etc.**—We have already had occasion to speak of some cipher machines, or cryptographs, with reference to the Saint-Cyr sliding strips, certain disks, the Bazeries device, etc. Devices of this type are legion; still more of them patented in Paris in 1919, differ from the Saint-Cyr sliding strips made with two paper bands on which the alphabet is written, only in structural details, levers, punctuation signs, etc. Then, too, we must realize that often disk devices, particularly with disks yielding variant values, are nothing more than making a circle, we might say, of a table which we might inscribe on a malleable substance and whose lateral sides we might join, keeping the table flat.

There is a long list of devices with rings or cylinders which amount to nothing but these very tables rolled around a spindle, or these disks stamped on a cone having its summit in their center, the summit being considerably extended. Just putting alphabets on rings instead of putting them on the rows of tables yields a patentable device; however, in the majority of cases, it does not interest the cryptanalyst.

**Wheatstone device.**—Among the classic disk devices, we will cite that of Wheatstone. It has two concentric fixed disks: One with 27 cells containing the normal alphabet plus a word separator; the other of 26 cells containing a random alphabet. About these disks move two pointers coordinated by a system such that, when the large one is shifted, the small one, keeping behind, shifts more slowly. When the large pointer has made 27 revolutions, the small one has made 26. The alphabets of this particular disk system keep one behind the other (it is just as if the first cipher row in the Vigenère square were slid with respect to the table, or after having enciphered with the column corresponding to the key letter, we were to encipher with the column next to the one which corresponds to this key letter; then with the next one, etc.). (Thus it is brought about that the key changes constantly, by replacing its letters by letters farther away from the beginning of the alphabet.) However, the number of letters of the text which correspond to these 27 revolutions and, hence, to a shift of $n$ letters of the key, may be very variable. Almost a whole revolution is required from B to A without enciphering a single letter in between; the same movement takes the encipherer from B to A, even though we encipher CDEF . . . Z in between. There is no relation between the changes of the key and the number of letters in the text. For a long time, this system appeared indecipherable. Then Kerckhoffs made the observation that the number of alphabets afforded by the device is limited, and that the cryptograms could be treated as polyalphabetic substitutions based on a long key. Moreover, by enciphering known messages by this method, we ourself observed that 27 revolutions correspond to an average of 50 letters. Other peculiarities have been recognized; for example, a doublet in the cryptogram is equivalent to two consecutive clear letters in reverse order (BA clear yields MM in the cipher). Thus, we actually get repetitions of isomorphisms (for example, in an instance cited by Wheatstone himself, POUND may have the encipherments MMCMS and IIXIA—the repetitions of I being symmetrical with respect to the repetitions of M). We have, therefore, methods of solving Wheatstone ciphers, particularly when we have several in the same key, with an identical starting point for the pointers.

A device of the same type, but without pointers, in which the retarded movement of one of the alphabets with respect to the other is effected by the unequal length of the circumferences of the two disks, has been constructed by Mr. Lock. One of the teeth on the inner disk which has only 26 letters, each bearing a tooth, meshes with one of the recesses corresponding to the characters on the outer disk, when the interior point of contact of the two unequal circumferences bearing the alphabets is moved about by means of an eccentric pivot on which the smaller disk is mounted. The device is sturdy and light.

Certain modern disk devices, for example the one referred to by the Burg patent (1908), possess systems of catches or clicks moved by levers, regulating the shifts according to keys and capable of yielding rotations of 2, 4, 1, 5, 2, 4, 1, 5, . . . letters (or any other combination), etc. These devices are so constructed as to yield the decipherment as well as the encipherment.

As for transpositions, a search among the patents filed in Paris did not yield us a very fruitful harvest. It does not seem that this class of systems has interested inventors aside from a few sliding-strip apparatuses enabling us to number the cells of a table in which a message is inscribed by placing the strips "according to a key" and to transcribe the letters of the message in this order. An example of this type is the cryptograph used in the French Army in 1886.

**Cipher machines of the typewriter type.** We will pass rapidly over the devices of the above-mentioned types: cryptanalysts, before pronouncing on their value, must study them carefully; for (as we have shown in the case of the Bazeries instrument, and as we have just demonstrated in the case of that of Wheatstone) the theoretical number of possible combinations to represent a letter or a word is often far indeed from the real number, and when we know the construction of the device, some of these combinations present resemblances which are easily recognized and which make decrypting easy.

By analogy, perhaps, with the designation typewriting or calculating machines, we of the present day rather call "cipher machines" those which possess a keyboard and print a cryptogram when the plain-text keys are struck.

**Machines yielding simple substitution.** When the patents filed in Paris for several years on this subject are consulted, it is discovered that some of them relate only to arrangements of detail intended to disguise the letters written on the keys of an ordinary typewriter, so, for example, as to write an F on the A key, and let it still print A. We get a simple substitution: Clear F yields cipher A. A similar device, yielding F on the sheet of paper when A is struck, effects the decipherment. With strips of paper, we can equip any typewriter so as to get a like result.

**Machines yielding polyalphabetic substitutions.**—On the other hand, there are some machines which make polyalphabetic substitutions possible.

A fairly simple type (to which Mr. de Medeiros' machine belongs) consists of an arrangement similar to the one which substitutes capitals for the lower-case letters on ordinary typewriters. The keys yield several different letters, according to the height to which the characters are raised above the paper by a simple lever. Evidently the device should preferably be combined with a machine on which the characters which print are not on independent type bars, but on a printing cylinder; its ascending or descending motion suffices, therefore, for any particular alphabet among those engraved around the cylinder, one above the other, to come into contact with the paper and print a letter. By regulating this motion by means of peg-cams, we get a polyalphabetic substitution, depending on the peg-cam and on the composition of each alphabet. We might conceivably change the peg-cam and the printing cylinder. The decipherment may be gotten with a deciphering cylinder having the proper alphabets inscribed upon it.

In other machines (to which the device of Bamberg and Weinhold is related), the keyboard is wired so as to send a current from the plain-text to a contact placed at the circumference of a disk. Opposite this disk is found another, bearing contacts each connected with the apparatus which prints a letter. The disks are concentric and movable. In one of the original positions, the current of key A will run so as to print A; but if one of the disks is turned, the current of key A of the keyboard will no longer reach printing key A, but another key, M, for example, and M will be printed when A is struck. If the disks are turned regularly through equal angles after the printing of a letter, the same device without any change, will effect both encipherment and decipherment.

A machine patented by Mr. Burg in 1904 yields polyalphabetic substitutions by means of the following procedure: The characters intended for the cipher are placed on a cylinder or barrel arranged parallel with another barrel which prints the clear character struck on the key on another sheet of paper. However, the cryptographing cylinder may be rotated with respect to the cylinder writing the clear, so that a letter other than the clear is printed by it. This rotation arises from a hook acting upon the cylinder and operated either by hand by a lever moved before striking a key, or, in another model, by a deeper movement of the keys. The auxiliary media comprise a platen which causes the hook to rise in proportion to the shift it undergoes and whose movement is limited by pegs fixed in the holes of a disk which, for each key struck, advances through a constant angle. According to the position of each peg which is followed by a new one every time the disk advances, the hook makes the barrel turn one, two, etc., letters. After printing, the barrel has no backward movement.

The sliding of the cipher letter with respect to the clear letter depends, then, upon the total rotation of the barrel, due to the hook, so the system is a disk system in which the key regulating the unequal movements of the disk may have a score of terms (as many as the pegs on the disk). The position of the pegs on the disk may be changed, and thus the key, too. The device is reversible, and yields the decipherment by means of a sort of backward movement, causing the barrel to turn in reverse manner to that which served for encipherment.

Mr. Burg complicated the mechanism of his cipher machine very much in a patent of 1908. If we have rightly understood this patent, the type wheel which acts as a barrel is first subjected to a rotation similar to the one of the preceding machines independent of the lowered key, regulated by a play of pegs on the disk and not occasioning a backward movement after printing, so that the cryptogram which would correspond to this rotation would be such a one as would be yielded by a disk system with a key (possibly very long) to regulate its unequal shifts. However, this is not the cryptogram that the machine prints. When the type wheel has made the first move of which we have just spoken, it gets a second rotation, depending this time on the key struck, but which, after printing, is retraced by an equal contrary rotation. The method of getting this second movement is pretty complicated; we will not depict it. We will only say that the amplitude of the rotation depends first upon the force with which the key is struck. The key may be arrested underneath at a height regulated by a double play of notched bars yielding variable combinations, in such a way that each key may descend to a greater or a lesser degree according to the position of these notched bars. The keys are ranged in 7 rows of 8; in each row we can get different combinations (16 in number) by means of the bars, in order to pick the one which will go deepest, the one which will go shallowest, and the intermediate ones. Then, too, by means of levers whose length may be varied, the depth of the keys of a given row are more or less amplified before being transmitted to the type wheel. Thus, we get very numerous combinations (the keys going more or less deep with much or little amplification) to be designated by numbers borne on the index of 14 notched bars (8 positions for each) and of 7 levers which may each act in 8 different ways. They also cause a variation in the supplementary shifts which are printed by the type wheel when we strike a given letter according to the regulating of the machine.

It seems, then, that secrecy is much more assured than in the first Burg machine. However, we would have to examine the functioning of the machine, and compare messages with their translation in order to be absolutely certain in this regard.

A patent filed by Mr. Fuller depicts a very ingenious machine from a mechanical point of view and a very complicated one, if we are to judge by the description and drawings of it. On the eighth page of his long description, the author would have us know "that a very great number of combinations or codes may be used with a machine of the type which is objectified by the invention in question, and that it is practically impossible to decipher the simplest messages, since, in the course of a message, not a single enciphered letter representing a clear letter can ever serve again to encipher the same letter in the same message." Making every reserve for the manner in which we have understood the description, for we have not seen the device itself, we will describe the functioning of a machine which we consider analogous to the device in question, in order to show, once more, how we may, with our cryptographic ideas, try to classify the system resulting from a machine among known systems.

Outwardly, the machine has the appearance of a typewriter. When we strike a letter on the keyboard, we determine, by the closing of a set of contacts, the movement of a selective mechanism, which releases a letter to be printed different from the one struck. In order to understand the movement of the selector, imagine a fictitious nut winding along a screw, and marking off distances parallel to the axis which are proportional to the screw's rotation. This nut shifts opposite the levers of the letters to be printed, and its position determines the letter which is printed. Now, when a letter of the keyboard is struck, the screw is turned through a given distance, differing from letter to letter, and hence the nut is advanced through a given distance varying for each letter, the shift taking the nut 1, 2, 3, 4 letters further ahead than it was. This shift takes place in reverse order, from Z to A. We imagined an actual screw in this description. In reality, only the screw bar exists, in the form of an inclined spiral and the imaginary nut comes back into action at one end of the screw as soon as it has passed the last letter lever at the other end. The movements of the screw may be followed by the operator on a dial which it impels and which turns opposite a marker. The screw may be acted upon directly with the help of a flywheel in order to place it in any position, without interfering with its automatic movement when a key of the board is depressed, and when the whole machine is thus connected up with a small motor.

Let us suppose that the A key gives the selector no shift at all, that B shifts it one letter, C two, D three, etc., and that at the beginning of the operation, we put the selector at A by means of the flywheel. Let us strike a key, B for example. The selector recedes one place and releases the lever of the letter corresponding to $A-1$, that is Z. Now let us strike E; the selector recedes four places and yields $Z-4=V$.

Let us strike E again; the selector recedes four and strikes $V-4=R$, etc. The character that is printed depends, then, upon the position of the selector after the enciphering of the preceding letter and upon what clear letter is struck. We get an auto-key cryptogram in which the cryptogram itself serves as a key after the prearranged single-letter key which indicates the initial position of the selector has enabled us to encipher the first letter of the message.

The correspondents, having a machine of the same construction, in which the letters of the keyboard have the same influence upon the selector, that is to say, whose substitution alphabet is the same, adopt as a key for the initial position of the selector, a letter indicated by the coincidence of this same letter on the disk with a fixed marker. A second disk, with the avowed aim and purpose of increasing the number of combinations, may be placed between the disk connected with the selector and the marker, and, instead of directly indicating the position of the selector opposite a letter by the coincidence of this letter and the marker, we may indicate the letter coincidences of the two disks between them and the position of the second disk with respect to the marker.

If we go back to what we have said about auto-keys of the sort that the machine produced, it will be seen that, if the alphabet is known, the key has no importance in solution.

The cryptogram ZVR... was obtained by means of the key ?ZVR.

We write:

$$\text{Key} _____ \ ? \ Z \ V \ R \ . \ . \ .$$
$$\text{Cryptogram} \_\_\_\_ \ Z \ V \ R \ . \ . \ . \ .$$

What letter corresponds to V in alphabet Z? E does. To R in alphabet V? E does. As for the first letter, we guess it from the context.

Decipherment with the machine is a little more complicated than encipherment. During encipherment, all we have to do is strike the keys of the board successively. During decipherment, we have to return each letter to the marker on the disk before striking the one that follows it. Starting with the key arranged as during encipherment, we strike Z. The selector which is at A recoils 25 spaces and gives B. We return the selector to Z and strike V; the selector recoils 21 spaces and gives E; we return the selector to V; placing V at the marker on the disk, we strike R; the selector recoils 17 spaces and gives E, etc.

As we have just said, if the cryptanalyst knows the alphabet, he does not need to know the original position of the selector, that is to say, what the key letter for the cipher is. Now, he may know this alphabet, for example, by means of plain text which will enable him to reconstruct it, a message which may be reduced to the result produced by the keyboard alphabet. Type-writing errors, perhaps not sufficiently appreciated by the lay personnel to whom the machine may be entrusted because of the ease with which it is used, and capable of occasioning repetitions of messages, will aid the efforts of the cryptanalyst. However, without even resorting to this assistance, he may notice that every letter of the cryptogram is enciphered with an alphabet whose indicator is known (the preceding letter). He will separate out all the cipher letters belonging to a single alphabet, that is to say, all those that follow a given cipher letter, A, B, M, etc.; they issue from an identical alphabet, and we will hence make use of considerations of frequencies, of digraphs, and of symmetry of position in order to reconstruct the basic alphabet.

Whether like the one patented by Fuller or not, it does not seem to us that the machine whose functioning we have described should yield "practically indecipherable" cryptograms. Perhaps secrecy might be increased by changing the alphabet frequently. It does not seem to us that it would be easily possible to change the combination which coordinates the lever of a key on the board with the selector, but perhaps we might be able to make substitutions among the letters occurring on the keys of the board. With long messages this precaution, also, would not prove very efficient.

A patent obtained in 1920 by Mr. Hugo Koch would seem to correspond, if our information is correct, to a machine sold under the name of "Enigma", of German make.

The application of the principle of the patent, which we will describe hereafter, leads to one machine yielding substitution, to another yielding transposition, and to a third yielding a superimposition of the two systems.

Let us imagine, on a fixed plate, 10 electric contacts corresponding on a typewriter to 10 keys (the numbers from 0 to 9, for example) (the description would be analogous for N alphabetical signs instead of 10). Let us suppose that these contacts are arranged on a circle at equal distances from one another. At a certain interval, opposite this plate, let us place another similar plate, on which the contacts are connected to the printing device. In the interval between the two plates a hollow disk bears on each face 10 contacts, which can connect respectively with the 10 contacts on the "key" plate and the 10 on the "character" plate. Each contact of one face is connected, in an entirely arbitrary fashion, to one contact of the other face and to only one.

If we turn on the current by depressing key 1, it will run, for example, from contact 1 to a contact connected with the one which touches contact 7 of the "character" plate and we will print 7. So far we get only a simple substitution.

However, if we cause the hollow disk to turn, the contact of the "key" plate disk beside it, which will come opposite the contact of key 1, will perhaps no longer connect to a contact which will be found opposite contact 7 of the "character" plate. If the wires are suitably interchanged in the hollow disk, instead of getting 7, we will get 5, for example, and if the disk advanced one notch each time that a key is depressed, we would get a polyalphabetic substitution with a periodicity of 10.

We might conceivably shift the disk in an irregular fashion; then we get a polyalphabetic substitution of the disk type with a random alphabet (in cases involving ideas of this kind, it may be left motionless for several letters). We know that the length of the period of the key is then 10 equal shifts (or 26 for 26 letters), of which each may be formed of several unequal shifts each corresponding to the striking of a key (if the disk shifts each time a key is struck). This may make a very long period.

In the place of the "character" plate, let us imagine a fixed plate such that the contacts go through the insulating material at different places, and that the plate presents 10 contacts on each face, exactly corresponding to one another. Let us interpose between this plate and the "character" plate, conveniently distant for this purpose, a second hollow revolving disk on which the contacts of one side are arbitrarily connected with those of the other.

If the two disks remained stationary we would superimpose two simple substitutions, one from the "key" plate through the intermediate plate and one from the intermediate plate through the "character" plate, and we would get only a simple substitution.

If the two disks revolved with the same speed, the same regularity, and in the same direction, the second would add only a simple substitution to the result of the first. We would get the results obtained from a disk type substitution of which we have spoken above.

However, if the two disks turn according to different laws, we get the superimposition of two-disk substitutions. This yields a periodicity equal to the least common multiple of the key periods of each disk. As we may increase the number of disks, it will be seen that by superimposing a number of disk type substitutions, we may reach a periodicity practically longer than any cryptogram.

We will not dwell on the mechanical arrangements enabling the various disks to revolve according to different laws. Cogs or meshing wheels with teeth and recesses produce advances by jumps, equal to one or more contact intervals, so that a contact may always be connected with the contacts of the plates, and so that the current may always pass from a key to the motive device used in printing. The inventor, it is true, describes his apparatus not with electric functioning but with pneumatic functioning; however, the principle is the same. The fixed intermediate plates between the movable disks are, moreover, left out of the machine and the disks touch each other contact to contact, yielding multiple combinations.

Markers indicating the original positions of the movable disks, enable us, with similar devices, to set the key in order to begin enciphering. We may easily change the disks and the cogs if we fear that an inquisitive person has a machine permitting decipherment.

A reversal of the direction of the current enables us to return from cipher to clear. We take all the transformations "hind part before" starting from the cipher letter.

Such is the arrangement for substitution. At first thought, all that I could say, unless I examined the machine, is that it seems to be a very secure system.

For transposition, let us fancy a device placed at the edge of a fixed sheet of paper. It comprises a series of parallel styli, separated equally (or by groups of 5), and advancing alternately over the paper in any order whatever, with the single purpose of showing at what point on the paper we write a letter of the message. If, for example, we imagine these styli numbered from 1 to 10 and from left to right, and that stylus 7 advances first over the sheet of paper, we will write the first clear letter on the point thus marked. 7 recedes and 3 advances; on 3 we write the second letter, etc. The order of the movements of the 10 styli will give us, then, a key of 10 digits for the inscription of the first 10 letters of the text. Now, with a single key, sending the current to a single contact on a "key" plate, connected to a movable disk by means of any one whatever of the 10 contacts on a "styli" plate, we will make the 10 styli move about in an order depending on these connections. If there is only one disk, the same series will be taken again for the 10 letters following; however, if there are several of them as in the foregoing device, we will have a new series, and the period may be long indeed. The machine is keyed for starting by means of indicators borne on the disks and by means of markers. But the author does not say in his patent what happens when, in the same series, the same stylus is put into motion several times, which does not seem impossible.

The same objection arises when we come to the machine superimposing substitution and transposition. It comprises two adjacent mechanisms; each time a key is pressed, on one hand, the substitution mechanism of the key, and on the other hand, the single contact mechanism of the transposition are actuated. The letters are borne on a barrel, and the printing mechanism makes the barrel revolve through an angle, starting with zero, corresponding to the character to be printed (the cipher character). The barrel returns to zero after each printing, so that the preceding character does not influence the encipherment of a new character. This barrel shifts along its axis, and, when a character is going to be printed, leaves an end of this axis and runs along in front of the paper until the moment when it is stopped by one of the styli of which we have spoken. This locates the letter for transposition. The paper is then pressed upon the character, then separates from it, and the barrel returns to the end of the axis. When a line corresponding to the number of the styli is printed, the paper is shifted to present another line to the barrel.

Such is this cryptograph which, at first thought, seems to us extremely secure from a cryptographic point of view. We do not believe that the machine is actually constructed in practice with a transposition. It will, however, give enough work to cryptanalysts with its substitutions alone. This is especially true if they do not have a device with the set-up used by the encipherer, and if they have not only to determine the key and the original positions, but also the different substitution alphabets.

The machine patented by the Patent Developing Co. functions, with a different mechanism, after the same principle as Mr. Hugo Koch's substitution machine, which was patented before it. Here again a hollow disk contains electrical connections connecting in a variable manner the contacts where the current from the key ends with the contact connected with the motor device of the letter lever. According to the description of the patent, which is rather confusing, it seems to us that the wheel shifts only with a regular movement, and the sketch presents only one wheel. In this case, we would not get anything but a system with mixed alphabet disks. This gives problems hard to solve, but less complex than those of Mr. Koch's appear to be. We might add that the patent provides for the use of several disks.

In order to facilitate decipherment, the connections and the alphabets are set up in such a fashion that we get reciprocal alphabets; if H becomes C for one position of the disk, C becomes

H for the same position. To decipher, all we have to do is to treat the cipher as we treated the clear, and each cipher letter becomes a clear one.

The hollow disk is easy to remove in order to change it, or, on occasion, to start at a new position.

The patent taken out by Mr. Henkels in 1922 (German) concerns a device for enciphering which does not print but only reveals the cipher letter which we copy elsewhere.

This device comprises a certain number of similar and adjacent arrangements. First, we will describe just one of them: A series of axes bear disks in a plane perpendicular to these axes. On these disks are inscribed the letters of the alphabet preferably in a normal order so as to facilitate setting the key and *setting the clear* of which we will speak further on.

These disks are free on the axes; they bear two adjacent sets of teeth on their circumference; one, turned by an intermediate pinion between the disk being considered and the preceding one, has teeth all along its circumference; the other, turning the following disk through the medium of a pinion, has such interruptions as to yield quite different rotations, engendered by successions of movements and pauses for three successive disks. If the first disk turns the second a tooth per letter for the first 15 letters, and then leaves it stationary for the last 11, the passage of these first 15 letters in front of a marker will correspond for the second disk to successive shifts of from 1 to 15 letters, from an original position on and, from this moment on, the shifting will not be modified until the first wheel, having made a complete revolution, is taken up again, and the first wheel brings about a shift of 16, etc. The third wheel will undergo the shifts of the second modified by the empty spaces in its set of propelling teeth.

We have said that the disks were movable on the axes, but that the whole system was drawn at once by pinions which transmit the movement from one disk to the following. Let us push all these pinions aside so that they will no longer face the disks; we break the solidarity, and each disk can turn freely. Let us next place disk 1 in such a manner that a certain chosen letter (a letter of the key) may be opposite a marker; then let us place disk 2 in such a way that another letter, for example, the first letter of the clear, may be opposite the marker on the disk; then let us place disk 3, by setting another letter of the clear (the eleventh, for example) at the marker, etc. Let us bring the pinions back into play, then, by means of a wheel with a mesh propelling disk 1, and whose handle turns before a circular marker; let us turn the series of coordinated disks. Let us agree to turn the handle through two twenty-sixths of a revolution. By hypothesis, the first disk will rotate to the same degree, and 28 letters will pass before the marker. The second wheel will turn, at first; then remain still for an arc of disk 1 corresponding to 11 letters; and then start out again (supposing that we did not commence with a void without meshes, we will get a shift of at most 17 letters), etc. Each letter will be replaced by another letter of the alphabet in front of the marker on the corresponding disk, and those will be the letters which we will write in the cryptogram.

The complete device is composed of a certain number (10, for example) of similar systems juxtaposed. The shifts of the 10 disks on the same cylinder may be entirely different, because the cylinders do not turn, but only the disks, drawn by like disks of the same series perpendicular to the axes. The markers are windows, so to speak, perforated in the box which contains the mechanism, and the letters are seen through them.

The movements of the disk for setting the machine or for deciphering are accomplished by means of a key for each disk. The top of the box bristles with these keys.

On what does each cipher letter depend? On the first letter of the disk appearing at the marker and on the rotation of the disk. Now, the disk is carried along by the preceding disk, but with intervals of starting and stopping. So the respective initial position of the 2 disks intervenes: If the preceding disk is shifted only 3 letters, for example, and if the letter at the marker of this disk is such that at this moment the intermediate pinion is not moved for a shift of 3 letters, the letter of the disk under consideration is not modified. On the other hand, if the pinion is in play, it will be replaced by the one three spaces ahead of it; the intermediate cases are possible if the pinion is at the juncture of a toothed section and of a smooth section. Since the encipherment of a letter depends on those that precede it, the starting point is set by agreeing on a keyword which is placed at the marker on the first disks. A knowledge of this keyword and that of the degree of rotation yield the means of translating the cryptogram; the first disks are set according to a key with the handle at its original position, and the handle is turned in the manner agreed upon, the other disks being disengaged; the cipher letters are set opposite the marker and the handle is turned in the reverse sense. The meshes work in the direction reverse to that of encipherment and rotate the disks through equal angles. The clear reappears.

The clear is divided up into sets equal to the number of the enciphering disks, say 40 disks, mounted by 10's on each axis, and one extra axis for the 10-letter key.

The first 10 letters will depend entirely on the keyword if we return to the key for each set, without using a key of more letters than there are adjacent disks, and if we always turn the handle in the same manner. The rotation of each disk on the first axis of the enciphering disks will always be the same, and the substitution will then be a polyalphabetic substitution in the Vigenère system.

In the case of the enciphering disks on the second axis, the degree of rotation will depend on the initial position of the preceding disk, and on the rotation that this disk itself receives from the key disk. The handle will rotate considerably without moving this second disk, either because the key disk will not mesh with the first, or because the first will not mesh with the second. This peculiarity runs on increasingly from disk to disk, and requires that the rotation of the handle be considerable in order to be sure that the letters of the last disk are modified. However, the cumulative effect of the influence of the initial positions of the preceding disks appears of such a nature as to complicate singularly the law of equivalence for the letters of the last disks.

We do not have the machine itself nor any messages produced by it for study. However, all we can see as a method of solution is an examination of the beginnings of telegrams in the same key (or the beginnings of sets when the length is known), enciphered by the Vigenère system.

Once the first set is found, if we have enough messages, we can make an attempt to connect up the letters of the two sets enciphered with an identical disk and an identical letter of the first set, and which, consequently, comes from an equal rotation. We can, at the same time, make trials on the letters of the same disk enciphered with letters alphabetically adjacent in the first set; the shift will be the same save in the case where we find ourselves at the juncture of a toothed and a smooth meshing sector. These methods, however, do not seem so practicable, and, just from the description of the patent, we fancy that the encipherments gotten by means of the device will be of such a nature as to give interceptors plenty of yarn to wind up.

We will now mention the machines constructed by Aktiebolaget-Cryptograph, of Stockholm, which are based upon several patented principles, according to their different types.

Mr. Damm has applied one of these principles to several machines of different forms, described in a patent of 1915.

Let us imagine an alphabet in which we read the clear letter, and opposite it a table of $n$ alphabets slid one space with respect to one another (a vertical set of $n$ columns of a square table— "Vigenère" or a similar one). Each clear letter may be represented by any one of the $n$ letters found on the same row. To encipher, we bring opposite a marker the letter of the clear and, consequently, the corresponding row of the table. In front of this table, let us imagine a screen checkered in such a way that each checker square covers a letter of the table, a single checker square being open on each line so as to form a window enabling us to read a letter of the row; this is the letter which will be substituted for the clear letter. (The checkering does not exist; we introduced it to clarify the arrangement of the windows.) Depending upon whether we raise or lower this screen before the marker to which we have brought the clear letter, the position of the aperture corresponding to the row of this letter will vary, and the letter to be substituted will be modified in consequence. If the screen were unlimited and if the holes therein presented themselves in the same order, after a period of $n$ shifts in the same direction, we would get a polyalphabetic substitution, the first, the $n+1$, the $2n+1$, etc., letters being read through the same window, and therefore, in the same alphabet, etc.

Such is the principle. The real machines are made with cylinders or disks. In the case of the cylindrical type, for example, let us consider the above table as rolled around a mandrel and passing in front of a bar, fastened to the structure, in which an aperture is perforated to serve as a marker. The screen has a total length greater than the length of the circumference of the table cylinder; and being flat would have a height of some 30 checker squares since the table would have 26 letters. Once its extremities are hooked securely together, it envelops the table cylinder, but does not keep in contact with it. If the cylinder drew the screen along directly at the same speed, we would have a device of the Wheatstone type (on which one of the alphabets shifts backward one letter each time the marker is passed), the succession of the alphabets being regulated by a law into which the number of letters separating two successive clear letters would enter, and the total period would be, save in case of error, the product of the length of the cylinder's circumference by the length of the disk. However, the screen is drawn by a system of click wheels, which make it move in one direction or the other according to the directions of a chain key characteristic of the system. This chain presents links of equal length, but of two different thicknesses, slipping on a guide under the end of a rod. The thin links let this rod down, which connects the screen with a wheel turning clockwise; the thick links lift the rod, and the connection of the rod is then produced by a wheel turning counter-clockwise. The chain key may be easily made up by hooking together the links, thin or thick, and putting it on the machine; the prearrangement for the correspondents is given by a number or a word indicating the succession of the links. Let us, besides, note that, the screen forming a continuous surface, we may get, by a direct rotation equal to its length less $n$ letters, the same result as by a reverse rotation of $n$ letters. Consequently, it seems that the wheel will return to its first position at the end of a period equal to the product of the number of links of the chain by the number of windows, and as this period may not coincide with the period end of the cylinder, it will still be necessary to multiply the result by 26 to get the length of the cipher key (if there are no factors reducing this result).

In another arrangement, the alphabets of the table are traced on radii of a disk. The clear alphabet is on its periphery, and the windows are located in another and smaller screen disk superimposed upon a part of the table disk, which is capable of movements in both directions according to the influence of a chain key. The marker gap is located on the common radius of the two disks.

As concerns these two models, the alphabets of the clear and of the table are thoroughly interrelated, but a special handle causes the chain key to advance, and by means of transmissions, directs the movements of the screen. Strictly speaking, therefore, it seems that we might regulate the movements of this handle as a key superimposed upon the system; however, this is not spoken of in the patent.

In a third type, we come to a machine which, from its exterior appearance, looks like a typewriter, with keys. Each of these keys is located opposite an alphabet written on the circumference of a cylinder. The totality of the alphabets, of which one is shifted one letter with respect to its neighbor, form a rolled-up square. The cylinder itself is submitted to rotary movements forward or backward according to the shape of the links of the chain key. Each depression of a key makes the chain advance one notch. The cipher letter is read on the marker gap, opposite the key which, under pressure, actuates a little shutter uncovering the part of the gap in which we are interested. Therefore, the movement of the chain is now connected up with the number of the letters; considering the alphabets on the cylinder, it seems to us that we get the same movement as with a disk device, advancing by irregular jerks each time a letter has been enciphered. The alphabets of the imaginary disks would be respectively that of the table and that of the series of keys in the order of the windows. By means of the chain key, we get a period longer than it would be practicable to use with a hand disk; however, we no longer get the security afforded by the period difference between the rotation of an exterior disk of more than 26 cells and of an interior disk of 26 cells (screen and disk or cylinder) and the irregularity of the window positions.

Thanks to the introduction of electricity, this very apparatus becomes a printing device. Following the diagonals of our table, on which the same letter occurs on each row and in each column, let us place a contact on each equivalent of this letter, and let us join all these contacts with a single wire conducting the current to the apparatus. This will make the printing lever of this letter work. Let us arrange all 26 letters in a similar way. When we press the key of the clear letter, instead of opening the window through which we read the cipher letter on the cylinder in the preceding model, we let down a contact which conducts the current to one of the contacts we have just spoken of; the striking of the key will cause the letter we were reading a minute before to be printed. The contact cylinder will always be moved forward or backward, being regulated by the chain key.

Let us point out in passing that the chain key has been utilized in a pocket cryptograph. In this device, the shifts of a strip bearing the 26 letters and the reading window are transmitted by means of a string to the motivating pinion of the chain key and to the table-bearing cylinder which turns in one direction or the other. The reglet is pulled from below before each reading in order to advance the chain key one link. The movements of the table cylinder are, therefore, as in the last types mentioned, directly related to the number of letters of the message. It seems to us that fundamentally we get a disk system.[1]

The prospectus of Aktiebolaget-Cryptograph leads us to imagine that, if the principle of the link chain has remained the same, some changes of detail have been brought to bear upon the finished product. The device, put on sale in 1922, has keys, and prints the clear and two copies of the cipher on three bands. The drawings present a series of 25 disks, each bearing in relief on its periphery a sector of a twenty-fifth of the circumference where a letter occurs. This enables us, by stringing these disks on an axis in a chosen order, to get the equivalent of a table,

---

[1] It is believed that the author is here referring to the A. B. Ing. Firman "Teknik" cryptograph. In this device, a strip bearing the 26 letters is located under the reading window and is caused to take one of two possible positions at irregular intervals. The fluctuations of this strip are controlled by the chain key. When this strip is in one position, the plain text letters are found on it and the cipher letters are taken from the strip on the alphabet drum; when this strip is in the other position, the enciphering operation is reversed and the plain text letters are taken from the alphabet drum sequence and the cipher equivalents are taken off the strip. The operating lever is pressed down and pulled back to the starting position before each reading in order to advance the alphabet-bearing drum one step. This lever, at the same time, actuates a wheel holding adjustable pegs which engage and operate the motivating pinion of the chain key at irregular intervals determined by the keyed setting of these pegs on the periphery of the wheel.

but easy to change, thanks to the modification of the alphabet of this table by a new arbitrary mixing of the letters. With these alphabets and these chain links (of which the total number and arrangement may be changed) we arrive at possible numbers of combinations in the decillions for one machine to differ from another. Finally, the automatic periodic movement seems, according to the prospectus, capable of being broken at the encipherer's will. When we begin the messages with the same chain key and the same initial position of the elements, this would enable us to change the period from the very beginning.

The device bears markers, corresponding doubtlessly to position indicators for the starting elements. It serves to encipher and to decipher, without precise indications being given in the description concerning the decipherment.

In 1920 the same Swedish firm had a machine patented in which the components are motivated by electricity by means of electromagnets, actuating ratchets which advance certain wheels each time that the current flows and in this case only.

Two disks turning in opposite directions, between which contacts are mounted, establish a connection between the wires connected with the letter keyboard and the wires connected with the keys. Each of them is moved by a mechanism actuated by a current which passes through an interrupter composed of a wheel making or breaking the contact according to the teeth located on its circumference (or projections located in the disk forming the wheel). This wheel advances through a constant angle each time a key is pressed. Therefore, if the teeth are such that when we press a certain letter the current passes into one of the interrupters and not into the other, only one of the disks shifts. If the current passes into both interrupters, the two disks turn in opposite directions and their shifts *are added together*. Each interrupter gives the disk a periodic movement, the period equaling, at most, a turn of the interrupter wheel. Suppose we combine the periods of the interrupters in such a fashion that they do not end together save at very great intervals. Let us have one of them act more forcibly upon one of the disks so as to advance this disk several letters instead of one at each passage of the current. Thus, we will succeed in getting a very long period for the displacements of the disks. If, for example, the interrupter wheels have 17 and 19 teeth, their total period will be $17 \times 19 = 293$ keys struck, and it will be necessary again to multiply this product by the common number of the letters on the disks to return to the beginning of the period, provided the shifts have been well chosen, and provided that we do not happen upon the beginning of the disks after less than 26 times 293 shifts.

A single alphabet (which does not seem to be the normal alphabet) is on the disks in direct order on one and in reverse order on the other, the rotation being regulated so that a simultaneous movement of one space by both of the disks prints a letter two letters distant from the one struck on the key. That is, of course, providing it is in the alphabet of the disks. Hence, we would get a disk system, with unequal but periodic movements. The problem presented by the machine is complicated by the following artifice: When a certain letter, called the influencing letter, is struck, the electric current is broken between the interrupter wheels and the disks, so that no shift takes place and the wheels stay still even in the case where, in their normal period, they would have shifted. As the interrupter wheels have continued to turn, when the following key is struck, the shift is the same as would be produced in the arrangement in question. However, comparing the device to a disk system, the enciphering disk has kept behind the clear disk, and retardations of this nature are produced according to only the occurrence of a single given letter in the clear; that is to say, without any law.

To clarify our ideas, let us suppose that one of the disks is propelled by its interrupter according to the key 11010 and the other according to 2200 (for this example, we choose extremely short keys). For the shift of the cipher letter with respect to the clear there will result a period each term of which is gotten by adding the shift of the first disk to that of the second, a period which will have 20 terms (4×5).

$$1\ 1\ 0\ 1\ 0\ 1\ 1\ 0\ 1\ 0\ 1\ 1\ 0\ 1\ 0\ 1\ 1\ 0\ 1\ 0$$
$$2\ 2\ 0\ 0\ 2\ 2\ 0\ 0\ 2\ 2\ 0\ 0\ 2\ 2\ 0\ 0\ 2\ 2\ 0\ 0$$
$$\overline{3\ 3\ 0\ 1\ 2\ 3\ 1\ 0\ 3\ 2\ 1\ 1\ 2\ 3\ 0\ 1\ 3\ 2\ 1\ 0}$$

If the influencing letter comes out the sixth and the ninth in the course of a message whose encipherment corresponds to such a period, we will get

$$3\ 3\ 0\ 1\ 2\ 0\ 1\ 0\ 0\ 2\ 1\ 1\ 2\ 3\ 0\ 1\ 3\ 2\ 2\ 0$$

(with 0 shifts for the sixth and the ninth), and while the regular period gave the following as shifts between the clear and cipher letter (supposing them not shifted at the beginning of the period):

$$3\ 6\ 6\ 7\ 9\ 12\ 13\ 13\ 16\ 18\ 19\ 20\ .\ .\ .\ .\ .$$

the influencing letter yields

$$3\ 6\ 6\ 7\ 9\ 9\ 10\ 10\ 10\ 12\ 13\ 13\ .\ .\ .\ .\ .$$

So the encipherment is absolutely different.

On decipherment, which is done like encipherment, the striking of the cipher letter keys printing the clear, the interruption of the current occurs on the type bar of the influencing letter. This influence of one letter (or even of several) succeeds in increasing in a large measure the already great security of the device, save in case of error or peculiarities of construction.

To differentiate the machines, changes of interrupter wheels are provided, enabling us to modify both the periods and the elementary shifts of the disks which play the role of disk systems known under that name.

It seems that modifications have been brought to bear upon the machine in the present-day commercial application of the patent. The influencing letter has disappeared. On the other hand, there are now four exterior marker signs corresponding to interrupter disks with indentures or projections making or breaking a contact and a fifth disk (or rather an ensemble of four disks—one for each of those preceding) which break the current or make it again according to its proper period. Upon encipherment this removes influence from or gives influence to each one of the first four disks. The initial positions of these five disks are indicated by means of 5 letters on the markers.

A few other devices aim to transform digit groups (charged for at the rate of five digits per word by telegraphic companies) into consonant-vowel or vowel-consonant letter groups, charged for at the rate of 10 letters per word. Some always give the same syllable for the same group, for example, by a method which makes these two elements appear one beside the other in the window of a cover. Among others there exists an easily portable one. By means of concentric crowns to which a key may be applied, this device replaces a number of five digits by a group of 4 letters, by means of an agreement enabling us to fix the order of reading the numbers of 2 and 1 digits occurring on these crowns and to form numbers from 0 to 99999, according to the order of the vowels and the consonants. We must say, however, that applying this system is far from the simplest thing in the world. Still another comprises, for the first 100 numbers, a table of 20 columns and 5 rows, opposite which rulers are shifted around their axes. On the faces of these rulers occur different lists of the 20 consonants and the 5 vowels; the syllable formed by the vowel of the row and consonant of the column replaces the number. The key is given by means of numerals indicating the faces of the two rulers to be used.

Aktiebolaget-Cryptograph has also constructed a device of this class. Combinations of 5 vowels with the first 10 consonants represent the first 50 numbers, and those of the same 5 vowels with the last 10 consonants represent the last 50. The vowel in the syllable, for example, always represents the tens, which gives the groups a characteristic appearance. Levers like those of some cash registers shift before sectors on which digits or letters occur. This enables us to form numbers on encipherment and groups of 2 letters on decipherment. Letters and digits are both in relief on the set of printing wheels, joined two by two and shifting at the same time. However, these printing wheels are slid one with respect to the other in the course of encipherment by means of a chain key similar to the one we described with reference to the cipher machine of Aktiebolaget-Cryptograph. The same two-figure group is therefore represented by different letters. The letter representing a given tens or units number changes constantly in the course of the operation.

The use of these devices requires a second operation after the encipherment which gave numerical groups. To us they do not seem very interesting in that they cannot be set up at a very low price; for correspondents, having a personnel intended to encipher with codes, and able to obtain, in addition, funds for superenciphering machines, seem rare to us in actual practice.

However, we have mentioned these machines in order to point out that the transformation of numerical groups into pronounceable groups of 10 letters is in vogue, and is not lost sight of by inventors.

Here we will stop the descriptions of machines taken from the patents prior to 1923. From some of the examples given, our readers have already seen that we cannot always depend upon the awe-inspiring numbers for different combinations presented by inventors in support of the excellence of their machines, but that we have to analyze the work, with the instrument in hand, in order to see whether some observation such as we made for the Bazeries device will not change the data of the problem. We have to consider the consequences of an error in striking a key, and see what the second version would be if the first is untranslatable for the recipient. It is necessary to consider whether or not there is a possibility of getting numerous cryptograms enciphered with components which will enable us to study them together. We do this according to the facility of changing the keying elements. In any event, the workings of a machine enable us to effect complications of systems that we would never dare to impose on a human encipherer. We must anticipate that the use of cryptographing machines will present new and interesting problems to cryptanalysts.

# Chapter XVII

## FINAL CONSIDERATIONS

Here we will bring these elementary studies in cryptography to a close. We have reproduced most of the simple systems; we have described the known methods of solving them; and we have even made incursions into domains in which the complexity of the systems made the actual labor and the imaginative efforts of the cryptanalyst more arduous. We have not feared to give many examples, and sometimes to protract some unattractive explanations in order to enable the reader to comprehend certain systems in detail. We have done so, too, in order that he may feel out, in the midst of the labyrinth in which we enwound him, whether or not his cryptographic calling may be of such stature as to resist the boredom of meticulous and bewildering calculations. We beg indulgence for any mistakes that may be found in the book, either as a result of uncorrected typographical errors or errors in encipherment in the exercises.

As you have seen, we have described only a fairly limited number of systems and methods in the foregoing pages. In brochures, reviews, and works on cryptography, you can find many of them which have not been mentioned here at all. This comes most often from the fact that among the thousands upon thousands of ciphers that have passed through our hands, we have never come across the use of these systems, and that the sometimes successful studies in their decipherment did not seem to us to belong in a work intended for beginners in cryptography. Besides, some of them amount only to variations or combinations of those we have mentioned, and, in the cases of some of them, the authors have piled up complexities in forming and designating keys, alphabets, and the order of letters without fundamentally changing the long-known methods. Such methods may be excellent, and form a precious reserve of weapons for correspondents anxious about the secrecy of their telegrams, yet they might be much less valuable on the day when they were put to use in an army in the field. In any case, we have not described them in detail here. We leave the care of dissecting these methods to our readers, if they wish, when they come across the descriptions published by their authors. Nor have we dwelt in our book for students upon methods used in late years. These systems are usually combinations of several classic methods, which have occasioned labors of great ingenuity and of lively interest. We would have had to appeal to very late history for explanations and examples. Doubtless, it is hardly time yet to treat of subjects of this nature.

In this connection, we might, however, make the following observation:

Immediately after the war of 1914–19, cryptographic studies seem to have sprung into new life. On the one hand, the systems are getting more and more complicated: two-part codes with superencipherment seem currently used. The same may be said about superimpositions of alphabetic systems. People no longer hesitate to burden encipherers with heavier labors than heretofore. Then too, they seek to baffle cryptanalysts by changing keys and systems frequently.

On the other hand, powerful organizations, private or public, have taken up cryptography in the period mentioned. They have compared notes; expressing the wish to dissect the complicated methods in order to be able to entrust a material part of the labor of decrypting, and then of deciphering, to clerks, the latter, possibly beginners in cryptography or even laymen. And these studies have occasioned proposals for new systems, avoiding the weak points of the old ones.

As a result of all this, besides difficulties due to the perfecting of systems, we have a much harder time than we used to just recognizing what systems are used. It is harder than it used to be to distinguish code systems from substitution and to differentiate between codes, because of the disappearance of the "earmarks" which indicated what code was used and because of the increase in the number of groups representing the same word (variants).

Hence, the cryptanalyst has much more trouble getting results than he used to.

Under these conditions, we could not recommend too strongly that you let no possible information escape you and that you set great store by statistics. We will not dwell upon the help we may seek to get from the outside, in particular from newspapers chock full of information that is still fresh. However, in the study of ciphers, we have more and more often to seek information from a comparison of messages. This is particularly true in seeking to discover what system is used when the lists of frequencies and linguistic peculiarities alone fail to furnish this information. For these detailed comparisons, we will advise transcribing the whole cryptogram on one big sheet of paper, or at least parts of the messages, especially the beginnings, and sometimes the ends or common sequences. In the formulae of groups and in repetitions, we will have to look for information which frequent changes of the key in a single system will seek to mask. We will have to make daring assumptions and undertake labors sometimes without any solid foundation.

The cryptanalyst's attitude must be that of William the Silent: No need to hope in order to undertake, nor to succeed in order to persevere. Some studies will last for years before bearing fruit. In the case of others, cryptanalysts undertaking them never get any results. But, for a cryptanalyst who likes the work, the joy of discoveries effaces the memory of his hours of doubt and impatience.

Over and above perseverance and this aptitude of mind which some authors consider a special gift, and which they call intuition, or even, in its highest manifestation, clairvoyance, cryptographic studies will continue more and more to demand the qualities of orderliness and memory. The lists must have references in order that each letter or each group may be found without any trouble on the more and more complicated messages we will have to study, and whose study will, therefore, require more and more data. Likewise, in a single list, we must endeavor to take precautions against including elements of codes or different systems. The most efficient way, to our mind, is a system of detailed references, enabling us to eliminate at once everything relative to documents which have become uncertain in the course of our study. Tabs may aid the memory to recall either peculiarities in certain cryptograms or the events or the names that may give rise to assumptions on the content of the messages.

The author terminates this study here. In spite of the dryness of the subject and the faults of the book, he hopes that the reader may follow the unfolding of the text. If, by this compilation of data coming from various sources, the author has been able to save persons desirous of studying secret writing the labor of researches in works sometimes hard to find, and if he has been able to impart to them a love for the work which has occupied a good part of his own life-time, he will deem himself happy.

THE END